DADDY'S PROMISE

DADDY'S PROMISE

BRENDAN T. HOFFMAN

Order this book online at www.trafford.com
or email orders@trafford.com

Most Trafford titles are also available at major online book retailers.

Printed in the United States of America.

ISBN: 978-1-4669-1741-5 (sc)
ISBN: 978-1-4669-1740-8 (hc)
ISBN: 978-1-4669-1739-2 (e)

Library of Congress Control Number: 2012904991

Trafford rev. 03/27/2012

 www.trafford.com

North America & international
toll-free: 1 888 232 4444 (USA & Canada)
phone: 250 383 6864 ♦ fax: 812 355 4082

Dedicated to my daughter,
Dawn

SECTION 1

CHAPTER ONE

NEVER IN MY lifetime would I have imagined losing one of my girls. I had heard stories about friends of friends of friends and read about losses in the paper, but the thought never crossed my mind that I could be that friend of a friend. My loss was not an easy one to overcome—not that any loss is—but mine was definitely unexpected and devastating. Even when I found out in November 2008 that my twenty-eight-year-old daughter Dawn had terminal brain cancer and was given six to twelve months to live, I didn't let it sink into my brain.

Those final months of her life were very hard for her and very hard for me to watch. Once we were given her prognosis, we woke up every day not knowing what to expect. Every day the same thought crossed my mind: *Oh God, it's one day closer.* I know I shouldn't have thought that way, but I did. Many nights I tried to put myself in Dawn's situation. What were her thoughts every new day? Sure, I know each and every one of us is going to die, and each new day is closer; however, when you're given a time frame, it's much different.

When the girls were little, how many times did I say, "I'm going to protect them from everything"? As a father, you are their knight in shining armor. Then the unthinkable happens, something that no parent ever wants to face—one of your children is terminally ill. With that news, you lose all bearings. You lose all track of reality. You are no longer normal, and you never will be again.

3

With all the promises I made to my girls when they were little, they used to ask me, "Daddy, will you protect me from things that can hurt me?" It hurt so bad knowing I couldn't keep the promise that I'd made to Dawn. All that kept crossing my mind was how I was going to defeat this cancer. I knew deep down that I needed more than just medical treatment. I needed prayers on end with a miracle to follow.

One day in June 2009, Dawn and I were sitting out on the lanai drinking coffee and reading scriptures from the Bible. We were asking each other questions when Dawn said, "Daddy, you have to promise me that you will continue studying the Bible."

You see, with my busy schedule, I had drifted away from God and his church. Dawn knew that and told me I needed to get back with the church and have a relationship with God. "I promise, Dawn," I said. "I will continue to read and study the words, and I will start going back to church."

After a few minutes of talking about the Bible, she said, "Daddy, after I'm gone, you have to write your thoughts and feelings down. You have to make this promise to me. Will you do this?"

"Dawn, hon, I can't write," I told her.

"Yes, you can, and I'm going to tell you how," Dawn told me. "You reach deep down into your heart, and you pull those feelings out and just add them to your thoughts. Daddy, you must do this, because it will help you after I'm gone, and your words will also help others."

"Who will they help?" I asked.

"Trust me, Daddy," she said. "They will help others. Promise me you will do this. Promise me right now."

"Okay, hon, I promise you," I agreed. These were just two of the many promises I made to my girl.

"Let the word of Christ dwell in you richly in all wisdom, teaching and admonishing one another in psalms and hymns and spiritual songs, singing with grace in your hearts to the Lord." (Colossians. 3:16)

It was a beautiful fall afternoon in Ponte Vedra, Florida. It was Saturday, October 18, 2008. I was watching the Ohio State versus Michigan State game when Dawn came over for a visit. During her visit, she told me about a knot that was in her right groin area. I told her she needed to have it looked at by her doctor. Dawn told me that she had gone to two different emergency rooms, and both times, she was told she had a hernia. Both ER doctors told her to go home and put heat on it four times a day. Her first visit was in January 2008. Her second visit was in May 2008. I told her she needed to return to an emergency room. She told me she was heading over to her mother Linda's and spending the day and night with her. The next day her mother took her to St. Vincent's emergency room, where they decided to admit her and do a biopsy. This was Sunday, October 19. When they performed the biopsy, Dawn was informed it would take forty-eight hours for the results. She was given a room, and the waiting game began. I went to visit her Sunday evening, and we walked around for a bit.

"Daddy, I don't feel good about this biopsy," she told me.

"It will be okay, babe. Don't worry," I assured her. I had to go out of town the next day but told Dawn that I would drop by when I returned in the evening. I spent Monday in the Gainesville area doing inspections. My mind was not on work at all. All that came to mind was Dawn telling me she didn't feel right about the test. I had the same feelings. I can't tell you why, but I just didn't feel comfortable with it. I was so worried about my girl.

On Tuesday, October 21, I was at work and scheduled to leave for the day at two o'clock that afternoon. I told Dawn I would be at the hospital no later than two thirty. My phone rang, and I recognized the number as being from Dawn's hospital room. When I picked it up, I noticed that she seemed calmer than I'd ever remembered her being.

"Daddy, when are you coming here?" she asked me. I told her I would be there in an hour and a half. "Daddy, my doctor is here, and I need for you to talk with her. I want my doctor to tell you the results of my biopsy." I didn't like what I was hearing. If the results were good, Dawn would have told me the biopsy results herself.

The doctor came on the line. "Mr. Hoffman, my name is Dr. Smith. Your daughter wanted me to inform you that her biopsy results are in, and it isn't good news. The results, Mr. Hoffman, show your daughter has stage-three melanoma cancer." The doctor went on to say that she would be around on the floor to talk to me more when I arrived. She then gave the phone back to Dawn.

"Daddy, please come now," Dawn begged me.

"I'm on my way, hon," I said. "I'll be there in thirty minutes." I hung up the phone and just stood there. I couldn't move. It was like I was frozen to my desk chair. *What did I just hear?* I thought. *No, that is impossible. My daughter couldn't have stage-three melanoma cancer. No way.*

After about two minutes, I walked into my boss's office. Normally, I would ask for time off, but this time I didn't. "Mike," I said, "I just received a call from Dawn and her doctor. I have to go. I don't have time now, but I will explain everything tomorrow when I see you."

The only words Mike said were "Just go. Oh, are you able to drive?"

"Yes, Mike. Thanks," I assured him. So I turned around and headed to the parking lot.

St. Vincent's was only eight miles from my work, but I had to go through town to get there. All I kept thinking about was getting held up in traffic downtown. As I was approaching downtown, I had a straight shot. There are four lanes of traffic, and the lane I needed was open—I mean, no cars in it at all. The other three had plenty of vehicles. All the way to the hospital I didn't catch one red light—sixteen red lights, and every one of them stayed green for me. I made it to the hospital in seventeen minutes.

As I was approaching Dawn's room, I noticed the door was closed. I knocked lightly on it and heard Dawn tell me to come in. As I walked in, I noticed that the doctor was still with Dawn. Dr. Smith said she didn't want to leave her alone. "She told me you would be here in no time," she said.

"Dr. Smith, I'm Brendan, Dawn's father," I said, introducing myself. "Please tell me what is going on."

"Mr. Hoffman," Dr. Smith began, "your daughter has stage-three melanoma, and its point of origin is the right groin area. We will need to start her on chemotherapy right away."

Then she continued, "Mr. Hoffman, there is something else you need to know. Dawn will need chemotherapy treatment five days a week for the first month. Then three time a week for the next eleven months. This isn't good, Mr. Hoffman; Dawn has three to five years with this advanced stage of melanoma cancer. You won't have any problems with her health insurance in covering this extensive treatment."

"Well, Doctor," I said, "she doesn't have any medical insurance. She is coming off a nasty divorce and was just laid off from work two months ago."

"Oh," Dr. Smith said, pausing for a second, "I'll have to get back with you. Please let me assure you that we will not put her out on the street. We're not like that here at St. Vincent's. Something will come up, and she will get this treatment. St. Vincent's gets donated money that could possibly be used for her treatment. I will contact the financial office and have them contact you. Please believe me—we're not just going to discharge her and not treat her."

The doctor then turned to Dawn and proceeded to tell her the severity of the cancer. She explained that because it was at a stage-three level, Dawn was looking at a five-year life expectancy. She went on to say that the upcoming treatment would slow it down but would not totally cure her. After the doctor left, Dawn and I talked about what had just transpired.

"Daddy, she is saying I have no more than five years to live," she said.

I was totally speechless, but Dawn wanted to hear from me. I told her that a lot can happen in five years. The doctors could find a new treatment during that time. Did I believe that? I sure did try to.

Dawn looked at me and said, "Daddy, age thirty-three isn't a bad age to die."

I looked at her and said, "Thirty-three is way too young."

"Daddy," Dawn said, "Jesus died at thirty-three."

I stayed with Dawn until ten o'clock that evening. I told her I would be back around eleven the next morning, and we could have lunch together. The next morning at nine o'clock, I received a call from Dawn.

"Daddy, they're sending me home without any treatment," she said. "How can they do that?"

"What? They can't do that," I told her.

"Daddy, the man from the finance office is standing here right now and says I'm being discharged," she insisted.

I told Dawn to let me talk with him. "I'm sorry, Mr. Hoffman," the man said, "but we can't treat anyone without insurance."

I told him I would be right there, because I wanted to talk to him in person. Needless to say, when I got there, he was nowhere in sight. I even went to his office and was told he was out; the secretary didn't know when he would return. At three o'clock that afternoon, just twenty-four hours after finding out she had three to five years to live, Dawn was discharged from the hospital.

We asked the discharging doctor what our options were. "Mr. Hoffman, Dawn, I am so sorry this hospital is doing this to you," he said. "Patients without insurance need to use Shands Hospital off of Eighth Street downtown. I don't know if it will help you guys, but I made a couple of calls to Shands Hospital in Gainesville. They have a wonderful cancer center, and I explained the situation to them. They gave me information to pass on to you if you elect to use them."

Wow, I thought to myself. *I found a doctor at St. Vincent's who was actually more concerned for the patient than insurance.* We were very grateful for his assistance in getting Dawn treatment.

On Wednesday, October 22, I called Colleen, the head nurse at the Oncology Department at the Davis Cancer Center at Shands Hospital in Gainesville. Colleen asked me several questions about Dawn's condition and then told me that the earliest they could see her was November 6. She explained to us that two weeks might sound like a long time considering Dawn needed treatment right away.

Before St. Vincent's found out that Dawn didn't have insurance, they told us that her treatment wouldn't start until Monday, November 3. Dawn asked me what we should do, but what choice did we really have other than to wait? We told Colleen we would take the one o'clock appointment for an MRI and then the two o'clock with Dr. Friedman.

On Halloween day, I received a call from my niece in Ohio telling me her stepfather had passed away. A viewing was scheduled for Saturday afternoon, and then there would be a private service with burial on Tuesday with immediate family only. I made a flight up to Ohio first thing Saturday morning. Soon after I picked up my rental car, I received a call from Dawn.

"Daddy, my head really hurts, and it's not a migraine," she said. Dawn experienced her first migraine when she was five years old.

"Are you sure it's not a migraine?" I asked.

"Yes, Daddy, I'm sure it's not," she said.

"Just take it easy and go lay down," I told her. Over the next three days, I received eight calls from Dawn telling me about headaches. On Tuesday, I told her she needed to go to the emergency room, because she'd had this headache for three days.

It was Election Day, and I was at the airport heading home. Before I got on the plane, I told Dawn that she wouldn't be able to reach me off and on. She did tell me that she still had her headache. The first thing I did when I arrived at the Jacksonville airport was call Dawn. It was three thirty in the afternoon, and I couldn't reach her. I went straight to my precinct to cast my vote and then tried calling again. Still, I couldn't reach her. I called her sister and asked if she knew Dawn's whereabouts. She told me she hadn't heard from her all day.

After dinner, I still couldn't reach Dawn. Her phone was going straight to voice mail. So, I sat down to read the paper. I know was eight o'clock, because I turned the TV on to watch some of the election results right before the phone rang. When I picked it up, there was a lot of noise on the other end. I finally heard Dawn's voice. She was crying hysterically asking me to come to her.

"Dawn, where are you?" I asked. "I can't understand you with you crying. Where are you?"

At that point, I heard another voice say to me, "Mr. Hoffman, this is the Orange Park Emergency **room**. We have your daughter here. I think you need to come immediately."

I was off the phone and on my way within five minutes. I lived approximately thirty minutes from the hospital in Orange Park. I don't know how I did it, but I was in the parking lot walking into the emergency room within twenty minutes. When I finally found Dawn, she was sedated, and the doctor was still in her room.

"I'm Dawn's father. What is going on? What is Dawn here for?" I asked.

"Mr. Hoffman, your daughter came in earlier today complaining of headaches," the doctor began to explain. "We were finally able to perform a CAT scan and an MRI. Mr. Hoffman, I am so sorry to tell you this, but we found four tumors on her brain."

I thought my legs were going to give out. I had to grab hold of the bed next to me.

"Mr. Hoffman, Dawn said she has an appointment soon in Gainesville," the doctor continued.

"Yes, Doctor," I confirmed, "she has one on Thursday."

"Try and get her in tomorrow if you can," the doctor said.

What am I hearing here? I thought to myself. *This can't be really happening.* About that time, Dawn's mother arrived and told me she was taking Dawn home with her. Before they left, I told Dawn that I would contact Gainesville and would get back with her first thing in the morning. To this day, I don't remember driving home that night. One thing is certain, though—I didn't get any sleep that night.

I was on the phone at exactly eight o'clock the next morning. I spoke to Colleen at the Cancer Center and told her what had happened the day before. She asked me for names and phone numbers and said she would contact Orange Park Hospital and have them fax down the paperwork for her to review. Colleen told me she would call me later to advise me on our next steps. About two hours later, Colleen phoned to say she had the paperwork and the findings were confirmed. She told me that Dawn couldn't be seen at the clinic that day but recommended that I take her to the ER in Gainesville. "At least now they will be able to give her something for the pain," Colleen said.

So off we went to Gainesville—Dawn, Cathy, and I headed to the ER. Cathy is Dawn's stepmother. We arrived at eleven o'clock in the morning. By the time Dawn was seen and we were heading home, it was midnight. If we had brought a change of clothes and things, we would have stayed in Gainesville, because Dawn had her two appointments the next day.

CHAPTER TWO

DAWN STAYED AT her mother's that night, and I told her I would pick her up at nine o'clock the next morning to head to Gainesville. First thing Wednesday morning I phoned Dr. Friedman's office and spoke to Colleen. I faxed down the test results from the night before, and she had them reviewed. She phoned me back and told me that the likelihood of Dawn's recovery didn't look good. I was over at Dawn's mother's house when I received that call, but I never told Dawn what Colleen had said. I told Linda and Kristie Lynn, (Dawn's Sister) and that was it. Cathy went to Gainesville with us that day.

On our way home that night, Cathy said she would drive, because I have trouble with oncoming lights. The roads to Gainesville are all two lanes, and that bothers me. Shortly after getting out of Gainesville, I closed my eyes to take a nap, but with everything that went on I couldn't sleep at all. Cathy and Dawn thought I was sleeping, however, and started to play this game. You pick a letter and find something along your trip that starts with that letter. At nighttime, it's very hard, because you can't see very much. We were on State Road 16 heading toward Green Cove Springs, just past Camp Blanding. We came up on State Road 24, which takes you into Middleburg. As we passed the exit, the two girls were on the letter *K*.

Dawn yelled out, "Knife."

"What are you talking about?" Cathy asked.

Dawn explained that there was a knife in the road.

"It's not a knife in the road; it's a fork in the road," Cathy corrected. They got to laughing so hard that I started to chuckle too.

Dawn said, "Cathy, listen to Dad. He sounded like a pig snoring." I did it again, and we all started to laugh.

We arrived home at midnight, and we knew it would be a short night. I told Dawn that we would have to leave no later than nine o'clock again in order to get there early enough to eat lunch.

No matter where I go I always have an Ohio State hat on. I realize Gainesville isn't the best place to wear it, because of their feelings toward us. They beat us in football and basketball to win the national championship in January 2007, but they were still pretty nasty toward Ohio State. I really don't know why they felt that way. I don't know how they would feel if we would have won.

When we arrived at Shands, Dawn and I went to the cafeteria to eat lunch. We had forty-five minutes before her appointment. When we finished, we walked out into the atrium to look at the booths that were set up. We came up to this one that had dolls on it. There was one doll in particular that looked so much like Dawn when she was little—long blonde hair in pigtails and blue eyes. Dawn kept looking at it like she had to do something with it.

It was time to check in for her MRI. When we got there, we were told they were about forty-five minutes to an hour behind. We explained that Dawn had a two o'clock appointment and were told they would notify the doctor that we would be late getting to his office. We sat down next to a lady who had her twelve-year-old daughter with her. The little girl had a tumor of some sort on her brain that made her revert back to a five-year-old. The mother told us that her daughter would always be that way. Dawn got to talking to the little girl, and a few minutes later, she told me she would be right back. Dawn left and was gone for about fifteen minutes. When she returned, she had that little blonde-haired doll and gave it to the little girl. Dawn had gone and bought it for her. How sweet was that?

The little girl's mother had told us that just a month before her daughter had become ill, she had given away all of her dolls. She had told her mother that she was too old for dolls. The mother went on to say that the little girl liked playing with dolls but didn't have any. That is why Dawn went and bought the doll for her. It was like the first time Dawn saw that doll she knew she was going to do something with it. The smile it put on that little girl's face was priceless. The smile it put on Dawn's face was also priceless.

It was finally Dawn's turn to receive her MRI. By now, it was two thirty, and we were told that the test would take an hour. She was scheduled for a full skull MRI, which is why it would take so long. Dawn was given some medication to relax her, because of the tunnel-type atmosphere of the machine. She was told to take it forty-five minutes before her scheduled appointment, but by the time she got in, they had to give her more.

Dawn came out at 3:45, and we headed back into the hospital to see Dr. Friedman, the neurologist. This whole time Dawn would point out my Ohio State hat to people, and I would get some looks and some comments. I told Dawn to stop, but she would just laugh. We checked into Dr. Friedman's office and didn't have to wait long, because he was through with all of his patients for the day. We were sitting in the exam room and in walked the doctor. He had on a light blue jacket and an orange tie.

Dawn said, "Look, Dad. The doctor is wearing your favorite colors."

Dr. Friedman stopped writing and looked to see what he was wearing. He looked at me and asked me if I liked the Gators. Dawn said, "Oh no, Doctor. He likes Ohio State."

The doctor looked at me and said, "So do I. I graduated from Ohio State." I thought Dawn was going to fall off her chair laughing.

The majority of the time specialists have no bedside manner whatsoever. They are very short and don't like to answer questions. Dr. Friedman fell in love with Dawn. He started to joke with her about the colors and trying to get me in trouble. He then went on to say that he reviewed the MRI and was sending us over to the Davis Cancer building to see Dr. Amdor. He told us that he had already spoken to him, and he would wait for us to show up. That scared me. I asked Dr. Friedman if he would talk to us about the MRI, but all he would say was that Dr. Amdor would go over it with us. This entire time Dawn stayed positive about the whole ordeal. If it was bothering her, she sure didn't show it. This was the beginning of a major change I started to see in her. I probably would have been hysterical.

We left Dr. Friedman's office and had to catch a shuttle over to the Davis Building. When we arrived at the check-in desk, the receptionist was expecting us. She called for one of the nurses, who came and took us to one of the exam rooms. One of Dr. Amdor's assistants came in and proceeded to tell us he would go over some things before Dr. Amdor joined us. Now, I should note that Shands is a medical school hospital, and this assistant was finishing up his degree. He was one of the ones I talked about before—no bedside manner, no patience, and very rude. Dawn even asked him what his problem was.

He asked some questions and then told us that Dr. Amdor would be in. When he left the room, both Dawn and I looked at each other and made that same comment: "What a jerk." A few minutes later in walked Dr. Amdor, and we knew immediately that he had no sense of humor. He had on a bow tie, and Dawn kept looking at me and making faces. I motioned for her to stop, but she kept going.

Dr. Amdor sat there for what seemed to be several minutes looking at Dawn's chart. Finally, he broke the silence by asking Dawn how she felt. Dawn told him about her headaches and then asked what they'd found and what could be done. The doctor tried to avoid the question Dawn was asking. In that moment, I saw another side of Dawn.

"Doctor, I want it up front," she said. "Don't sugarcoat anything. I want to know what is going on."

At that time, Dr. Amdor told Dawn that they had found eight tumors on her brain from the MRI. He then proceeded to tell her that they needed to start radiation treatment right away. He told her she could start receiving treatment the next day. Dawn looked at me and asked if that was all right. I told her it was, and then the worst question was asked—the question that turned Dawn's life upside down and started this nightmare.

"What does the diagnosis look like?" Dawn asked.

"Well, Ms. Hoffman, you do have eight tumors," Dr. Amdor began, hesitating.

"Doctor, I want to know the diagnosis," Dawn prodded.

"Ms. Hoffman, it isn't good. You have terminal brain cancer," he said.

I thought we both were going to drop down to the floor.

"How much time do I have?" she asked. The doctor told her six months to a year. We both just started crying. The doctor got up and left the room, and Dawn and I stood up and held each other. Neither one of us knew what to say until Dawn put her hands on my arms and stepped back. The next thing she said totally shocked me. "Daddy, I am so sorry, I know how much you love me, and I know this will break your heart."

This girl was worried about me. Why wasn't she worried about herself? We cried and hugged each other for a long time. I didn't want to let go of my baby girl. I felt so horrible for her.

The doctor came back in and told us that her treatment would start at three o'clock the next day, which was November 7. He gave us paperwork to take to the Hope Lodge to see if they had a room available. The Hope Lodge is place run by the American Cancer Society that has rooms where patients receiving treatment can stay. Dawn was scheduled to receive ten full skull radiation treatments every day. After the ten treatments were completed, she had to wait six weeks, and then Dr. Friedman would perform laser brain surgery on her. He had invented the procedure, and Dawn was looking forward to it.

Waiting six weeks after treatment was a necessity, because we were told that the radiation treatment continues to work that long after the last treatment. We were told they needed to try to shrink the tumors before the surgery could be done.

By the time we left the Davis Cancer Building, it was six thirty in the evening. Neither one of us was looking forward to the drive home. It was a very emotional journey home. We cried for more than half the drive home. The conversations that Dawn and I had began a relationship between the two of us that would make us inseparable.

Dawn and I both knew the rough road she was facing, the mental anguish she would have to face on a day-to-day basis, and the strength and courage she would need to find. But most of all, she knew she had to strengthen her faith. As we were leaving Gainesville, Dawn called and told her mother the news. She then called and told Kristie Lynn. They talked for a few minutes and then Dawn asked me if we could meet Kristie Lynn at the Walgreens in Green Cove Springs. Kristie Lynn had asked Dawn to spend the night with her, and I agreed to meet her.

The talks that Dawn and I had were very deep—conversations I would have never thought possible between a parent and a child. We talked about dying, a subject no parent ever wants to be confronted with. Later on in this story, I will tell you some of the conversations we had. I have to lead up to them as the time is right.

When we arrived at Walgreens, Kristie Lynn was waiting for us. She had her mother and the kids with her. We talked briefly in the parking lot, and then we both left. As I was leaving, I told Dawn I would pick her up at noon to head to Gainesville, because we had to go to the Hope Lodge before her first treatment. As we were getting ready to pull away, Dawn asked me to contact her ex-husband Erik and let him know what was going on. I told her I would and that I'd let her know what he said. We then both went our separate ways.

The remaining twenty miles I had to drive home was the longest journey I have ever made by myself because of the things that were going through my head. In no way could I even begin to imagine what was going through Dawn's head. I had promised Dawn on our trip home that I would be there for her every day. I would not leave her side. I promised her that we were going to fight this with everything we had. We promised each other that we would be each other's rock and that we would lean on each other when we needed to. We promised each other that we would be strong for each other and lift the other person up when need be. I was not going to let her down. I was going to give it all I had to stand by her side, just like she had asked me to.

On my way home, I realized that Dawn would not be able to live in her home in St. Augustine because she didn't have a car and could not get back and forth to Gainesville. I decided to talk to Cathy when I got home to see if Dawn could move in with us. Cathy met me in the drive way when I arrived home. As soon as I got out of the truck, Cathy and I grabbed each other and started to cry.

"We have something we need to talk about," Cathy said. We went in the house, and Cathy explained, "I want Dawn to move in with us, so we can take care of her."

I told Cathy that I wanted to bring it up, but she beat me to it. So we both agreed that after Dawn's treatments, she would move in with us.

Needless to say, Cathy and I didn't get any sleep that night. Who in their right mind could sleep after hearing that kind of news? I kept thinking about all the treatment Dawn would be receiving and the rough road she had to face. She would not have to face them alone—I had promised her that.

CHAPTER THREE

THE PHONE RANG early, and I couldn't think who it could have been. When I answered, it was Dawn wanting to know what I was doing. I told her I was sitting on the lanai thinking. At no surprise to me, she hadn't gotten any sleep either. I told her I would pick her up, and we would have lunch before checking in at the Hope Lodge. As we were eating lunch at Applebee's, I asked Dawn if she would move into our home so we could take care of her. She smiled and said, "Thanks. I was hoping you would ask."

After lunch, we went to the Hope Lodge and met with Jackie, the assistant manager. We filled out the paperwork, and she showed us what a room looked like. The room was pretty nice; it was large with a table and two chairs for you to eat meals or do work on. There was a sofa, end tables, and a coffee table. They had a phone with an Internet hook up. Then there was the bedroom, which had two twin beds, and the bathroom. It was a real nice setup for the patient and a family member. Jackie also gave us a tour of the building and the grounds. The setup in the kitchen area was pretty neat. They had six little kitchens and all of the pots and pans to go with it. The refrigerators were divided up, so each room had its own section. Everyone was assigned cabinet space, which came with a lock and key.

Jackie then told us we couldn't start staying there until after Dawn's second treatment. That wasn't so bad, because we were planning on going home after her treatment on Friday and not coming back until her Monday treatment. We told Jackie we would see her on Monday after Dawn's treatment. The Hope Lodge was four blocks from the main hospital and three-quarters of a mile from the Davis Cancer Building. All of Dawn's treatments would be done at the Davis Building. There were shuttles that ran all the time to these places, but Dawn and I decided to drive. That way we never had to wait, and if needed to go to a store, we could just go.

We left the Hope Lodge to head over to the Davis Cancer Center. All of a sudden both Dawn and I became very quiet. As I told you before, I started seeing a change in Dawn from the moment they told her she was terminal. Her actions and conversations were comforting to others. She never talked about herself or what she was going through.

Here is a good example. As we were driving to her treatment, Dawn said to me, "Daddy, are you all right?"

"Yeah," I told her.

"Then why do you look so worried and aren't talking to me?" she asked. "I'm going to be all right through this treatment. You don't make yourself sick, because you promised to be by my side."

At that moment, I looked into her eyes. The look I got was concern but also peaceful. I knew then that I wasn't dealing with the normal Dawn. If it was, then her whole upbringing wasn't her.

Let me explain. When Dawn was growing up, she would tell us all the time that she didn't feel good. "I have a headache." "My stomach hurts." "I have a hangnail," she'd complain. But since she'd found out about her cancer, I had never heard her complain about not feeling well. Not one time did she say that she was in pain. What was happening and making her different? All of a sudden, Dawn had more strength and courage than I had ever seen in her.

We arrived at the Davis Building and checked in. Dawn was her cheerful self and talking with everyone. The lady at the check-in counter asked Dawn to fill out some paperwork. Now this lady didn't introduce herself to Dawn, but Dawn looked at her name tag and said, "Good afternoon, Ms. Harriett. How are you doing?"

I guess the woman wasn't used to that, because her whole attitude changed and she became very close to Dawn. Every day

Ms. Harriett would be looking for Dawn to check in to talk to her and find out how she was doing. That was very sweet of her. Ms. Harriett told Dawn she shouldn't have to wait too long and continued to talk with her. About five minutes went by before a radiation nurse came out and called Dawn's name. "Hi, Ms. Hoffman. My name is Cooki."

Out of nowhere, Dawn said, "Hi, Cooki. I like cookies better than crackers."

I thought, *Oh my gosh, what are you doing?* Then Cooki started to joke around with Dawn. The two of them became friends and stayed in touch through MySpace.

Cooki then proceeded to tell Dawn that her treatment would last anywhere from six to ten minutes. Her first treatment would be longer, because they would have to set everything up to match the location of her tumors. She was in the treatment room for thirty minutes. When she was finished, Dawn was totally drained, but not one negative word passed those lips.

When Dawn's treatment was complete, we headed home. She said she felt fine and wanted to go home. Dawn spent the weekend with us. We didn't have to be back until Monday at three o'clock. We would then check into the Hope Lodge after her treatment. When we arrived, we were both pretty nervous but stuck by each other for support. Dawn said she was going out to smoke a cigarette, and I thought I would go with her. When we got outside, there were a couple of patients already there.

One of the patients was a man named Jim. Jim was in his midthirties and had a tumor on his brain. He didn't have hair, although it was gradually growing back but very slowly. He saw how nervous Dawn was, so he broke the ice and started a conversation with her. He told her she had a right to be scared and nervous being in a place she wasn't familiar with. He then told Dawn that everyone was there for the same reason, so she shouldn't feel sorry for herself. Everyone needed to help one another out, and each day would get a little easier than the day before. I could see Dawn was relaxing more as Jim talked to her. They became very close and supported each other.

About a year before Dawn's illness, she talked to me about going back to church. She told me she had been going to an all denominational church at the University of North Florida. I didn't know too much about the church, but I had heard that the younger group was going there. It never bothered me that people attend different churches. We have one God, and we worship the same God no matter what church we attend. I told Dawn that I was glad she was going back. She would meet friends there. What better place to meet friends?

Dawn's illness did not get her to return to church. Dawn's illness brought her closer to God. We went and purchased a Bible, and she bought a notebook. She began to read the Bible from cover to cover. During this time, she would write notes. The notes she wrote were unbelievable. She would read and take notes for hours.

Our conversations changed from her illness to talking about God. She would ask me if I knew this or that. It wasn't much later that she was quoting the Bible. Each and every day I saw her faith get stronger and stronger.

My work was being wonderful. They let me work from four o'clock in the morning until noon. I would then leave and head to Gainesville to attend Dawn's treatment with her and spend the evening. There were times I would just take the whole day off and spend the night with her.

One night I was at the table working on a project from work, and Dawn was on the sofa using the Internet. I asked her what she was doing, and she told me she was on MySpace. I asked her what the heck MySpace was. She started laughing and then told me it is a website that you could use to stay in touch with friends. I went over to the sofa, and she showed me how it worked.

"Modern technology." That's all I could say. I then went back to the table to work, and a few minutes later Dawn started asking me all kinds of questions. Questions like, "What college fight song do you like? What's your favorite color? What this, and what that?" I didn't think anything about it, because Dawn was always the quizzing type.

About thirty minutes later Dawn said, "Hey, Daddy. Come look."

I went over to the sofa, and Dawn had created a MySpace page for me. It had the Ohio State background, and when you pulled it up, it played the fight song. She even had me hooked up with several of her friends.

"I have no clue how to use this," I told her.

"I'll show you," she said.

I do have to admit that it was pretty addicting at first. I think Dawn realized she wasn't going to get her computer back for a while.

The days were coming and going, and during this time, the pain in Dawn's groin area was getting worse. They couldn't do any treatment on that area, because they were more concerned about her tumors. Dawn mentioned to Dr. Amdor that her groin was bothering her. The doctor sent her over to see Dr. Mildenhaul, who was a general surgeon. Dr. Mildenhaul reviewed her notes and told Dawn she should have those lymph nodes removed. This was Friday, November 14, and the doctor scheduled her surgery for Friday, November 21.

I brought Dawn home after her treatment on Friday. She felt up to traveling, so we headed home. A few days after her treatment all she wanted to do was lie down, because moving made her sick. I think on Friday she was sick but just wanted to go home. I would make a couple of stops for her to get out and walk around. I would stop in Waldo, Starke, and then Green Cove Springs.

We had a quiet weekend at home. Kristie Lynn came over and spent the day with Dawn. On Monday, Kristie Lynn set up a page on the CaringBridge website for Dawn, although I'm not sure how Kristie Lynn first learned about the site. And what a wonderful site it is. Dawn loved it. Individuals would write in and give Dawn encouraging words—comments to build her inner strength. After a couple of days of people writing in, Dawn would look and read each entry every night. Dawn asked me, "Daddy, where is your entry?" I would tell her that mine was always the first and always the last in the day. She would just laugh.

I would like to share Some of Kristie Lynn's journal entries with you. These are the actual entries made and the dates she entered them.

Welcome!!! I setup this site so all of Dawn's amazing friends and family can come visit and see how she's doing everyday! Be sure to read the latest in the journal, view the photos and drop us a line in the guestbook. Please join me on my mission and let's show Dawn how much we love her!!!!! ~Kristie :)

Background Story

I just created this site for Dawn today, 11/17/08. As soon as Dawn can, I know she will write out her story and start leaving daily updates. In the meantime, I will start :)

My name is Kristie Wooten, I am Dawn's sister. She is my everything and has been ever since she was born. No matter what Dawn and I have gone through in the past, as her big sister, I have always been soooo protective of her and have wanted to fight anything that hurts her. So, here I am now FIGHTING with her to kick this cancer's butt!!!!!!

Dawn, I love you Baby Girl!!!!!!

Always,
Kristie :)

Once everyone got wind of the site, it took off. People who didn't even know Dawn were making entries.

I watched Dawn, and each and every day I could see the determination in her eyes that she was going to fight the cancer with everything she had. One of the many conversations Dawn and I had was about how we were going to fight this. We would stay with one another and give support every minute of the day. We would continue to talk about God, love, and family. If one of us got down, the other would boost the mood up. Most of the time it was Dawn boosting my mood back to the positive side. Dawn might have had a lot on her mind, but she never showed it on the exterior.

When Kristie Lynn informed Dawn about the CaringBridge website and the purpose of it, Dawn was okay with it. It didn't take long for the word to get out that Dawn's friends could follow up with her and her status. Kristie Lynn faithfully kept the site updated with Dawn's condition.

For the first several months, Dawn would pull up the site before she went to bed. She would read every posting that was made that day. One night when neither of us could sleep, we were sitting out on the lanai talking.

"Daddy, I see you on CaringBridge every day," Dawn said to me. "You are normally the first entry of the day and the last for the day. Can I tell you something?"

"Of course you can," I said.

"Those postings give me strength," Dawn told me, "and they give me encouragement to fight this cancer.

"Dawn, I am so glad to hear that," I told her.

Then it got to the point to where Dawn couldn't read the website's posts anymore. "Daddy, please read CaringBridge to me," she said. I would read them to her every night before she fell asleep. When I was finished, she would thank me and have a little smile on her face.

I started to see another side of Dawn that I never knew she had. I saw this young lady full of strength, courage, and faith. I also started to see and hear how inspirational she was to others and how she got them to return to church or start going. Dawn was acutely changing me. You see, I had pretty much stopped going to church. I never stopped believing in our Lord Almighty; I just stopped going to church. Dawn sat me down one night on our lanai at home and told me that if we were ever going to be together again, then I had to start getting more involved with God and his most holy words. Dawn would read me scriptures and then explain them. I could honestly picture her teaching the words of God in church or some Sunday School. She was really getting good.

As time went on, my writing started to change on CaringBridge because of Dawn. Instead of writing the normal, everyday stuff like "hope you are doing well today," I started posting prayers on her site. These were prayers from the deepest part of the heart.

It was time for her surgery, which was scheduled for one o'clock on Friday afternoon. We were told to check in at eleven o'clock that morning. The whole morning Dawn asked me to stay by her side. Dawn was finally acting like a normal human being—she was nervous about the surgery.

Because Dawn would not be able to make her normal three o'clock treatment, her appointment was moved up to seven thirty in the radiation department of the hospital. We left a little early, because she just had to have her Starbucks coffee. She would get it right there in the atrium of the hospital. The girl loved her flavored coffee. When her treatment was over, she didn't want to go back to the Hope Lodge right a way. She never told me why, but I knew the reason. Dawn and I were too much alike. She didn't want to go back, because then she would just sit around and get more nervous about the surgery.

We arrived at the Lodge at ten o'clock so we could get the bag she'd packed. She was told she would be an inpatient for four to five days. Before we left for the hospital, I told Dawn I had something for her to read. I wanted her to know some things before we left. I'd written a letter to her a couple of days before and wanted her to know how I felt.

My Dearest Dawn,

This is the fifth day since we heard the devastating news. I honestly thought my heart was going to jump out of my body. It hurt so much for you; all I wanted to do was to take it right out of your body and put it in me. I wish the Lord would let me do that. You are my baby, and I am not suppose to let you hurt.

I truly saw where your heart is. Not even five minutes after you found out your illness you made a comment to me. You were more worried about me then your own self. You made the comment, "Daddy, I am so sorry. I know you love me, and this is going to break your heart." Dawn, what a warm heart you have. Yes, this is breaking my heart, but we are going to fight every day. You are going to get stronger every day. You are going to eat properly; you are going to get plenty of rest.

I know that each day you are going to feel sick from the treatment you are receiving. Please fight each day, take you medicine, and you can bounce back like you did last night (Monday November 10). Write down a journal about each day you have a treatment. List the complications you have and how long they last. List everything that helps combat this problem.

Dawn, when you were five weeks old, we almost lost you. We thanked every doctor who cared for you, and each one stated that they didn't save you. Two things saved you. 1) You fought; you never gave up. If you can do that as a five-week-old baby, then you can do it as a twenty-eight-year-old. 2) A miracle—if it happened once, it can happen again. God tests us all the time. This will make you a stronger person. Think of yourself first; fight for yourself. Then think of those two beautiful kids of yours whom you will get back one day soon.

There is so much to say. I do want to put it in writing first and then go over this with you the next time I spend the night. I want us to talk about every sentence of this letter. Do promise me that we'll do this, because I have to get some things off my chest other than by this letter. I will get them off by this letter, but I also want to talk about them.

You have opened my eyes to several things this past ten days. You have made comments that I did not even realize I was doing or did. You have told me things that I feel horrible about, and I have to live with it. What you told me was true, and I honestly did not do it purposely.

You told me that I was always harder on you then Kristie Lynn. If you believe I was, then I must have been. I truly did not realize I had done that. I took you under my wing the minute you were born.

I, in no way, meant to hurt you. Please forgive me for making your life harder. I never meant for that to happen. I wish I could go back in time and change all of that. I wasn't fair to you. I am so sorry.

You pointed out another thing this past weekend that I will work on changing. I need to practice what I preach. I have told you over and over that you do not need extra stress in your life. What have I been doing? Adding extra stress in your life. How stupid I am to not see what I have been doing. I am so blind.

I promise I will not rush you in any way. If I walk away, please believe me I am not rushing you but letting you have your time. Sure I wish you would stop smoking, but I also understand why you are. I promise I will not hurry you in smoking a cigarette. I will make the time for you. I do wish you would let someone hold them, so you could cut down. I will make sure you are on time for your appointments but not an hour early. Dawn, that is my makeup I have had since my military days. Those days are behind me, and I should not be forcing my lifestyle on you. I have always had a saying that I would rather be an hour early than a minute late. I don't think I have ever been late for anything. I promise I will work hard on this problem of mine. I am sorry for not practicing what I have been preaching.

I want to get this to you, and I will so you can read it now. Please, Dawn, you have to continue to fight. You will get through this, and I will always be by your side.

You are my love.

Daddy

I thought I had to write this to her, because I was being a total jerk. I was getting on her case about smoking and the amount she smoked. What gave me the right to tell her she should not be smoking? Heck, several of her doctors told her to go right ahead. No one could put themselves in her shoes and know what she was going through.

28

Another thing was being at an appointment early. I thought I had to explain myself to her. Then I realized she really knew how I was and didn't have to explain. I just felt better knowing that she knew I would try to change.

We checked in at eleven o'clock, we were told they were running about an hour behind. We weren't too surprised by that. The time was ticking away, and by now it was three o'clock and still no word on when they were taking her to pre-op. Dawn was getting very tired from sitting in those uncomfortable chairs in the waiting area. Short-term, they're not bad, but long-term, well, you are in trouble if that happens.

Five thirty came, and Dawn's name was finally called. Dawn asked me to go to pre-op with her. Once we got up there, we talked to one of the doctors who would be assisting with the surgery. She told us that it shouldn't take more than ninety minutes. Finally, at six thirty they took Dawn into the operating room. She was still conscious, but they had her heavily sedated. I went back down to the waiting room on the first floor. Cathy was there alone with Kristie and the kids. No one had eaten all day, so we thought we would get something in the cafeteria. We knew we had at least ninety minutes.

We went and ate and arrived back at the waiting area with thirty minutes to spare. The ninety minutes passed, and it was now nine thirty. Dawn had already been in the operating room for three hours. I called up in the recovery area and was told she wasn't out of surgery yet. Ten thirty came and still no call from the doctor. Once again, I called recovery.

"Mr. Hoffman, when Dawn is brought here, I will give you a call," the woman at the desk said.

Finally, at eleven forty-five, I received a call telling me Dawn was in recovery and that she did fine and will be fine. Recovery told me I could come up to see her.

When Cathy and I arrived in recovery, we could hear Dawn giving someone hell. When we came around, Dawn was telling the nurse she wanted something to eat. "I have not eaten since six o'clock this morning," Dawn yelled. The nurse told her she shouldn't eat, but

Dawn insisted. The nurse finally told me I could get her something. I told Dawn that Subway was the only place open downstairs because it was midnight. She told me she wanted a roast beef with lettuce, tomato, onion, and mayo. I looked at Dawn and asked her to repeat it. Dawn repeated to me what she wanted, and I looked at Cathy and walked away.

I arrived back with her sandwich and soda; the girl was starving. It didn't take her long at all to eat that and the cookie I brought her. When she finished, she wanted more, but the nurse told her not to push it. By now, it was almost one o'clock in the morning. Cathy told Dawn that when they took her to her room we would leave. At one thirty, they got her settled in her room on the fourth floor. Cathy and I went back to our hotel room.

It was a very long day, and it didn't take Cathy and me long to fall asleep. We set the alarm for six o'clock the next morning, because we wanted to shower and then get some breakfast before we went to the hospital. We arrived at Dawn's room at nine, but when we went in, there was no Dawn. The nurse told us she had gone downstairs. Cathy and I could not believe she was up and around. We went downstairs, and sure enough, there was Dawn outside drinking a cup of coffee. She looked really good compared to what she'd looked like last time we'd seen her.

I asked Dawn if she had eaten breakfast, and she said no. We went into the cafeteria, and the only place open on Saturday morning was Wendy's. As Dawn was eating her breakfast, I commented on how fast she'd eaten her sandwich the night before. "What sandwich?" she asked. I told her what she ate and what was on the sandwich. She said, "There's no way I ate that, because 1) I don't like roast beef, 2) I don't eat tomatoes and onions on a sandwich, and 3) I don't like mayo." But I assured her thats exactly what she ate, even though she didn't like anything about that sandwich. We all got to laughing about that.

We could not believe how good Dawn looked. Now she wasn't walking around; she was in a wheelchair, and being pushed around. The surgery went well, although they were not able to do the complete surgery they had wanted to do. They only removed the lymph nodes in her groin area. The doctors told us they couldn't remove her ovaries and uterus. If they had done all of that, the doctors explained, Dawn would not have had enough strength to make it through the surgery. She had two drains attached to her groin area, which she would need for several weeks.

When Dawn's treatment started, she asked Dorothy, who was the radiation technician, if she would lose her hair. Dorothy told her she probably would. On our way back to the Hope Lodge after Dawn's first treatment, we were talking about her hair. She was a little upset, because she had the most beautiful blonde hair. When Dawn found out she was terminal the crazy nut went out and dyed her hair red and got her nose pierced. She told me she never would have done this if she weren't terminal.

When we got back to the Lodge, Jackie heard us talking as we walked by. A few minutes later there was a knock on the door. I answered it, and Jackie asked to speak with Dawn. Dawn came out of her room, and Jackie gave her a couple of caps. She told her she could pick a couple more out if she wanted. Dawn ended up with five of these caps of different colors. Jackie also told Dawn that the American Cancer Society would give her a wig of her choice.

When Dawn and I were eating dinner that night, losing her hair was still on her mind. I told Dawn that when she lost hers, I would shave mine off too. She looked at me and asked me why I would do that. I told her to make her feel better. She got a smile on her face and agreed.

A week went by, and Dawn started to notice a little bit of hair here and there was coming out. The hurt I had for her was unbelievable. I know how much she loved her long hair. The Monday after her surgery I was in her room when all of a sudden Dawn started to cry. I was reading the paper and looked up to see Dawn holding a handful of her hair. Within five minutes, 90 percent of her hair was out. About that time the nurse came in and saw how upset Dawn was. She left the room, and a few minutes later she came back and told Dawn that a hairstylist would be up soon to make her look prettier.

That evening Dawn was still pretty upset. I had to head home, because I had to work the next morning. I had just arrived back in Waldo when Dawn called me. "Daddy, I'm scared," she said. As soon as I heard that, I turned around and went back to Gainesville. I couldn't leave her by herself that Monday night. On my way back to Gainesville, I phoned Cathy and told her I wouldn't be home and explained to her what had happened. I then phoned Mike and told him I wouldn't be in and that I would call him in the morning.

CHAPTER FOUR

DAWN WAS DISCHARGED from the hospital around one o'clock Wednesday afternoon. This was the day before Thanksgiving. We went back to the Hope Lodge to get some things that she wanted to take home. We planned on coming back Sunday evening, because Dawn had a follow-up appointment first thing Monday morning. On our trip home, Dawn asked me when I was going to start decorating for Christmas. I normally start putting up the outside lights Thanksgiving weekend, but I told her I didn't feel like decorating and probably wouldn't. We normally put up six to seven Christmas trees. Each tree had its own theme—a traditional tree, a fifties tree with ornaments from when we were little, a sports tree, a grandkids tree, and a military tree. I told Dawn that I would probably only put one tree up. She asked me why, and I told her with all that was going on, I didn't feel like Christmas. Well, I could just see her head turn.

She said, "Daddy, this is probably my last Christmas. I want to have a Christmas party." I told her I didn't want to hear her talk that way. She said, "Dad, you know this will probably be my last." Deep down I knew what she was saying, but I didn't want to believe it. Who would want to believe that this would be my baby girl's last Christmas?

Dawn and I had some very deep conversations. Sometimes I didn't want to hear them, but I knew I had to. Dawn was very open about her condition. She asked me if I would contact Erik. Erik had been deployed in Iraq for the past eighteen months but was due home sometime in December. I told her I would try emailing him when we got home.

We started heading home, and the feeling we both had was wonderful. Just knowing that we were going to spend Thanksgiving at home was beautiful. Dawn didn't want company, so the only ones who were going to be there for dinner would be Cathy, Dawn, and Dawn's friend Shawn, and me. Kristie Lynn had already made plans months earlier to go to her boyfriend Jason's father's house for Thanksgiving. When we arrived home, Dawn was ready to lie down. The trip wore her out. I told her to lie down, and I would let her know when Cathy got home from work.

We had two bedrooms downstairs, but Dawn didn't want them. She wanted to stay upstairs in the bonus room, which was better known as the sports room. I could understand why she wanted to stay up there, because it only had a forty-two inch TV hanging on the wall, a refrigerator, and its own bathroom. I didn't really care what room she slept in. All I cared about was that she was comfortable. We didn't have a regular bed, only a sofa bed. Dawn said that would be fine. Dawn was excited about being home, because she wanted to help Cathy prepare for Thanksgiving dinner.

We had a very peaceful evening just sitting around talking. It was so wonderful having Dawn home. Shawn spent the night, so he and Dawn went upstairs to watch a movie. Me, well, I went into the garage to start pulling Christmas decorations down from the attic. At first I wasn't excited about this ordeal, but when Dawn told me she wanted it, I was all for it. I had set my mind to do whatever she wanted. She was far from abusing it, but she knew I would do whatever she wanted.

One of the conversations we held on the night of November 6 was that we were going to make life as easy as possible. The doctors told us that is was important to keep stress out of Dawn's life, so I promised her I would make her life as stress free as possible. It wouldn't be an easy promise; however, I did my best.

It was a beautiful Thanksgiving morning in the low fifties. We were all out on the lanai drinking coffee and eating breakfast when

Dawn asked me when I was going to start hanging lights. I told her after breakfast I would start putting the lights out around the roof. Shawn said he would help me, so we went and got started. We started out front and worked our way to the back. It probably took me about forty-five minutes to get to the corner of the house in the back when I heard Dawn crying. Cathy was talking to her, so I went to see what was wrong.

When I opened the screen door, Dawn looked at me. "Everything is all right. I am crying because this is the happiest I have ever been in my entire life," she said. She was sitting there with her Bible and taking notes. I sat down with her, and we started talking about verses in the Bible.

Once again, we talked about Dawn after she was gone. She asked me to keep all of her Bible notes and to one day give them to her kids. She looked at me and asked me to start getting more involved with the Bible, church, and God. I promised her then that I would carry on where she left off.

She got me crying when she said, "Dad, do you realize from here on out that this is the last of everything for me?"

God, I hated hearing her talk that way, but it did make me think about things. I would never tell her that it very well could be. After about an hour sitting with her, I went out and finished putting up the lights on the house.

Dawn wanted to help Cathy make Thanksgiving dinner; however, she couldn't be on her feet long. She had those drain bags on her leg and couldn't stand for long periods of time. We weren't planning on eating until about three o'clock, so around eleven o'clock Dawn said she was going to lie down and watch a movie. When she went upstairs, I went out in the garage to sort through the rest of my outdoor light. All kinds of things ran through my head about what was said earlier in the day. I just sat on the tailgate of my truck and cried. I cried because I more than likely would not have Dawn at our next Thanksgiving. I already wasn't looking forward to it.

As we all sat down to eat, Dawn asked if she could say the blessing. I wish I could remember the exact words she said, but I can't. She did thank God for us four to be able to have this wonderful meal, and she thanked God for allowing her to spend it with us. There weren't too many dry eyes sitting at the table. Then Dawn's humor came out. "Okay, guys, no tears in the potatoes or gravy," she ordered. She always had a way to put a smile on our faces.

I think everyone has the same Thanksgiving tradition—a turkey sandwich later in the day. I think it was only three hours after we ate when Dawn asked us when we were going to have our sandwiches. At that time I was still full from dinner. One thing I have to say is that Dawn had a healthy appetite. She was told early in her appointments to try and eat three meals a day. We were very happy with her, because she was.

Another one of our traditions since Cathy and I've been married is to go to Garden Ridge on Thanksgiving night. On several Thanksgivings in the past, Dawn had gone with us. Nothing was said all day about going to Garden Ridge, because we didn't think Dawn would be able to go. Wrong. She said to us, "When are we leaving for Garden Ridge?" We went but made sure she wasn't on her feet long. Dawn had told me Thanksgiving morning that she wanted everything to be the same. She didn't want any special treatment. Believe me, she would tell you, "Do not patronize me."

I started to see another side of Dawn. Dawn never wanted to talk about her illness to just anybody. Dawn didn't want everyone to know how bad she really was. She wouldn't try and face this alone but only with certain individuals. That is where a lot of our one-on-one conversations came in. Throughout this story, I will put notes, letters, and emails that reveal Dawn's thoughts. She asked me to write down notes and to one day write a paper. She knew that people had questions about her health but were afraid to ask. During so many of the conversations Dawn and I had, she would ask me to take notes. I want people to know and to never forget how brave she was. Her strength was growing stronger every day. Her courage to face her horrible illness got stronger every minute, as did her faith. It blossomed into one of the strongest faiths there could be.

The rest of that Thanksgiving weekend Dawn just relaxed as much as possible. She didn't want to overdo it and start having problems with her surgery area. We made a couple of trips to the Redbox for her to get some movies, and that is what she did the rest of the weekend. She knew she had to get her strength back from her surgery.

CHAPTER FIVE

ON SUNDAY, WE decided that we would leave for Gainesville around five o'clock. Dawn had an eight o'clock appointment Monday morning, and neither of us felt like getting up super early to head down there. Sunday afternoon we went out to eat at Applebee's before Dawn and I left. We had a nice dinner, and then Dawn and I told Cathy we would give her a call when we got to the Lodge. It was a rainy day, so we wanted to take our time getting there.

Everything seemed to be okay when we first arrived back to the room. Dawn was on the computer reading her CaringBridge site, and I was doing some work at the table. Dawn told me she was going to lie down. I looked at my watch, because it was early for her. I didn't say anything to her; I thought I would just keep an eye on her. When she went and lay down, I kept the bedroom door open in case she needed me. About thirty minutes later Dawn called me and told me she was having chest pains. I immediately called the front desk and told them to call 911. It certainly didn't take long before six EMTs were in the room. They were so kind and gentle with Dawn. They sat with her for almost an hour until she didn't have the pains anymore. They contributed the chest pains to anxiety and stress. The poor girl had enough on her plate, but how could she avoid anxiety and stress?

She did fall asleep before the EMTs left and was out for the entire night. I was told to watch her and check and listen to her breathing every so often. When they told me that, I knew that I wouldn't get much sleep. I had to watch out for her. I was there to take care of her. I had promised her that, and I wasn't going back on my word. I loved her so much.

I did fall asleep at some point. The last time I remembered looking at the clock it was four o'clock in the morning. Did you ever have the feeling that someone was watching you when you were sleeping or just lying there? I did, and when I opened my eyes, there was Dawn sitting on the side of the bed.

"It's about time you woke up," she said. I asked her what time it was, and she told me that it was six o'clock. I immediately jumped up and asked her how she was. She told me she felt drained, but overall, she was feeling fine. She asked me if I wanted a cup of coffee. I told her I did and offered to go and make a pot.

"I already did," she said. "You have to get up pretty early if you're going to get one on me." I started laughing, because that is what I told the girls all the time.

As we were sitting down in the kitchen drinking coffee, several patients and caretakers came over to ask Dawn how she was feeling. Dawn was a very personable person. She talked to all of the patients. Dawn was the youngest patient there, so many of the patients and caretakers looked up to her. Dawn would talk and give them all words of encouragement. She would get them coffee or whatever they wanted. They all loved her very much. I lost track of the number of times people would come up to me and ask me how she did it. I would ask them what they meant, and they would say, "How does she stay so positive?" She was always in good spirits.

There were dozens of patients and caretakers who looked up to Dawn. Everyone would walk away feeling better about themselves when they finished talking to Dawn. One day we were outside when this lady came out to smoke. Dawn knew she was new there, because she saw her check in. Dawn went up to her and gave her the same speech that Jim had given her. I just stepped back and listened to Dawn tell this lady she would be okay. I was so proud of her. She was giving back what she had learned from Jim.

After Dawn's treatments ended at the Davis Center, she had to check out of the Lodge. She could stay home until she had appointments, which I would take her to. My work still let me stay on the schedule of four o'clock to noon. We scheduled all of her appointments for late in the day. It worked out pretty well with getting her to the appointments.

CHAPTER SIX

DURING THE DAY, Dawn filled out her invitations and mailed them out. She scheduled her Christmas party for December 13. I stayed busy in the evenings putting up all the Christmas trees, while Cathy decorated the interior of the home. Dawn made her menu list out, and we were set for the party. Dawn invited friends from her high school days, as well as some current friends. Cathy and I invited the neighbors. We all talked and agreed that Dawn would have her party downstairs, and Cathy and I would have ours upstairs.

Dawn asked Cathy and me if we would take her out to buy a dress for the party. I'm not the best to go shopping with, so Cathy and Dawn went alone. When they returned, Dawn had a beautiful black dress. She looked amazing in it. She put her wig on and said she felt like a lady again. Dawn would either wear her hat or have her wig on. She didn't want anyone to see her bald head. It wasn't too long after that she would let me see her bald head. Even though I'd told her that when she lost her hair, I would shave mine off, she wouldn't let me. I just didn't want her to feel alone. She told me that she liked my hair and wanted me to keep it.

The turnout was wonderful. Dawn had more than sixty-five guests come to her party. All of her friends from her school days knew me. All the girls used to call me Dad. As the neighbors left for the night, Dawn and her friends asked for Cathy and me to stay downstairs and party with them. Dawn was enjoying herself immensely; however, as the night went on, I could see she was getting tired. I went up to her a couple of times and asked her if she was okay and if she wanted to lie down. She didn't. The party continued with Dawn.

It was midnight, and several of her friends were still at the house. They were out on the lanai joking around and reminiscing of their high school days. Dawn looked totally exhausted, and finally, around twelve thirty I told the remaining friend that Dawn had to go to bed. Even Dawn didn't argue this time around. The next morning over breakfast all she talked about was how much fun she had.

Before Dawn found out about her illness, Cathy and I had planned on spending Christmas in Maryland. It had been several years since Cathy spent Christmas with her family. When Dawn became so ill, there was no way I could leave town. Dawn got a little upset with me because I told her I wasn't leaving her. I told her I didn't want to leave. Cathy and I had agreed that she would go to Maryland, and I would stay at home with Dawn. Cathy left for Maryland the evening of the twenty-first. She was to return home the day after Christmas, and we would have our celebration on the twenty-sixth.

Dawn decided that we should do something together. So we put our heads together and came up with the idea of seeing A Christmas Carol at the Alhambra. We decided to go on Christmas Eve, just the two of us. So, I purchased the tickets online to pick up at the box office. We were both very excited about doing this together and were looking forward to it. Dawn joked around about going on a date with her daddy. Everybody thought it was funny the way she said it.

I was leaving to take Cathy to the airport on December 21 when Dawn asked if she could stay with her mother that night. She asked me if I would pick her up on the evening of the twenty-third. I told her there wasn't any problem, and she could just call me when she wanted me to pick her up. By the time I got back from the airport, Dawn was gone. I probably became overly protective, but it sure was strange not having her home. It was just me and Phoebe, the dog.

Speaking of Phoebe, Dawn always liked her. She is a golden retriever, so what's there not to like? Before Dawn became sick, she would pet Phoebe when she came over, and Phoebe would then go and lie down in her favorite spot. From the beginning of Dawn's illness, Phoebe wouldn't leave her side. If Dawn went out on the lanai, Phoebe had to be with her, lying next to her. If Dawn was in her bedroom, Phoebe was either at the foot of the bed or at the door. Phoebe knew Dawn was very ill.

As previously mentioned Cathy and I have had multiple Christmas trees for years. Dawn has always loved the different themes. One night Dawn said to me, "Daddy, why don't you have an angel tree?" I looked at her and told her it was because I didn't need seven trees. We both laughed and changed the subject. About forty-five minutes later while sitting on the lanai, Dawn said out of the blue, "Daddy, make it a purple one."

"Make what a purple one?" I asked.

"The angel tree," she said. After telling Dawn that they don't even make purple Christmas trees, she looked me in the eyes and said, "Trust me. You will find one." I didn't give it any more thought, and Dawn never brought it up again.

CHAPTER SEVEN

THE AFTERNOON OF Tuesday, December, 23, I received a call from Dawn. When I saw the number on the caller ID, I thought she was calling to tell me when to pick her up. When I answered, she sounded terrible. I asked her what was wrong, and she told me she wasn't feeling well. She said she was running a fever and that the leg she'd had surgery on was swelling. I knew exactly why it was swollen—she hadn't stayed off of it. I asked her what she had been doing, and she told me she was at the mall. I didn't say anything to her about it. I told her to go lie down and call me in a couple of hours. We would then see if she felt better and was ready to be picked up. That was around three o'clock. I didn't hear anything from her until eight o'clock that evening. When I answered, Dawn told me she was in the emergency room of the Orange Park Hospital. The first thing that came to mind was the surgery she'd had on her leg. She told me it was a combination of the leg, fever, and a test the doctors wanted to perform. I told her I would be there within thirty minutes.

On my way of to Orange Park, it kept crossing my mind that they were going to admit her to the hospital. I just knew they would do that. I, of course, did not tell Dawn that. When I arrived and went to Dawn's room, Linda was there. Linda told me that she'd brought her to the emergency room because of her fever. She then went home.

Dawn had told me that the doctor had already been in to see her. She ordered X-rays of her leg and said they may take the drains out. For them to take the drains out they would have to make her an inpatient. The doctor never said that, but I remember them telling us that at an appointment in Gainesville. The ER doctor came in and told Dawn she was going to admit her. Dawn told her that she couldn't be admitted, because she had a date with her dad the next night. The doctor told Dawn that she would most likely be in the hospital for two, maybe three days. That meant Dawn would be in the hospital until the day after Christmas. I felt so bad for Dawn, because she was going to miss the Alhambra dinner date seeing *A Christmas Carol*. Dawn was also upset because she knew she would have to be in the hospital for what she said would be her last Christmas.

Dawn wasn't taken to her room until midnight, which meant we were in the early morning hours of Christmas Eve. After they got here settled in her room, Dawn looked at me and asked what I was going to do for Christmas. I looked at her like she had three heads.

"I am having Christmas wherever you are," I told her. "If you are here, I'll be here." Dawn fell asleep shortly after getting to her room. Around four o'clock that morning, I told the nurse that I was going to run home, shower, and change clothes. I said I would be back within two to two and a half hours. The last time I'd eaten was around noon the day before, so when I left to go home, I stopped at IHOP and ate breakfast. I ate, but I didn't really enjoy it. Everything that was happening to Dawn was really bothering me. I felt so sorry for her. I just wanted to take away all of her problems.

I did make it back to the hospital before Dawn woke up. I made sure to get back, because I didn't want her to think she was going to be there alone. I sat in the recliner they had in the room and dozed off. When Dawn woke up, she never knew I had left. There were tests scheduled for Christmas Day to see if they could remove the drains or if they would have to keep them in. They also said they may have to go in to see if an infection had set in where surgery was performed.

Dawn's morale was low, because of where she was and the time of year that it was. She told me that it wasn't fair she had to spend her last Christmas in a hospital. Kristie Lynn made a journal entry on the CaringBridge website about Dawn's status. That afternoon she had some friends stop by. They brought her some Christmas gifts and a small Christmas tree. We then decorated her room with the tree and other decorations that I went out to get.

Dawn was bummed out because we were going to miss seeing *A Christmas Carol*. I told her not to worry and that we'd see something different after the first of the year. Friends visited with Dawn off and on all day. Around six o'clock I told her I was going to run home and feed Phoebe, and I would bring dinner back for us. She told me to surprise her with something. After leaving home, I stopped at Applebee's to order take-out. When I got back to Dawn's room, she told me she didn't care what I got her because she was so hungry. I got her the teriyaki chicken rice bowl. After dinner, we watched *It's a Wonderful Life* on TV.

After talking to the doctors about the test they'd run, we were told that Dawn needed to see the specialist the next day, which was Christmas Day. I found it hard to believe that a specialist would come in on Christmas Day for a routine visit. Later we were told that the scheduled test could not be done, because the specialist wasn't there and they needed him to remove the drains. Overall, the day was a total waste of time, because nothing got done. That made both of us even more frustrated. Several times during the late afternoon we asked the nurses to have the doctor come in because we wanted to know what was going on. Not one time did the nurses call for the doctor.

I was sitting in the recliner Christmas morning playing solitaire when Dawn woke up. I wished her a Merry Christmas and gave her a kiss. She said, "I'm hungry. Can we eat breakfast in the cafeteria today?"

I was already dressed and ready to go, and it didn't take Dawn long. She didn't have to worry about makeup. She got to laughing when I told her that. On weekdays, the cafeteria opened at six o'clock, but on weekends and holidays it didn't open until seven. Dawn and I didn't mind, because we only had to wait five minutes. There was a shelf hanging on the wall next to where we were standing; it held a lot of different brochures. Dawn was going through several of them and collecting some of them. I didn't see what she was getting, and

I've never been the nosey type. I thought she would tell me if I needed to know.

Well, I guess I needed to know, because after we got our food and sat down, Dawn said to me, "Dad, if it comes down to this, would you help me with it?"

It was a hospice brochure. I thought my heart was going to stop. "We'll talk about it later," I told her.

"No, Dad," Dawn insisted. "We need to talk about it now."

"All right," I agreed. "What do you want me to do?"

"I don't want to die in hospice. I don't want to die in a hospital. I want to die at home. Is it okay? Can I?" she asked me.

"Dawn, hon, if that's what you want, then that is what you get," I assured her.

She then started reading to me about the different programs hospice had and what they offered—some before but most afterward. They had lots of counseling sessions for all members of the family. I never could figure out why most sessions were for after your loved one passed away. But who am I? I'm not a counselor.

Kristie Lynn stopped by and told us that she was putting Christmas dinner on hold. We were scheduled to go to her house at two o'clock for dinner. She said she would start it later and eat later just in case Dawn would be discharged. When morning came, I asked the oncoming nurse to let the doctor know we wanted to talk with him. He told us he was getting ready to make his rounds, and it wouldn't be long. The hospital floor wasn't that busy. Nobody goes to the hospital around Christmas. I stood at Dawn's door looking out to watch for the doctor but never saw him. At ten o'clock I asked the nurse where the doctor was and was told he'd gone home and would be back later.

"I thought you told me he was making his rounds," I said.

"He was," the nurse told me, "but then he left."

At one o'clock the doctor came in. I didn't have to start asking questions, because Dawn beat me to them. The doctor told us that the specialist wasn't coming in and that Dawn could be discharged. He went on to tell us that the specialist wasn't scheduled to come in and that the nurses' station had been told that the day before. They had also been told that Dawn could be discharged and was supposed to follow up with her doctors in Gainesville. These orders were never received or looked at by the nurses' station. The doctor told us that he hadn't come in that morning because he thought we had been discharged late the evening before.

I thought the two of us were going to come unglued. Dawn told the doctor, "Do you know that this is the last Christmas I'll be alive, and you guys kept me here? That was totally wrong. Someone really screwed up on this."

I phoned Kristie Lynn and told her we would be leaving the hospital around three o'clock and would head over to her home for dinner. I started taking things to the car, while they were finishing up with Dawn. It's unbelievable the things that accumulate in two days. Well, she did have gifts brought to her.

As we were pulling out of the parking lot, Dawn phoned Kristie to tell her we would be leaving shortly and to expect us in about forty-five minutes.

I thought, *It's not going to take us that long to get there.* "Dawn, why did you tell her forty-five minutes?" I asked.

"You'll see," she said. "Oh, when you turn on Blanding, there is a Dunkin' Donuts on the right. Stop there so I can get a coffee."

Well, we got that, and I thought, *Okay, that was less than five minutes. What else does she have planned?* As soon as we pulled on to Blanding, Dawn started talking about when she died. I told her I didn't want to talk about it. I then got in the far left-hand lane on Blanding when she told me to get in the far right. As soon as she said that, I knew what she was up to. We were coming up on Jacksonville Memory Gardens, and she asked me to pull in. I did, and she asked me to stop and park. She then asked me to make her arrangements at that cemetery. I started feeling very sick.

I said, "Dawn, please, I don't want to talk about it."

"We have to," she said. "Promise me you will do it for me."

"Yes, hon, I will do it," I promised her." Do you want to be with me when I do it?"

"No, Daddy, I trust you. You know I never liked cemeteries," she said.

The things that were going through my head as we pulled out on to Blanding were mind-boggling. How could I make funeral arrangements for my baby girl? There's no way I could do that. Then I remembered what she asked me at breakfast about hospice. *Damn, girl,* I thought. *What are you doing to me? Merry Christmas to you too.* I decided to let it slide for a day or two and then bring up both subjects to her.

When we arrived at Kristie Lynn's house, dinner was just about ready. All she had to do was carve the turkey and mash the potatoes, and it was time to dig in. That was good timing on everyone's part. We didn't have to wait long, which was a good thing, because Dawn and I hadn't eaten any lunch. The last we'd eaten was breakfast, and I'd gotten indigestion from it because of our conversation. I was surprised I didn't get indigestion from dinner with the conversation we had on the trip over to Kristie Lynn's.

I didn't stay long after dinner, because I was mentally and physically tired. All I wanted to do was get home and relax. Dawn stayed with Kristie Lynn, and they had their little Christmas together. Dawn said she would be home early the next afternoon, because Cathy would be home from Maryland. I got home, grabbed an adult beverage, and sat down. I tried to contemplate the two favors Dawn asked me to do for her. Sometimes I am really stupid. Out of the blue that light came on, and when it did, I realized why Dawn asked me to do this for her. I won't write it down, because it was a personal conversation we'd had just the two of us. Please trust me on this. I then felt very honored to have been asked to do it. It would be very hard, but I would get it done for her.

I sat in my chair trying to put myself in Dawn's shoes. No one on this earth can even imagine what was going on in her mind and the pain she was in. The people who say "I can imagine" are clueless unless they have been there. I have always had the upmost respect for Dawn, but watching her those two months after her diagnosis had given the word respect a whole new meaning. With the way that girl handled herself both physically and mentally, I was truly seeing another side of her. It was a side I always knew she had, but I didn't see it often and not as strong as it was.

I thought I would get a good night's sleep in my bed on Christmas night, but things don't always work out as planned. I fell asleep in my chair, which isn't something new. I did sleep through the night and woke at five o'clock the next morning. Almost every morning when I woke up, I hoped that everything going on with Dawn was a nightmare. Not one time had it been one.

I didn't do anything in the morning; I knew I had to leave for the airport around ten thirty. Cathy's flight was due in at eleven o'clock from Baltimore. Dawn wasn't going to be home until two o'clock, so I thought Cathy and I would stop and get some lunch. Her flight was on time, and I was really glad to have her home. I know she was pretty upset that she had been in Maryland while Dawn was in the hospital. She told me she was going to try to get a flight home when Dawn was admitted, but I told her not to. There wasn't much she could have done. We had a nice lunch at Longhorns and then went home.

We hadn't been home even thirty minutes when Dawn arrived. Dawn and Cathy just hugged each other and cried in each other's arms. They were both very happy to see each other. It wasn't long after that Dawn said, "Okay, it's time for our Christmas."

Dawn was always a little kid when it came to opening up her gifts or, for that matter, when she gave presents to others. She could never keep a secret for long. She would buy someone something, and before it was time to give it to the person, she would have already told the individual or individuals what it was.

CHAPTER EIGHT

IT WAS A pretty quiet week between Christmas and New Year's. Not much was going on at all except enjoying the time off. Dawn asked Cathy and me what we were going to do on New Year's Eve. I told her that we don't do anything; we just stay at home. Dawn asked me if she could go and do something with some friends. I told her if she felt up to it, I had no problem with that at all.

So on the morning of New Year's Eve, Dawn had talked to a couple of her friends—Crystal Campbell and Angie Pennington. I didn't know what was planned, but later that afternoon, Dawn said she was going to Angie's. She mentioned something about them going out to a farm in south Middleburg and building a bonfire. I really wasn't too crazy about that idea, because it was cool and damp. I certainly didn't want Dawn getting so sick that they wouldn't be able to do her laser surgery on January 13. On the other hand, how could I tell her I didn't think it was a good idea? The girl just wanted to have fun.

On New Year's Eve, Cathy and I just stayed home and watched a movie. I didn't want to wander off just in case Dawn called or came home. I guess I was that worried old dad. We didn't even stay up till midnight; lights were out by eleven o'clock. The phone did ring. It was Angie telling me that Dawn was running a fever and throwing up. I asked her if she was able to be moved and brought home. Angie said that she wasn't but assured me that she was in the bedroom with Dawn and would remain in there with her for the rest of the night. If anything came up, Angie said she'd call me immediately. I didn't hear anything until around nine in the morning. I wanted to call earlier, but I didn't want to wake up Dawn if she was still sleeping. Angie told me she would have her phone with her in the bedroom.

Dawn did make it home around five o'clock that evening. She still was feeling pretty bad. The week before Christmas Dawn was given Temozolomide, which is a pill form of chemotherapy. The medication is taken in four-week cycles with three weeks off in between each week of pills. It was set up to where Dawn's second cycle would begin two days after her laser surgery. She was told that the medication could make her sick, and they weren't kidding—it did. Dawn came into the house and went straight upstairs to her bed. Cathy made her some chicken broth, because she couldn't keep any food down. She drank some of it and then fell asleep. I stayed upstairs with her in case she needed me in the middle of the night.

There were times when Dawn would mention to me that I was being overprotective. Can you figure? After we talked about it, she could see my side, and I could see hers. She would tell me, "Daddy, I am dying. Let me have some fun." That sure opened my eyes to a lot of things. What was I going to do, just keep her cooped up? She had a very valid point. Let her do what she can do. Let her be as happy as she can be. She told me that she knew her limit, and if she had trouble with something, she would let me know.

It was the same reason she wanted to stay up in the bonus room. She loved it up there because it had everything she needed—a full bathroom, a refrigerator, and a large-screen TV on the wall. She joked around with me about it being her room, and I would have to ask permission to enter it.

She knew that one day she would not be able to climb the eighteen steps. Before I even said anything, she told me, "Daddy, one day I won't be able to come up here. I will let you know when that day is." It was very hard to imagine what was going through her head. Here was a twenty-eight-year-old who was full of spunk starting to feel her body shutting down. What willpower she had. What strength to face everyday head on. Her will to live was unbelievable.

At this time, it was January, and Erik hadn't brought Jordan who was Dawn's three year old daughter. I phoned him, and he told me he couldn't make it in December. He told me he was trying for the end of January. I then told him I would inform Dawn of that. Well, January came and went, and Erik never came to Jacksonville.

CHAPTER NINE

DAWN WAS SCHEDULED for a three-hour MRI the day before her laser surgery. Can you image a three-hour MRI? I have trouble with a forty-five minute one. That stressed her out until they told her they would give her a valium to calm her down. I wish they would have given me one. Dawn's surgery was scheduled for Tuesday, January 13. She had to check in by six thirty in the morning.

We left home at ten thirty the morning before Dawn's surgery to drive to Gainesville. Cathy had to work, so she was meeting us at the hotel later in the day. Dawn and I got to Gainesville and ate lunch. Her appointment for the MRI was scheduled for one thirty, but everyone knows you never get in on time. Try being late yourself, and they tell you, "Sorry, you weren't here at your scheduled time."

I felt so sorry for Dawn, because she had problems having MRIs done. She would become claustrophobic in the machine. Have you ever heard of a three-hour MRI? She did ask the doctor if they could put her under for the test, but they told her they couldn't, which is why they gave her the medication.

We had hotel reservations at the Cabot Lodge for two nights. The doctor didn't want Dawn going home the night of her surgery just in case something might come up like a fever, bleeding from the radiation halo, or a couple of other complications they mentioned.

They weren't too late in calling her back. She went back at 2:15, and the test was done at 4:30. Thank God it was shorter and not longer. When we were done, we went and checked in at the hotel.

Dawn said she would lie down until Cathy got there, and then we would go out to dinner. Cathy left work a little early, so she arrived at five thirty. It was a very cold, rainy day in Gainesville. I suggested that we should order something in, but Dawn wanted to go out. She said she would be cautious not to get sick.

So, off to Texas Roadhouse we went. Dawn had a ton of choices, and she decided on tilapia. The poor girl was still heavily sedated from her test. A couple of times we thought she was going to fall asleep while she ate. During the meal, she told us that when we got back to the room she was going to bed. I told her that was fine and said I'd drop her off at the hotel before going to Walmart to pick up some things I needed. It was like I'd said we'd won a million dollars. Dawn raised her head up and said, "I want to go." Dawn loved Walmart. It was still raining out, but Cathy had an umbrella for Dawn to use. It was always fun watching Dawn shop. She would look at everything that was on sale. If the price was still high, she would let you know it. She always told us she was a bargain shopper. She also used to tell us how frugal she was. We would just laugh at her. She really did look to see how to stretch that dollar.

When we returned to the room, Dawn wanted to take a shower and go to bed. We had an early rise time and a very long day for Dawn. We knew the time we had to be at radiation, but we didn't know the exact time of her procedure.

Morning came, and I woke up Dawn. She was moving a little slow for a couple of reasons. One, she didn't feel well, and two, her nerves were acting up because of what she was about to go through. I went downstairs and got her a cup of coffee. The girl loved her coffee.

We arrived at the hospital at 6:25 and checked into the radiation department. The receptionist told us to go around the corner and through the first door on the left to the waiting area. We about flipped when we entered the room, and there were twelve people ahead of us. Terrie was the nurse in charge of setting up the patients and sending them back for their halos. Terrie loved Dawn, and the two of them talked all the time. Everyone, visitors and patients alike, was fed breakfast. So Cathy and I went up to the cafeteria and brought Dawn down something to eat. It was soon after she ate that Terrie came to get her for her the X-ray and the halo. Terrie told Cathy and me that it would be at least forty-five minutes before Dawn would be back out.

I didn't know anything about the procedure they had to perform for the halo. I had asked a couple days before but never expected to see what I did when Dawn came out. It was now eight thirty, and she came around the corner with a halo on and three screws in her head. The pain she was in was unbelievable. Then the news came that Dawn wasn't scheduled until three o'clock. They said her surgery was so late because hers would take the longest due to the fact that she had eight tumors to try and shrink while all the other patients only had one.

Dawn was also the only patient who'd undergone radiation treatment and had no hair. Everyone else was going through this procedure hoping that they wouldn't need any other treatment. Everyone felt so sorry for Dawn. They all knew she wasn't feeling well, and none of them wanted her to wait that long. They all loved her, and they had just met her that morning. When she entered the waiting room at six thirty, she started joking around with everyone, and they just fell in love with her.

Dawn wanted to go have a cigarette, so I asked Terrie if I could take her outside. She said normally she'd say no, but because it was Dawn, she'd let us. We were only gone about twenty minutes when Terrie was waiting for us to return. She told us that all the patients went to her and said they wanted Dawn to go next. Dawn was so happy to hear that. We all went into the waiting area and thanked everyone. They all hugged Dawn and wished her luck. It was about fifteen minutes later when Terrie came to get Dawn. It was now ten thirty in the morning.

They told us from the beginning that Dawn's procedure would take approximately three hours. At about eleven o'clock, Cathy and I went to get some lunch. Terrie had my cell number in case they needed to reach me. I told her we would only be gone about thirty minutes. When we returned, Terrie told us that the procedure was going well and might not take the whole three hours. After two and a half hours, they brought Dawn out on the bed. The halo was already removed, and I knew she was happy about that. We were told that she would have to remain flat for at least an hour. We were then able to leave the hospital, but they recommended that we stay in town in case of any complications from the procedure. I had already reserved our room for two nights just in case.

After I got Dawn's prescription filled, we didn't get back to our room until three o'clock. Dawn was really worn out from her long day. I asked her if she wanted something to eat, but she wanted to take a nap first. She was out like a light in no time. Angie and Larry, who were good friends of Dawn, stayed for another night also, so I had someone to talk to while Dawn was resting. Cathy went on home after we got back to the room. She had to work the next day, so I wanted her to get home before dark. It was another rainy cold day in Gainesville, and I didn't feel like going back out in it. Before Dawn fell asleep, she asked if we could eat in the room. I told her that was fine with me.

After talking to Angie and Larry, we decided to order pizza. I knew the kind Dawn liked and thought we would order it around six. That way, she would have a good couple of hours of rest. Well, with the medication they gave her, we could not wake her up for anything. So I let her sleep. I was just getting into bed around eleven o'clock when Dawn woke up. First thing she wanted was a cup of coffee, then a cigarette, then food. I couldn't really find freshly made coffee at eleven o'clock at night, so she had to make do with what I found her. She told me it wasn't Starbucks, but it would do. I then went outside with her to smoke a cigarette. She wasn't very sturdy on her feet. The medication really had her drowsy. Then it was time for her to eat. She ate three large slices of the three-meat pizza.

When Dawn finished eating, she wanted another cigarette, so I took her back outside. It was pretty cold out by now, so we didn't stay out long. When we returned to the room, Dawn took a shower and went back to bed. I thought she might have trouble sleeping, but

I was wrong. She took one of her pain pills and was out again. At least this time when she woke up in the morning I would have her fresh Starbucks coffee.

We were staying at the Cabot Lodge in Gainesville, which was a very nice hotel. They had an agreement with Shands Hospital to give a discount to guests who were being treated for cancer. The normal checkout time was eleven o'clock, so I wasn't in any hurry to wake up Dawn. Everything was packed and ready whenever she was.

I was down eating breakfast when the hotel manager came up to me and said, "Excuse me, are you Mr. Hoffman?" I told him I was, and he asked how my daughter was doing after her treatment. I told him she was pretty tired. He then told me that he'd already let the front desk know that we didn't need to check out by a certain time. And on top of that, he said if Dawn didn't feel like traveling when she woke up to let him know, and the night would be on him. How many hotels would do that? I thought that was great.

Dawn woke up around quarter after nine, and I had a fresh coffee for her. She asked what time we had to check out, and I told her about what the manager had said. You know what she did? She put her coffee down and said, "Good. I'm going back to sleep," and smiled at me. She did too; she slept for another two hours. Angie, on the other hand, had to be out of the room by eleven and was going to ask Dawn if she wanted to ride home with her. I would have preferred her to come with me just in case of any complications, but I remembered that I had to loosen those reigns.

We left the hotel at twelve thirty, and it was a ninety minute ride home. I got home a little after two and knew Dawn would be about an hour later. They told me they were going to stop and eat some lunch. She got home around three thirty and was definitely glad to be home.

We were told it would be about six weeks before we knew if the laser surgery had been successful. It would take that long for the tumors to shrink. All we could do was sit and wait.

February came, and there was still no Erik. I phoned him again, because Dawn wanted to know when she would see Jordan. When I spoke to Erik, he informed me that he wasn't coming to Jacksonville, and he wasn't bringing Jordan to see Dawn. He said Jordan wouldn't remember any of it anyway. I told Erik that the visit wasn't for Jordan; it was for Dawn. He then proceeded to tell me he couldn't afford to fly down to Florida. He stated he didn't have any money or leave time. He was an individual who spent eighteen months in a war zone with tax-free money. His mother watched Jordan free of charge, and he received thirty days of vacation a year. What was wrong with this picture?

He told me that if Dawn wanted to see Jordan, she would have to travel to Kansas. I told him that the doctors informed her she could not travel. For one thing, she couldn't travel on an airline because of the eight tumors on her brain. The pressurization in itself would kill her. She couldn't travel by car, because it was fourteen hundred miles. His comment was "Oh well, I guess she doesn't get to see her."

CHAPTER TEN

A WEEK AFTER her laser surgery, Dawn told us that the lower part of her head and the upper part of her neck were hurting. We scheduled an appointment to see Dr. Staal, and he wanted us to bring her in right away. Dawn was scheduled for an MRI that same day. With all the new technology, the doctor had the results right away. The MRI showed a massive tumor on the base of her brain stem. He ordered radiation treatment starting that Monday, and it was already Friday.

Dawn's cousin Alisha came to Florida every other January during the week of her birthday to spend time with Dawn. She had her trip planned to come down this year even though she knew Dawn was ill. The last-minute radiation treatment was scheduled the week Alisha was coming, so I contacted her. I explained to her that Dawn would have to stay in Gainesville the whole week for treatment. Alisha asked me if she could stay with Dawn and take her to all of her treatments.

Sunday night Alisha arrived at the house around eleven o'clock. Dawn was already sleeping, and Alisha was worn out from the all-day drive from Ohio. I woke them up before I left for work, because Dawn had to be in Gainesville by nine o'clock that morning. The Hope Lodge was full, so I had to get a hotel for them. Because the Lodge was full, the American Cancer Society paid 75 percent of the hotel stay.

I left work on Tuesday and drove to Gainesville to spend some time with the two girls. We went out to dinner and sat in their hotel room and talked. Alisha had to leave to head back to Ohio on Friday morning, so I told them I would be back very early Friday so Dawn didn't have to be by herself. I know when Friday came Alisha sure hated to leave Dawn. Those two were always so close.

After Dawn's treatments were complete, the doctor ordered another CT scan. The scan showed that the radiation treatment didn't work very well for Dawn. It seemed every time there was news, it wasn't good. The scan showed the tumor on her brain stem had gotten bigger. The diagnosis wasn't good, and the doctor was beating around the bush. Dawn flat out told the doctor that she didn't want any sugarcoating and to tell her what to expect. Dr. Staal stated that he would like to try a very strong chemotherapy treatment, which he'd already scheduled for the next day. He explained that it was two treatments of different chemo medication that would last six hours—three hours for each medication.

We arrived for the treatments first thing in the morning, and the nurse told me I needed to stay in the room with her. She said that the first chemo medication could have some serious side effects, including stopping the patient's breathing. I sure didn't want to hear that.

About fifteen minutes into the first treatment, Dawn wasn't looking good. Then all of a sudden, she started calling my name. She couldn't breathe. I had everyone available in that room in no time. They asked me to leave the room, but Dawn wouldn't let go of my hand, so they let me stay. It didn't take them long to stabilize her, and she was breathing normally within a few minutes. They gave her an injection to counteract the chemo medicine. I could not believe the hell this girl was going through. After about an hour, they proceeded with the second treatment, and she had no problems with that one. When the treatment was over, Dr. Staal came in to see Dawn. He told me that I might want to contact Moffitt Cancer Center in Tampa to see if they had a clinical trial Dawn could get into. He explained that Moffitt was the second largest cancer center in the country.

When Dawn and I got home from Gainesville, I called the Moffitt Cancer Center. I spoke to the individual who Dr. Staal had referred me to. I was informed that Dawn would have to see a doctor first, but there wasn't an opening for two months. I told them Dawn couldn't wait two months and then added that the system really sucked.

The next morning I was sitting at my desk when a coworker came in to see how Dawn was doing. I told him what had happened and that they recommend Dawn go to the Moffitt Cancer Center. I then told Zeke that they informed me that it would be two months before a doctor could see Dawn. Now, we were having this conversation at six thirty in the morning. Zeke pulled his cell phone out and made a call. He didn't tell me who he was calling or anything.

I could only hear Zeke's side of the conversation. "Morning, Nancy. This is Zeke. Is the old man still at home, or did he leave for work?" There was a few seconds of hesitation before Zeke said, "Yes, I'll talk with him . . . . Hey, Bill, I was wondering if you could do me a favor. I have a coworker here whose daughter has terminal cancer, and they found a new spot on the stem of her brain. The doctors in Gainesville told her to contact Moffitt, which he did, but he was told it would be up to two months before she could be seen." Another pause. "Yes, I will have him call you in an hour. Thanks, Bill. I'll see you in a week or so."

Come to find out, Bill worked at Moffitt and had a lot of pull. He used to work for Zeke when they were in the Navy. Zeke was the best man at Bill's wedding. That hour seemed to take forever to pass. I was just about to call Bill when my phone rang. It was Bill. He told me he'd called Zeke back and asked for my number. I was on the phone for almost forty-five minutes answering questions about Dawn. When we were finished, he told me I would get a call from Colleen within an hour. About an hour later, Colleen called and asked me if I could have Dawn down in Tampa on March 4. I told Colleen I would have Dawn down that day if she wanted me to. Now get this, this happened on February 26. What a far cry from the two months I was told before. Bill got Dawn in to see a doctor, and not a regular doctor but the head doctor of radiation, in less than a week. Once again, we found that it really takes knowing someone to get things done.

I couldn't thank Zeke enough for what he'd done. Dawn asked me to invite him over, because she wanted to meet him. Come to find out, he was going to be in Tampa the same time we were scheduled to be there. Because Dawn's appointment was early in the morning, we went down the day before. We couldn't see getting up and leaving at four in the morning.

Once again, the hotel we stayed at was wonderful. They also had arrangements with the Moffitt Cancer Center for patients. Check-in time for patients was one o'clock. We got to Tampa at eleven, because we planned on eating lunch before we checked in. The trip totally wore Dawn out. I pulled up to the hotel to see if we could check in early, and they took us in immediately. When we got into the room, Dawn said she was going to lie down and asked me to get lunch and bring it back. I went to Panera Bread and brought it back to the room. Dawn wasn't feeling well at all, so I let her sleep for a little longer. She woke up, ate, and lay back down. Zeke and I had made arrangements for the three of us to go out to dinner. Dawn was really looking forward to that.

I had called and left a message for Zeke to tell him what room we were in and to call me when he finished for the day. He called around five, and we planned to leave to eat at six. Dawn was still not feeling well and asked me if she could just stay in the room and have dinner brought back to her. I told her that wasn't a problem. I even told her I would cancel going out with Zeke. She didn't want me to do that, so Zeke and I went out. Zeke did come to the room and met Dawn. They hit it off very well, joking and cutting up with each other.

We left for dinner, but I told Zeke I didn't want to be gone long. We went to Longhorns, which was a mile down the road. We ate and came right back. Dawn wanted some broccoli cheese soup, so I brought her some back. She was awake when we arrived back into the room. She talked to Zeke for about an hour. She then asked if she could go down and smoke a cigarette, so the three of us went outside. When we got back to the room, Dawn took a shower and was out for the night.

I was glad to see that Dawn went to bed at a decent time. I knew the next day would be a very long one for her. We were planning our return around her. After her appointment, if she felt up to the drive, we would head home; if not, we would stay another night.

We were only a half a mile from the University of South Florida where the Moffitt Cancer Center was located. What a beautiful campus it is. What a wonderful setup they had for cancer patients. Everything was color-coded to tell you exactly what section of the hospital you had to be at. The same was true of the parking garages; you just pulled up, and it was valet parking by color.

I could tell Dawn was nervous. She wanted the doctor to tell her she was eligible for a clinical trial. We arrived at the site of her appointment, and the waiting area was packed. We both thought we would have a very long wait, but we only had to wait fifteen minutes past her appointment time, which surprised us both.

First the nurse came in, and she and Dawn hit it off right away. I couldn't believe how fast they started joking around. It seemed everywhere we went people fell in love with Dawn. She had the brightest outlook on life and the most strength and courage you would ever find in a person.

A few minutes later, the physician assistant came in. She told Dawn that it was routine for the PA to see the patient before the doctor came in. The PA asked Dawn several dozen questions that covered everything from when she first noticed her problem to her pain level. Dawn was always in a tremendous amount of pain. Then the PA looked at me and asked me if I minded stepping out. I looked at Dawn, because she always wanted me present when someone was talking to her. Dawn asked the PA why she wanted me to leave, and she told Dawn she wanted to talk to her about something private. Dawn said that if it didn't have anything to do with taking her clothes off, she wanted me to stay. The PA started to object, but Dawn stopped her. "My dad is not leaving this room without me," she said. The PA looked at me then looked at Dawn. You could tell she was contemplating whether to say what she wanted to at first.

She started talking to Dawn about her pain, asking her if her medication was effective with her pain. Dawn told her that her medicine worked but didn't last long enough for her next scheduled dose. The PA then looked at me again and then asked Dawn if she ever thought about smoking marijuana. She told Dawn that it would help with her pain in between her scheduled doses. Dawn looked at me, and I know she saw a shocked look on my face. The PA then started to explain what marijuana could do for her.

Nothing more was said on that subject with the PA. She left, and a few minutes later the doctor came in. The doctor checked Dawn over, and then they talked. The doctor told Dawn that the next available clinical trial was a month away, but she didn't have time to wait for that. The tumor on the stem of her brain was growing at a fast rate. He told Dawn that she would need radiation treatment immediately and would recommend Shands in Gainesville to start right away.

Dawn had such a disappointed look on her face but still said she was going to fight. She wanted a clinical trial so much. Before we even left the room, the doctor came back in and told Dawn she had a scheduled appointment in Gainesville for the radiation treatment. It was the very next day.

We left the hospital and started home. At first, no one was talking. We were both trying to absorb what had just taken place. Then Dawn asked me the question about the marijuana. She asked me my thoughts on it, and I told her my beliefs about illegal drugs. I told her I had dozens of sailors either busted or kicked out of the Navy because of their use. However, after reading articles about it being used for medical reasons, I told her that if it relieved her pain, I would find it and buy it for her. She laughed, but she never went that route.

We were traveling on Interstate 4 when we were passing the Lakeland area. This time of the year was the strawberry festival. Dawn loved fruit, so she asked me to stop. We brought home more strawberries than you could imagine.

We started home from Lakeland when Dawn reached in the backseat and grabbed a couple of strawberries. I asked what she was doing,

"I'm going to eat them. What do you think I'm going to do with them," she said.

I said, "You have to wash them first."

"Dad, what's it going to do to me? Kill me?" she asked. She had a way with words, that's for sure.

I told her to stop eating them and offered to stop if she was hungry. So we ended up stopping and eating a meal.

By the time we arrived home, Dawn was totally worn out. She couldn't travel for more than an hour without it getting to her. When we arrived home, she went to her room and lay down. I asked her if she wanted me to wake her up for dinner, but she said no. She said she'd get something when she woke up. I told her that we would have to leave no later than seven o'clock for Gainesville for her to start her new treatment.

This treatment consisted of one major radiation treatment on the back of Dawn's neck. A normal radiation treatment lasts from three to six minutes per session. This one-time treatment was scheduled to last approximately fifteen minutes.

So, we were off to Gainesville at seven o'clock the next morning. Dawn was up most of the night, as was I. We sat out on the lanai and talked for hours. We talked about everything under the sun—or the moon, as was the case. Some things are open to discussion, and other stuff was personal—just between Dawn and me. Our trips together were always interesting. The conversations we had were priceless.

Dawn's treatment time was on schedule, and Dawn did fantastic during it. Her dear friend Dorothy in radiation always looked out for Dawn. Heading back home and knowing we didn't have to return to Gainesville for a couple of weeks was nice. That trip would put a toll on Dawn, but she never complained.

CHAPTER ELEVEN

DAWN HAD ALL of her belongings at Fort Riley, Kansas. After she found out Erik divorced her, she hung around Manhattan for about a week trying to talk with him and trying to see Jordan. With no luck and no money, Dawn had to return to Jacksonville without all of her belongings or Jordan.

During the first part of March, I spoke to Erik, and he told me that Dawn needed to get her things out of his house. I told him to box it up and to ship it to my house. Not one time did he tell me the amount of things she had. Then on Saturday, March 7, 2009, I spoke again with Erik. He informed me that Dawn's belongings had to be picked up by Thursday, March 12, 2009, because the movers were coming and packing his stuff up. That is when I found out what all Dawn had. There was no way I was going to let her stuff be left behind and lost.

Without much notice, I couldn't find anyone to travel with me to help. I asked Erik if he would pick me up at the airport, which was two hours away, but he said he couldn't get off. I then asked him if he would help me load the truck, and he told me he would do what he could. My neighbor Don said he would try to get off to help me drive back but later found out he couldn't get off the flight schedule. Don is a naval officer pilot and flies the H60 Helicopter. When he came home from work on Monday, he informed me he couldn't get off work.

So on Tuesday, March 10, 2009, I flew out to Kansas City International Airport. The whole flight out I was wondering how

I was going to load a sixteen-foot U-Haul by myself. I also knew it was going to be a very stressful visit once I arrived at the base. All I wanted was to get Dawn's belongings and visit with Jordan.

Dawn did not have a copy of her divorce papers, so we didn't know exactly what had been awarded to her by the courts. I asked Erik for a copy, and he informed me that I could get a copy from the Manhattan courthouse. I called them the day before I flew to Kansas, and they informed me that it would take up to thirty days to have a copy sent to me. I then asked them if I could stop by the courthouse and pick up a copy but was told they needed a couple days' notice. I explained to them that I was coming to town the next day and would be leaving the same day. I had no luck whatsoever.

I arrived in Kansas at ten thirty, and after picking up my luggage, I caught a shuttle bus to Manhattan, the town right outside of Fort Riley. The driver of the shuttle was a retired army soldier, and we had a couple of conversations before we departed the airport. He asked me where I was going, and I explained to him I had to stop at this U-Haul store in Manhattan. He told me he knew exactly where it was and would drop me off there. That was a relief.

I forgot to tell you that it was twenty-four degrees when I landed. Being from Florida, I didn't own a winter coat. The jacket I had on was my winter coat in Florida, but it would have been a jacket most Midwesterners would use in midspring. That was the least of my worries.

After getting my truck, I headed to Fort Riley. It was only ten miles from the base, and I just hooked up the GPS and headed to the base. Because I am retired military, it was a little easier to get on to the base. Once I got on base, I headed to Erik's home. When I pulled up, Erik was standing at the door. By now, it was three thirty, and he informed me he had been off since ten o'clock. He was still in uniform; I couldn't figure that one out. I know during my military days, if I got off early, I got out of uniform. Another thing—he told me he couldn't pick me up from the airport, but he was off. It cost me ninety-eight dollars plus a tip to get to his house from the airport.

There wasn't any small talk between us because I wanted to get the truck loaded and hit the road. I have never been a big fan of driving at night, because I have trouble with oncoming lights. Here I had a sixteen-foot truck, and after seeing all of Dawn's things, I didn't know if I would be able to get everything packed by myself. Erik helped me with the big, heavy items, and I packed the rest. All of the things were down in the basement, and I had to carry them up the steps, out the door, back down some steps, and to the truck.

Around four thirty, Erik told me he had to leave at five to pick up Jordan from the day care center. I told him I would stay behind and start loading the truck. I was putting everything outside the truck to try and pack things by size. When Erik left at five, I stayed behind and packed the items I had on the sidewalk into the truck.

About the time I finished, Erik arrived home with Jordan. What a beautiful little girl she was. She looked so much like Dawn at her age. Erik did stop at McDonald's and brought me back something to eat. I hadn't eaten all day and was starving. I knew I had a couple more hours of work to do, but I did stop working to eat my sandwich.

Jordan and I were eating in the kitchen, while Erik was in the basement sorting through boxes and putting aside the boxes I had to bring up. I knew I had several hours to go before I would have the truck loaded. There was one major concern that was always on my mind—I didn't want to be away from Dawn in case she needed me. I knew she was in good hands with Cathy, but it was that father instinct about getting home.

I wanted to spend a little time with Jordan, but I knew I had to get back on the road. I finally finished loading the truck at eight o'clock, and Erik asked me if I wanted to spend the night so I could spend time with Jordan. I told him my plans were to drive to at least Kansas City, spend the night, and hit the road first thing in the morning. I just knew I had to start heading east. I knew I wouldn't get far, but two hours was two hours closer to home.

So off I went. I hit the interstate not knowing how far I would make it. It had already been a very long day. By the time I got to Topeka, it was almost ten o'clock, and I thought I would stop for the night. I don't know why I did, because I sure couldn't rest. So at one o'clock in the morning, I got dressed and hit the road toward Kansas City.

The traffic wasn't too bad, and I told myself that if I started getting tired, I would pull over at a rest area. I wanted to get home, because I didn't want to be away from Dawn that long. With a loaded sixteen-foot truck, I sure couldn't move very fast. I ended up having to spend the night at the Tennessee-Georgia state line. I did at least get a little more sleep that night and was on the road by four o'clock in the morning. I needed to get through Atlanta before the morning rush.

I finally pulled into my driveway at noon, and Dawn was waiting for me with open arms. All I wanted to do was put my arms around her. That was one trip I will never forget in more ways than one, if you know what I mean. I was too tired to do anything with the truck and her things, so I just parked the truck and left it for the next day. On Saturday, I took Dawn's things to Atlantic Storage for her.

During my trip home, so much was going through my head. Most of it was about Dawn. How was she being so strong? How was she able to wake up every morning knowing her condition and still have a bright day? I can't think of anything that could have been said that would have been worse.

CHAPTER TWELVE

DAWN WANTED TO go through the things I brought back, so I would pick up around six to eight boxes from the storage unit for her to go through. This was a very sad time, because Dawn saw not only her personal items but also items that were hers and Erik's. The worst thing she found were gifts that she had sent for Jordan. These items were never opened. There were toys that were never played with. Most of the items were still wrapped and never looked at. That broke her heart. There was so much hatred in Erik's heart. Dawn called Erik and asked him why he never gave Jordan her gifts, and he just laughed at her. What a hateful person.

A couple days before St. Patrick's Day, Dawn asked me if I was cooking corned beef, cabbage, and potatoes. I told her it wouldn't be St. Patrick's Day without such a meal. Dawn loved that meal, so I thought I would get two large briskets. That way, we could have leftovers.

Normally, if St. Patrick's Day falls on a weekday, we would wait till the weekend to cook. If I did it after I got home from work, we would be eating really late. But because I was home during the afternoons to be with Dawn, we decided to cook it that day. Dawn wanted to help, so I let her.

I truly believe that corned beef and cabbage was one of Dawn's favorite meals. It was dinnertime, and the three of us sat down to eat. Dawn was sitting across the table from me, and Cathy was next to us both on the side. Cathy finished eating and said she had a few things to do. Dawn and I were still eating when we noticed that there was one slice of corned beef left on the platter. Dawn and I would both look at the platter and then look at each other. This went on for a couple of minutes. All of a sudden, the phone rang, and I got up to answer it. When I did, I heard Dawn laughing on the phone. I turned around, and there was Dawn with her cell phone, laughing. She had the slice of corned beef on her plate. I thought that was so funny. She did things like that all of the time.

I was so amazed and proud of Dawn. With all she was facing, she still kept a positive attitude. I can honestly say I don't know if I could have done it. About a year before she found out she was sick, Dawn returned to church. She went to the All Denominational church that was at the University of North Florida. She asked me if I minded, because she had been raised Catholic. I told her that I don't go to the Catholic church and hadn't for years. I told her I now went to the Methodist church. I then told her that in my opinion, it doesn't matter what church a person goes to, because there is only one God, and we all worship him.

Dawn had a friend named Larry (Flash they called him). Dawn helped him in his business by keeping his books. Larry was in the sign business. Well, Larry got Dawn to attend his church, which was Arlington Church of Christ. Dawn started to tell me about the minister of the church. "Dad, you have to meet Acie . . . ." Acie this, and Acie that. She loved Acie.

There were times Dawn would drive herself to church on Wednesday evening and on Sunday. She was still able to drive, so I let her go. She knew the time would come when she wouldn't be able to. Here was a twenty-eight-year-old, and she was dying. What was I to do, stop her from doing anything? I don't think so.

When the time came that she couldn't drive, I would take her. I finally got to meet Acie. What a wonderful man. I can't think of a kinder person in this world than Acie. I can see why she loved him.

If Dawn wasn't in church, she was reading or listening to the Bible. Cathy and I bought her the audio Bible. She would sit out on the lanai for hours at a time reading and taking notes, listening and taking notes. She asked me to pass the notes she took on to her kids one day. I will for sure do that.

Dawn used to read scriptures to me. I learned more from her about the Bible than I'd learned my entire life growing up. For five to six hours a day she would be with her Bible studying and learning the scriptures. She told Cathy and me that The Acts of the Apostles was her favorite book of the Bible. I had to laugh one day when she was talking about Job. I picked up her Bible and turned to that section and started reading it. She took the Bible and asked me if I had ever read the entire Bible. I told her I hadn't, and she told me that I should start at the beginning. I thought that was so funny. She would not let me read Job.

We are now at the end of March, and one Sunday I ran to the store to get Dawn some things. When I returned, Dawn and Cathy were sitting on the lanai. I went outside, and Dawn said, "Dad, we're having a party." I asked her what kind of party she had in mind, and she said it would be a spring party on April 11, the day before Easter. I told her that would be fine and asked who she planned on inviting. She said that it wouldn't be as many as she invited to the Christmas party. I told her she could invite anyone she wanted. So the next day I took Dawn to the store to buy invitations.

That night she sat on the lanai and filled out her party list and invitations. The next morning I went and got stamps and mailed them for her. She told me she wanted to go to the store with me to buy the food for the party. She knew I loved to cook out, so she wanted me to do chicken, ribs, and steaks. Cathy and I were going to make this a wonderful party for her.

CHAPTER THIRTEEN

ALL OF DAWN'S treatments were over for the time being. I was to take her back in the middle of April for some more tests. On Saturday, April 4, Dawn was feeling really sick. She told me her neck and back were hurting her more than usual. I phoned the Davis Cancer Center, and they instructed me to take her to the nearest emergency room. So off we went to Baptist South with instructions from her doctor in Gainesville.

After the MRI and CT scan were complete, the neurologist came into Dawn's room and told her some bad news. She said that the tumor that was located on her spine right above the shoulder blades was growing. The radiation treatment she'd had didn't do any good. The doctor then told us that Dawn had a tumor that was on her brain stem on the back of her neck. God, I will never forget that day. The doctor told Dawn that to contact Dr. Staal in Gainesville on Monday. They let me bring her home Sunday evening. The doctor asked for Dr. Staal's phone number and said she would call him first thing Monday morning.

Midmorning on Monday the phone rang, and it was Dr. Staal from Gainesville saying he'd just gotten off the phone with the neurologist from Baptist South. He then informed me that no more treatment could be given to Dawn, and I needed to contact hospice. He went on to tell me that the tumor on her spine had no reaction to the radiation treatment, which couldn't be given in the same place twice. Plus, the tumor on her brain stem would make her a quadriplegic.

I was totally speechless. The doctor asked me if I was still on the line. What could I say with the two sets of bad news he'd just told me? I then started asking him questions about hospice, and he answered my questions. I also asked him about her becoming paralyzed and was informed that it would be within the next week or two, because the tumor was growing so quickly.

The whole time I was talking to the doctor I was watching Kristie Lynn and Rena, a friend of Kristie Lynn and Dawn, talk to Dawn out on the lanai. *How am I going to tell Dawn this news?* I wondered. *How can I tell a person who is so active that she is going to be a quadriplegic within the next couple of weeks?* The doctor asked me if I wanted to tell Dawn the news or if I wanted to bring her to his office so he could talk to her. I told the doctor I would talk with her, and we hung up.

When I finished talking to the doctor, I just sat down to try and get my thoughts together. What was I going to say? Should I have had the doctor tell Dawn? Dawn knew I was talking to the doctor, because when he phoned, he asked to speak to Dawn. Dawn got on the phone and told the doctor to talk to me. She then went outside with the others. I knew as soon as she saw I was off the phone, she would start asking questions. *God, please help me*, I prayed to myself. *How do I tell her this? How could you make her a quadriplegic on top of all her other illness? Please, Lord, don't put her in a wheelchair for the short time she has left.* So for the next five minutes I continued to pray, pleading with God to not take her feelings away in her body.

I couldn't even think straight. I sat in the dining room after I prayed to God, and then Kristie Lynn came in to find out if I was still on the phone. As soon as she saw me, she knew it wasn't good news. Like Kristie Lynn used to say, every time Dawn got news, it was bad news. She could not catch a break on anything.

I then went outside and sat down. Dawn wanted to know what Dr. Staal had said. I hesitated at first, and then Dawn said, "Daddy, just tell me." She used to tell the doctors that all the time. "Don't sugarcoat anything," she'd say, "just tell me the facts."

I then proceeded to tell her exactly what Dr. Staal told me. There was no reaction whatsoever on her face. It was like she knew what I was going to say. She got up out of her chair, came over to me, and gave me a kiss. She then asked me to contact hospice as soon as possible, because she was going to need medication. She then told us that she was going to go lie down and needed some time alone.

I helped her upstairs, because she wanted to lie down up there and watch TV. After I helped her, I went back outside and talked to the girls. I then called hospice and informed them of what the doctors had told me. Dawn was already registered with them. They told me they would call back in a few minutes. It was about thirty minutes later hospice called and told me that an ambulance would be by to pick her up in about two hours. I told them I would take her, but they informed me that as a first-time patient, she had to come in by ambulance.

After I received the call from hospice, I went to check on Dawn. At first I thought she was asleep, but as I was leaving, she said, "Stay, Daddy. I need to talk to you."

I sat in the recliner, and she turned over in the bed. "Give me your hand," she said. "Daddy, you do know that God does things for a reason."

"Dawn, I—" I started to say, but she cut me off.

"Daddy, if God wants me to finish my life as a quadriplegic, then that is what I will do. God knows what he is doing, and it's not our place to question him," she said.

What a strong young lady. Could I have handled that news like her? I hope I would, but I just don't know if I could.

All the thoughts in my head were just unbelievable. Here I had Dawn who was facing the fact she was dying and had only months, if that, to live, and now she had to face the fact that she wouldn't be able to get around on her own. What faith she had to turn everything over to God. All that kept crossing my mind was her saying, "Daddy, God knows what he's doing."

We received a call from North Florida Community Hospice around two o'clock. They were calling to confirm that an ambulance would be at our house to pick up Dawn. For two hours, we all walked around in a daze, not knowing what to expect next.

Around four thirty in the afternoon, Liberty ambulance arrived. Dawn asked me if I would ride with her. There was no way I was going to leave her alone. Cathy told us she would follow us to hospice. As we were heading to the center, all kinds of things were going through my head. How could this be happening to my daughter? Then I realized it wasn't about me, and I began to think about how Dawn was feeling. What was going through her head? Here was a twenty-eight-year-old young woman. How could she be so calm? She was so strong. I kept looking at her, and she had on a stone face stare.

As we were sitting in the ambulance, we could see the cars behind us. We were on Phillips Highway and Old St. Augustine Road when out of the blue Dawn said, "Look, Dad, Eddie Fisher." I asked her what she was talking about, and she said, "Look. Eddie Fisher—you know, the ambulance chaser."

I just looked at her and busted out laughing. Dawn never lost her sense of humor. Even in a person's lowest moments, she didn't throw in the towel and give up. She fought every minute of every day.

We were all a bundle of nerves when the ambulance arrived. God, the things that were going through my head—all the stories I'd heard about hospice. It sounded so final, and I hated to think that way. Once we got into Dawn's room and the nurses left for a few minutes, Dawn said, "You know what, Dad?"

What?" I asked.

She said, "This is really real, and it's like the final part of the stage." Dawn and I thought a lot alike. Sometimes it could get pretty scary.

Earlier in the story I told you that Dawn never sat still. She was always on the move, always had to go places. I didn't know what she was going to do now that she was inpatient. They told her she would be there anywhere from three to five days. They had to get her medication regulated. Once they did that, then they would release her to return home.

Dawn smoked cigarettes before she found out she was ill. However, she only smoked three to four cigarettes a day. After she found out her condition, she started to smoke more. The doctors told us to leave her alone, because it helped her nerves. Besides, what were the cigarettes going to do to her? It wasn't long after Dawn got into her room that she asked the nurse if she could go outside and smoke. I thought the nurse was going to hit the ceiling.

"You can't do that," the nurse said. "You are sick."

Dawn told her she might be sick, but she wasn't dead yet. The nurses and Dawn clashed for a while, because the nurses weren't use to someone that young and that mobile being in hospice. Their typical patient was at least thirty to forty years older than Dawn.

Dawn and I would take walks around the lake and the entire perimeter. I didn't care how many times she wanted to go out. When she wanted, I would help her. She loved it outside. We had some wonderful conversations during our walks.

On Thursday, April 9, I brought Dawn home from hospice. She was now hooked up to an IV twenty-four hours a day. Because Dawn was in hospice, a nurse came out to the house every day to check her vitals and make sure the IV pump was working without any problem. Even in the middle of the night, if there was any problem whatsoever we could call hospice, and they would send a nurse out. We had to do that many times until Dawn's medication was stable.

Hospice informed us that with Dawn now on a twenty-four-hour IV someone would have to be within earshot of her at all times. With Cathy working an eight-hour day and me going in early, we would need someone to sit with her from seven till eleven in the morning. Kristie Lynn lived thirty minutes away and had two kids to get ready for school, but she still made it over at seven so Cathy could leave for work. We would alternate with others to help out.

Dawn was usually still sleeping at that time. Whoever was there when she woke up would fix her some breakfast and then play games with her or just talk to her. Dawn was never short on words.

Dawn's friends knew they were welcome anytime. Several of them would come and sit with her and talk. Most of them lived at least thirty minutes away, so I asked them to call first. Dawn got worn out fairly easy. She never had a set time to rest, so I would have them call first.

CHAPTER FOURTEEN

WITH DAWN COMING home from hospice on April 9, we had our work cut out for getting her party set up. We hadn't done any of the shopping yet. Dawn told me that she wanted to go with me to pick out the meat to cook.

So on Friday, April 10, I connected Dawn's IV to her backpack, and off to Walmart we went. "Dad, would you cook your ribs and chicken?" she asked. "And I want to pick out some nice steaks."

I told her I would cook anything she wanted. So the menu was set. I was to make my potatoes on the grill, the three different meats, and homemade baked beans. Other people also brought things to go with the meal.

The weekend before the party, I was at my neighbor Lyle's house talking with the guys. Don another neighbor was also there. The four of us were talking, and we got on the subject of Dawn. Like I said before, it was like Dawn was part of their families too. I told them that Dawn was going to get to the point where she wouldn't be able to go for her walks with me. Every day Dawn I would go for a walk. Lyle asked me if I was familiar with those electric scooters. I told him I'd seen the advertisement on TV but didn't know much about them. Not another word was mentioned about a scooter.

The day of Dawn's party was beautiful and sunny—warm but with a little breeze that kept us cooled off some. There were more than sixty people in attendance, and everyone was having a good time. We had games going on in the backyard, and people were roaming around having a good time. Then all of a sudden Ryan, a neighbor boy, came riding around the corner and through the backyard on a purple electric scooter. The neighbors had all chipped in and were renting it for Dawn. Dawn was sitting at the table I had moved outside, and Ryan drove it right up to her. Dawn was speechless and started to cry. Lyle went up to her and gave her a hug and told her she could continue her walks with me.

Dawn wanted to try it out, so Ryan took it around front for her. We all went around with her to see her on it. She got on it, received instructions on how to run it, and took off. We could not believe how fast that thing moved. Dawn was zipping around the cul-de-sac at a pretty good clip. Then all of a sudden she was gone. Down the street she went, and she disappeared. She was taking it all around the neighborhood. When she came back in sight, she was really moving on it. Cathy told the neighbors they were going to come home from work one day to find all of their mailboxes knocked down from Dawn wiping them out on her ride. Dawn was so grateful for all the neighbors' thoughtfulness. I was able to rig up a system with a pole to hold her IV bag.

The party was a success, and everyone thoroughly enjoyed themselves. Dawn had purchased plastic Easter eggs, and all of the kids had an Easter egg hunt. Dawn made sure everybody had something to do. She did a wonderful job in coordinating the party. She would get worn out so fast. She had to go and lie down and told me she felt bad because she couldn't help clean up. I told her she didn't have to worry about helping, because we had plenty of help already. So off to her room she went to rest.

The last of the people left around eight o'clock that night. Most helped us clean up, and after we finished, we all sat down to relax. It was a wonderful cookout with some wonderful friends. We were so happy that Dawn enjoyed herself and the party she'd set up.

The day before the party Dawn asked Cathy and me if we would take her to a dollar store. We both got to the point to where we wouldn't ask her for what. When we got there, she asked me again how many children were scheduled to come to the party. I told her fifteen. She purchased candy, little toys, and baskets with grass for each child. That evening she was feeling really sick but told us she was going to put the baskets together. Cathy and I told her we would do it, but she insisted on doing it. Tyler, who is Dawn's eight-year-old son, asked his Mommy if he could help her, so the two went into the back bedroom and did seventeen baskets—two more than needed, just to be on the safe side.

The next day at the party Dawn was rewarded by seeing all the kids with smiles on their faces. They had an Easter egg hunt with several golden eggs. She made sure that all the kids won some sort of a prize.

CHAPTER FIFTEEN

WHEN DAWN STARTED radiation treatment in November, the doctors told her she could have some problems with her teeth. She had beautiful, white teeth and only one filling. Dawn had always taken pride in her teeth. When the spring arrived, she started having some problems with teeth chipping. Then on May 20, one of her teeth split completely in half, leaving a nerve exposed. We called around to some dentists, but because Dawn wasn't already a patient, I could not get her in soon. Finally, on the afternoon of the twenty-first, I found a doctor who would see her the next day.

The office told me to have her there first thing in the morning. On our way down, Dawn asked if she could have the laughing gas instead of Novocain. I told her it was okay with me, but we'd have to check with the doctor because of the other medication she was on. We had about an hour to wait before they took her back. You know the old saying—hurry up and wait. When they did take her back, Dawn asked about the gas and was told they didn't see a problem with it. I stayed out in the waiting area, and when they were finished, they came and got me. They informed me that the gas didn't work on her, so they had to give her Novocain.

While we were waiting for her to be called back, Dawn and I were talking about Jordan. It was Jordan's third birthday that day. Dawn asked me again if I would contact Erik and see if I could talk him into bringing Jordan to Jacksonville. I told her when we got home I would either call him or send him an email.

When we were done, Dawn told me she was hungry. The dentist had told her that she could eat, but it had to be soft foods. We stopped at Wendy's in Riverside, and Dawn ordered a baked potato and a frosty. While we were there, she received a call from her mother wanting to know if Dawn would spend the night with her. Dawn told her she would be over later.

Dawn left for her mother's around five o'clock. She told me she would be back first thing in the morning. I didn't want her to go, because she really didn't look that well. But when Dawn got something in her head, it was impossible to change her mind.

She never did make it to her mother's. She went over to her aunt's house in Mandarin. About six in the morning Dawn came home. I was already up, and when she came in, she told me she was going to go lie down. She looked worse than she had when she left the night before. Around nine o'clock Cathy went to Dawn's room to check on her. Dawn was up and in the bathroom. She called out to Cathy and told her she wasn't feeling well and something was wrong. Cathy went into the bathroom and found Dawn sitting on the floor. I was outside and didn't know this was going on. When I came in, I heard Cathy yelling for me. I went to Dawn's room, and Dawn was having a seizure.

We were told back in November and December that seizures were a possibility, but because she hadn't had one, we all stopped thinking about it. I will never forget that morning. The first one lasted approximately a minute and a half. After it ended, I called hospice, and they said they would send someone out. Cathy then called our neighbor Bridget who was a nurse and asked her to come down until the hospice nurse arrived. Dawn had her second seizure about fifteen minutes later, and that one lasted about thirty seconds.

An hour passed, and the hospice nurse still wasn't at the house. I called again, and they said the nurse was in St. Augustine. I told them we were only ten miles from St. Augustine, and they told me they would call him and get back to me. About ten minutes later hospice called and informed me the nurse would be there within the next thirty minutes. By this time, it was already ten thirty. Eleven thirty came, and the nurse still wasn't at the house. I once again called hospice and told them they better get someone there now. About that time, Dawn had a major seizure, which lasted about two minutes. I had never seen anything like it before in my entire life.

Bridget told us that we needed to call 911 and get an ambulance to come take Dawn to the emergency room, so Cathy called. By this time it was noon, and we heard a knock on the door. I went and opened it up and found a nurse standing there with a Starbucks coffee in his hand. "I got here as fast as I could," he said. It took him more than three hours to get there. He knew he better stay out of my way.

The ambulance arrived and transported Dawn to Baptist South Emergency room. She had another seizure in the ambulance and the last one in the ER. She had a total of five in four hours. Then at around five o'clock the doctor came in to tell us that they had her stabilized and were calling for Liberty ambulance service to transport her to the Hospice Center. This whole time Dawn was not conscious.

I once again rode with her in the ambulance, and Cathy went home to get me some things to wear. I was spending the night with her. This whole time Dawn didn't know what was going on. Saturday night came and went. Sunday came, and she was still unconscious. On Monday, Dawn was still out. I spoke to the doctor at hospice, and he informed me that Dawn may never regain consciousness. Hearing that broke my heart. The nurses put a rollaway bed in the room for me, but I would pull the chair over to the side of Dawn's bed and sleep. I held her hand throughout the night.

Tuesday came and went, and I was really worried. When you are inpatient at hospice, they only treat you for pain. Dawn was not being fed through the IV. Hospice does not prolong life. It had been four days, and she hadn't had anything to eat or drink. I was constantly praying to God, asking him to help Dawn. It was around eleven o'clock, and I had fallen asleep holding Dawn's hand. Around three o'clock in the morning on Wednesday, I was awake and looking at Dawn. I started talking to her, and the next thing I knew she opened her eyes and said, "Daddy, is that really you?" I can't think of another time when I was happier. About that time, the nurse walked by the room, and I called her in. They took her vitals, and one of the first things Dawn said to the nurse was, "I'm hungry." Because it was so early in the morning, there really wasn't much to give her except soup and ice cream. Dawn told the nurse she would take both and then wait on breakfast. My Dawn was back, and she had her humor to boot.

Not long after that Dawn started to ask me when she was going to be able to go home. Hospice has a policy that you have to stay as inpatient for at least three full days to make sure your medication is regulated, and the days Dawn was unconscious didn't count. I told her we would have to wait and ask Dr. Santamarie when he came in.

That afternoon when the doctor came in to see Dawn, that was the first thing she asked him. The doctor and Dawn got to know each other spiritually the first time she was an inpatient. She didn't like what he told her. He said that she would have to stay at least until Monday, June 1. He recommended to me that she stay through the weekend, because they wanted to make sure she wouldn't have any more seizures.

A hospice team is assigned to a patient, and they pay the patient a visit every day when the patient is home. On weekends there is a nurse on call. The doctor thought it would be better for Dawn to wait until Monday when her team would be able to visit her. She wasn't happy, but there was nothing we could do.

Then on Sunday, May 31, Dawn had a setback. Her pain got worse, and they had problems getting it under control. I didn't tell Dawn, but I knew she wouldn't be discharged the next day. Like I said before, her pain had to be under control for at least seventy-two hours before they would send her home.

During our stay, we had met some wonderful families. I would sit out on the lanai when Dawn was sleeping. I would see families come and go. This one evening there was a young lady sitting out smoking a cigarette. I knew she was new there, because I had never seen her before. The first day I never say anything to new guests, because they have so much on their minds with their loved one being admitted to hospice. The next morning I was sitting out there drinking a cup of coffee and reading the paper when this young lady came out. I asked her how she was, and that broke the ice. She was there with her mother. Her name was Eve Bryant. She was such a sweet girl.

It wasn't long after we got to talking that I told her I had to check on Dawn. When I entered her room, Dawn was waking up and said she needed to use the bathroom. I helped her to the bathroom, and soon after she finished, she got her cigarettes and said, "Let's go." When we got out on the lanai, Eve was still there. Come to find out Eve was thirty-one years old. She and Dawn hit it off wonderfully.

I ended up being the gopher for the two of them, because they both wanted coffee and would send me. Believe me, I didn't care. I was happy that there was someone Dawn could talk to. Dawn had visitors all the time, but she and Eve hit it off. When Eve wasn't in her mother's room, she was in Dawn's room.

On Friday, June 5, Eve's mother passed away. On that day I saw six families lose a loved one in a three-hour period. It was such a depressing day. I could not even imagine what was going through Dawn's head. Even though Eve was leaving the center, she told Dawn she would be back to visit her. Eve kept her word and visited Dawn every chance she could.

Because of Dawn's setback on May 31, we knew she would be there for a while. It wasn't until late Tuesday when they got her meds under control. So I had a feeling they were going to keep her through the weekend again. Sure enough, they kept her and finally discharged her at noon on June 9. That was a very long seventeen days for Dawn.

I truly believe the staff never could get use to Dawn being so active. Before they discharged her, they told her she needed to do nothing. Dawn would look at them like they had their heads on backward. She would tell them that she wasn't dead yet and that she wasn't just sitting at home. They told her that she couldn't disconnect her IV, because it would screw up her medication. So, I came up with an idea. I planned it all out and then ran it by Dawn. What a smile she got on her face when I told her. She asked me when I was going to say something to the doctor. I told her I would when he made his visit in to discharge her.

We caught them all off guard, because he reiterated that Dawn couldn't go anyplace because she couldn't disconnect her IV. I then said to the doctor, "I have an idea and a demonstration." I then reached into a bag I had at the foot of my rollaway bed and pulled out a backpack. I then showed the doctor where I'd punched hole in the bottom of the bag and demonstrated it to him and the nurse. They said her IV couldn't be disconnected for a long period of time. I then proceeded to show them by disconnecting Dawn's IV, running the tube through the hole in the bottom, placing the IV pump inside the backpack, and reconnecting it. Dawn was good to go. It took less than a minute to do this transfer. You could see they weren't too thrilled about the idea, but the doctor said that if we could come up with a plan, then she could go places. They didn't think we could come up with something. Dawn was happy she could go places again. She loved Walmarts, as she called it. We used to get the biggest laugh out of her when she called it that.

So we were on our way home. Because Dawn was being discharged and having the hospice team visit her at home, I was allowed to drive her home. We didn't even get around the corner when she said, "Dad, stop at Starbucks." She loved her coffee.

Father's Day was approaching, and Dawn asked me if I would take her to the store. I asked which store, and she gave me this look that said, *Daddy, I would like to go to Walmarts.* How could I not have known that? She loved her Walmarts.

I asked her what she needed at Walmart(s), and she looked at me and said, "Daddy, it's no concern of yours. I want to get you something for Father's Day."

"Dawn, you don't have to buy me anything," I told her.

She then said, "Daddy, Father's Day is coming up, and it will be my last one with you."

It broke my heart to hear those words. Hearing them was one thing, but knowing what Dawn knew was another thing.

What goes through the mind of a person who is terminal and knows that each special occasion is the last? Dawn's strength and courage had been remarkable. I told her having her by my side was all I wanted for Father's Day. Then I got to thinking about the following Father's Day. It was totally breaking my heart. She insisted on me taking her, so off to Walmart(s) we went.

Once we arrived, she told me I had to go in another direction. Here was Dawn on an IV twenty-four/seven going through Walmart. She was a hard one to keep down. I'd learned several months earlier to let her do what she wanted.

We were only in the store for about forty-five minutes when we met up. She then asked me if she could get her eyes checked. The doctors told her that sooner than later her cancer would start affecting her sight. She got her eyes checked and picked out a pair of glasses. The worker there knew the situation with Dawn and told her he was going to put a rush on them. He told her normally they would take ten days to get back, but two days later Dawn received a call telling her the glasses were in.

She was so happy; if she wasn't reading and taking notes from the Bible, she was playing Sudoku. She was very good at that. She had the hardest version, while we had the easiest, and she would still beat us all. One day she asked her sister if she wanted to race to see who could finish first. Kristie Lynn took the easy book, and Dawn the hardest. Off they started. About five minutes later Dawn said, "I'm done with them both." She'd done two puzzles and still won.

Later that evening Dawn, Cathy, and I were sitting out on the lanai. We had just finished eating dinner, and Cathy got up to clean up. Dawn said, "Cath, where you going?"

"I'm taking the dishes into the kitchen," Cathy answered.

"Okay," Dawn said, "but come right back out."

While Cathy was in the kitchen, Dawn pick up where she'd left off with her Bible studying. Dawn was asking me question after question when Cathy returned.

Dawn looked at me and said, "I'm a little sad, Daddy."

"Why?" I asked.

"When I go to heaven, I won't be able to call you Daddy anymore." She went on and said that the Bible says there is only one father in heaven, and it's God. "What will I call you?"

Cathy was sitting there with the Bible and showed Dawn that we are all brothers and sisters in heaven. Dawn turned to me, looked me in the eyes for a few seconds, and said, "Daddy, you know I'm going to be in heaven way before you, so that will make me your big sister, and you will have to listen to me."

The girl was on a roll, because she came right back with that one. Ever since the girls were little I used to tell them that The Horseshoe football stadium at Ohio State was heaven. The same night that Dawn told me about being my big sister, she said to me, "Daddy, I have to tell you something. I asked her what it was, and she went on to tell me. "You know I'm going to heaven, don't you?"

"Of course you are," I said.

And her reply was, "And it's not The Horseshoe at Ohio State."

You could always count on some kind of humor from Dawn. Back in the 1970s, there was a TV program called *Kung Fu*. In this program. the master taught his students kung fu. Well, during the program, the master often said, "Grasshopper, it's time for a lesson." When Dawn had something serious to say, sometimes she'd start by telling us, "Grasshopper, it's time for a lesson. Come to Master for today's lesson."

I often wondered if God gives terminally ill patients a special gift. Does he give them the ability to see a little into the future? Does he allow for them to know a little of what will happen? I ask this because of some things Dawn had told me and what happened after her death.

Cathy got up and said she was going to bed. I told her I was going to stay up a little longer with Dawn. It was a hot, muggy night, but Dawn wanted to stay out on the lanai and talk about the Bible for a little bit.

"Daddy, you have made me several promises these past couple of months," she said. "Keeping these promises will keep you busy. Is that okay with you? You must always remember that each promise you made has a specific reason behind it. You may not know the reason at the time, but trust me—they all have a very important meaning. Daddy, don't you forget the most important promise you made, and that's to study and learn the Bible."

Dawn continued, "Daddy, as you know, I made my peace with God. God will welcome me with open arms soon. You must know God's words. You must accept him into your heart. Turn your Bible to John 14:1-6. Daddy, read this out loud to me and listen to every word you say."

I opened the Bible and read, just as Dawn asked me to. It said, "'Do not let your hearts be troubled. Trust in God; trust also in me. In my Father's house are many rooms; if it were not so, I would have told you. I am going there to prepare a place for you. And if I go and prepare a place for you, I will come back and take you to be with me that you also may be where I am. You know the way to the place where I am going.' Thomas said to him, 'Lord, we don't know where you are going, so how can we know the way?' Jesus answered, 'I am the way and the truth and the life. No one comes to the Father except through me.'"

When I was finished reading, Dawn said, "Daddy, do you know what Jesus just said? You have to trust in God and trust in Jesus. One day we will be together again; however, you must learn the words of God. Promise me, Daddy, you will do this. Promise me now that you will take God's words and put them in your heart."

"I promise you, girl," I agreed. "I too want to be with you again."

Luke 11:8 says, "I say unto you though he will not rise and give him, because he is his friend, yet because of his importunity he will rise and give him as many as he needeth. 'And I say unto you. Ask, and it shall be given you; seek, and ye shall find; knock, and it shall be opened unto you. For every one that asketh receiveth; and he that seeketh findeth; and to him that knocketh it shall be opened.'"

After about an hour of making small talk, Dawn said to me, "Daddy, there is no one on this earth who loves me more than you."

I looked at her and said, "You are right. There is no one who loves you more than me."

"Daddy, there is no one on this earth who knows me better than you," she added.

I said, "You got that right again." I should have seen what was coming, but I was blindsided by this.

"With that in mind, Daddy," Dawn continued, "I want you to write my eulogy."

"No, Dawn," I said. "I can't do that. Please don't ask me to do that."

"Daddy, listen to me. You can do it. You have it in your heart to do this," she encouraged me.

"Who is going to read it?" I asked.

"You are, Daddy," she said.

"Dawn, do you know what you are asking me? This whole ordeal has been—"

Dawn interrupted me. "Daddy, listen. Look at all the things you have done for me that I asked you to do. Things you said you couldn't do, like make arrangements for my funeral, my resting place at the cemetery, and many more things. Daddy, you set your mind to it, and you do it. This will make you a stronger and better person."

"Dawn, I can't do your eulogy," I insisted. "Do you realize what you are asking of me? I'm going to be a basket case when that day comes."

"What day is that, Daddy?" Dawn asked.

"You know what day I'm talking about."

"You mean my funeral, Daddy?"

"Yes, that day," I said.

"Say it," she said. "Tell me that day. That day is coming, Daddy, and you have to accept it."

"I don't have to accept anything," I said.

"What did you just read me about being together? Trusting in God is the key. By doing this, Daddy, you will make it through, because you will have extra strength on your side. Trust me. Now promise me you will do it," Dawn said again.

"Okay, I promise you," I agreed.

"Now that we are on the subject of writing," Dawn continued, "I want you to write after I'm gone. Write about what I asked. I want you to write your thoughts and feelings down."

"How do I do that?" I asked her. "You know I can't write."

"Do you remember two years ago and last year when you went to Cooperstown for umpiring?" Dawn reminded me. "When you returned, you wrote two stories about your adventure. How did you do that, Daddy? If I'm not mistaken, you wrote that from your heart, and everyone loved them. You do the same here. You reach deep down in your heart, and you pull those feelings out. You then put them in your thoughts and write them down. One day, Daddy, they will help you, and they will also help others."

"What others? Who will they help?" I asked her.

"Trust me, Daddy. They will help you and others. Class dismissed for the rest of the day."

"Dawn, you just can't—"

She cut me off again. "I'm the master here," she laughed. "Go, Grasshopper, and get me another cup of coffee."

CHAPTER SIXTEEN

IT WAS AMAZING to see all the help Cathy and I received from friends—friends who had their own busy schedules but still found time to help us. I honestly believe that God works in mysterious ways to help you get through troubled times. When a family lives in a neighborhood, you might have a family friend, if that. It seems everyone wants to keep to themselves anymore. This is not so in our neighborhood. I truly believe that God put us in Austin Park for a reason.

The love and support we received from our neighbors were nothing but miraculous. Not only did we get thoughts and prayers, but we received meals from them. They cut our lawn, cleaned our house, and even sat with Dawn when Cathy and I couldn't. One day when Cathy was at work and I was at hospice with Dawn, I received a call from Cathy. She told me she just finished talking to Bridget, and we needed to be home at six o'clock. Well, I refused to leave Dawn alone. I would get food and eat it in her room. I wasn't going to leave her. I then phoned Bridget and told her I wouldn't be able to make it home, because I didn't want to leave Dawn. She told me, "You will leave, and you will be home at six."

Dawn was pretty much out of it, so I thought, *Okay, I'll run home to see why they wanted me home.* Cathy and I got home about the same time. We walked into the house, and Bridget was there. She had cleaned our home, cooked a meal for us, and had fresh flowers and candles lit on the table. How wonderful was that?

One Friday afternoon when Dawn took her afternoon nap, I decided to run home and get the yard work out of the way. I pulled into the driveway and could see that the yard was cut and edged. Ryan, who was fifteen at the time, is Kevin and Bridget's son. He would come and do the yard work for us. I offered him payment, but he refused to take it. Spencer and Emily, who lived on the next street over, brought us five—and six-course meals. Michelle would bake cakes for us. Blaine had a variety of baked items she would bring over. Lyle and Julie would bring us baked goods. Someone was always doing something for us.

During the time of Dawn's illness, the lot next-door to us was under construction. We met the family who would soon be our new neighbors. One day they were touring their home when they saw us outside, so they had the opportunity to meet Dawn. Not a time that went by when they stopped to look at their new home being built that they didn't ask about Dawn. We have the best neighbors in the entire world.

Ezra 1:6 says, "All their neighbors assisted them with articles of silver and gold, with goods and livestock, and with valuable gifts, in addition to all freewill offerings."

Then we had this funny story with Don's wife Jennifer. Jennifer, who was almost eight months, she would come over in the mornings and sit with Dawn. They would watch two, sometimes three, movies together. This one day when I got home, Jen said she was going to make a snack for them to have the next day. She said it had Corn Chex cereal, chocolate, and other ingredients I can't remember. Jen made this huge batch that filled two large bowls. Of course, they had to try it out. Well, it was supposed to be refrigerated and be ready the next morning.

Cathy left for work around quarter to seven, so that was when Jen arrived at the house. They didn't hesitate in starting to watch the movies they'd picked out the day before. I normally left work at ten thirty to head home. This particular morning at 9:15 I received a call from Dawn. She was moaning and groaning, telling me that she and Jen were sick. I asked what was wrong with them, and I could hear them laughing. They said they were sick, because they ate all of the snack stuff. They both told me they couldn't eat another thing all day. I started to laugh and told her to go watch another movie, and the two of them would be fine.

"No," she kept telling me, "Daddy, you just don't understand. We are really sick and couldn't eat another thing." I told her I had to go, and I would be home at eleven. I hung up and went back to work. One hour and five minutes later I received another call from Dawn. I have caller ID on my phone at work, so as soon as I saw it was her, I picked it up and asked if they were okay. She said they were both fine. She then asked me what time I was leaving work and if I was coming straight home. I told her I was leaving work in ten minutes, and yes, I was coming straight home.

She said, "Good. Stop at Chick-fil-A and pick up two number five combos."

I then asked what the number fives were. Dawn told me she wasn't sure, but Jen said they were really good. "Oh, by the way, Dad, pick up some extra sauce. Jen said you need some extra sauce with this meal."

I said, "Dawn, I thought you two were sick from eating."

"Dad, that was an hour ago," she said. So, yes, I stopped and picked up two number five combos for them.

Every one of our neighbors contributed above and beyond. The funny thing about our neighbors is that we all moved into this new development within a six-month period. None of us ever knew one another before this, but we all lived in a five-mile radius of each other.

My work was wonderful. My immediate supervisor, Mike VonDolteren, was very understanding. His immediate supervisor was Pattie Mallon. Between the two of them, they made my life, which was a living hell, a little easier with my work schedule. When Dawn was in Gainesville, they would let me work from four o'clock in the morning to noon. I then had time to get to Dawn's radiation treatment at one thirty. Then, when she was home after the holidays, they let me work six thirty to ten thirty in the office and then eleven thirty to three thirty at home. That way I was always home when the hospice nurse would arrive in the afternoons. I can't say enough about how my work treated me.

On the other hand, Cathy's work was the total opposite. When we found out about Dawn's illness, the Practice manager told Cathy that it was a personal problem and to keep all personal business outside the doors. She was told not to bring them inside with her to work. Can you believe how some people are? Even some of the workers told her, "It's not like she is your daughter. She is only a stepdaughter."

They added so much more stress to her life than she already had. Cathy might have only been the stepmother, but the two of them got along wonderfully together. There were endless days when Dawn couldn't sleep and Cathy would sit up all night with her and then go to work. Cathy treated Dawn as if she were her own daughter.

CHAPTER SEVENTEEN

THE NIGHT OF June 30 Dawn was having serious problems with her medication. Her IV pump was acting up, and she wasn't getting her proper dose of medication. We had to call the night nurse with hospice to come out and look at the pump. Sally arrived about forty-minutes after we called. Sally had been out to the house in the past, and she and Dawn got along very well.

Once she looked at the pump and saw the amount of pain Dawn was in, she called the doctor on duty that night. Their recommendation was for her to come in for three to five days to get her medication regulated. Dawn was pretty upset, because of the plans we had for the Fourth of July. She told Sally she would go in on one condition—that she was home no later than the afternoon of the fourth.

The reason she wanted to come home was because a week or so earlier Dawn made the comment she would like to see fireworks. So the neighbors went and bought over fifteen hundred dollars' worth of fireworks. We were going to give her a firework display she would love.

After Sally got off the phone with the doctor, she informed us that we needed to check into hospice around nine in the morning. I know Dawn hated the thought of it, but she needed to get her pain under control. Neither one of us got any sleep that night.

We were told that before Dawn checked into the center, I needed to take her to Baptist South. The Hospice Center made arrangements with them to have a port put in her chest. They said the IV wasn't getting her the medication fast enough, so they had to put it through a port. We had to be at the hospital at eight thirty, and they took her back right away. She was only in the operating room for about forty-five minutes. When they were through, we left for the center.

As we were pulling out of the hospital parking lot, Dawn asked if we could stop at Starbucks. There was one right in front of the hospital, so I told her of course we could. She then asked if we could sit outside and drink her coffee instead of going straight to the center. I didn't blame her. I wasn't in a hurry to get her there as long as she wasn't in pain.

As we were checking in, Dawn went up to the nurses' station and told them, "Don't even put me in if I'm not going to get out by the afternoon of the fourth." They all looked at her and laughed and told her then she better get into a room so they could get started.

For the next three days, the nurses got Dawn's pain under control and her medicine regulated to where she wasn't having any problems. At one o'clock on the afternoon of the fourth, we walked out of hospice and headed home. No sooner did we hit the doors did Dawn say, "Dad, take to me Starbucks." The temperature was in the nineties, and Dawn said she was getting an iced coffee.

That morning Cathy and Dawn were talking about Starbucks, and Cathy told Dawn she'd never had an iced coffee. Well, when we pulled into the drive-through, Dawn told me she was buying Cathy one. On our way home, Dawn called Cathy and told her she needed to be in the driveway when we pulled in. Dawn wouldn't tell her why, but Cathy agreed. As we got about a mile away, Dawn called Cathy and told her to be outside. Dawn was so excited about the coffee she was giving Cathy. They both ended up going into the house drinking their coffee and talking.

The plan was to cook out over at the LaRoses' house. Dawn knew this and asked us if we could bring her home a plate. We had no problem with that. We were going to shoot the fireworks off over the lake, and Dawn could sit on the lanai and watch them. As it got darker, the whole neighborhood was getting ready for the fireworks display. I was going to help them with it all, but I told them I wanted to be with Dawn. So Cathy and I stayed home with Dawn. It wasn't long after that when Jennifer joined us. Jen was very uncomfortable because of her pregnancy.

When we started firing off our fireworks, there were a couple other families on the other side of the lake that were doing the same. Dawn had a wonderful time watching all the fireworks go off over the lake right in front of her. She had the best seat in the house. By the time it was over, Dawn was both physically and mentally worn out. It had been a very long day for her. As she was about to fall asleep, she opened her eyes and said, "Daddy, thanks so much for the wonderful fireworks. They were the best."

CHAPTER EIGHTEEN

RIGHT AFTER THE Fourth of July, we started to see a major decline in Dawn's health. She was having trouble getting around and losing major functions. I kept asking myself how she was so strong and was amazed at the courage she had.

She was so tired of just lying around in her bedroom that I moved my recliner from upstairs down to the family room. That way she could have a couple of places where she could rest. She loved the recliner, because she was more comfortable in that than the bed. We made it as comfortable for her as we possibly could.

Nancy, who was Dawn's hospice nurse, told her that she was going on vacation July 1 for two weeks. She told Dawn that a temporary nurse would stand in for her while she was out. On Dawn's first day back, which was July 5, Carol came and introduced herself to Dawn. From the very beginning, Dawn and Carol hit it off. They fell in love with each other.

Carol was a very sensitive, kindhearted person. Not only did she come to check Dawn's vitals every day, but she spent time with Dawn and talked to her about her kids and so many other different conversations. Their talks always brought joy to Dawn. Also, she would bring Dawn a Starbucks every day. The look on Dawn's face was priceless when Carol brought her the first one.

Dawn was in the recliner sleeping. I never woke her up for anything. Most of the time, the nurses could get all the information they needed whether she was awake or asleep. The second day that

Carol came Dawn was sleeping. When I opened the door, Carol had a Starbucks coffee for Dawn. I went up to Dawn and tried to wake her up. I said, "Dawn, Carol is here. Open your eyes." I had no luck in getting her to wake up. I finally said, "Dawn, Carol has something for you, and you will really love it." She opened her eyes a tiny bit until she saw what it was, and then her eyes were like silver dollars. Carol treated Dawn as a friend, not just a patient. That was very important to her.

Friday, July 10, was Carol's last day with Dawn. Nancy was supposed to be back from vacation on Monday, July 13. On the night of July 9, Dawn, Cathy, and I were watching TV. Dawn said to me, "Dad, you know that necklace I have that says we are friends?"

I said, "Yes. Why?"

She said, "I want to give that to Carol tomorrow. Do we have a gift bag?"

Cathy got up and found one for her. We put this little gift together for Carol when she came for the last time.

I was getting so worried for Dawn, because of the decline in her health. It was so hard to see my beautiful daughter suffer. The only thing we could do was make her as comfortable as possible. I prayed every day and asked God to relieve her pain. "Please, Lord, she is suffering. Please help her. Please take away her pain."

When Carol arrived that Friday afternoon, she came in and handed Dawn her coffee. Dawn could not wait for Carol to arrive. As soon as they saw each other, Dawn gave Carol her gift. Carol told Dawn she wasn't allowed to accept it. Dawn said, "You might not be allowed to accept it as my nurse, but you can as my friend." Carol opened it and started to cry. It was very touching for every one of us.

After Carol was through with Dawn and had checked all her vitals, Dawn was worn out. She fell asleep in the recliner. Whenever Dawn's medication bag had to be replaced, a second nurse had to be present. Suzy came a few minutes later than Carol that day, just enough time for Carol to check all of the vitals and stuff. When they put her new medication bag on, the three of us went out on the lanai. I had some questions I wanted to ask the two nurses. We could all see concern in each other's eyes. We all could see Dawn's health failing and failing fast.

I was told by the nurses that Dawn should probably go back into the center. Their reasoning was that her medication was constantly changing and having to be increased every four to six hours. I then told them my promise to Dawn about letting her die at home. Dawn did not want to die in the hospital or the Hospice Center. I told her that she could die wherever she felt comfortable.

Both Carol and Suzy told me that Dawn probably would not make it through the weekend at home. They told me they would more than likely admit her again. My heart was breaking. I could not believe this was happening to my baby girl.

I mentioned earlier in this story about Dawn asking me to make her arrangements. I could not believe what I was hearing. This was all wrong; a father isn't supposed to make funeral arrangements for his children. So after the holidays, I went to Jacksonville Memory Gardens and made the arrangements. Then one day in the spring Dawn and I were sitting on the lanai at home, and out of the blue she asked me where I wanted to be buried. I told her that I was going to be buried in the new National Cemetery out by the airport. She said, "Oh, all right." I asked her why, and she said she wanted me to be buried next to her, but dependants weren't allowed to be buried in the National Cemetery. Nothing more was said about this.

All night long that conversation crossed my mind. Dawn was worried about being alone. Even though I realized the dead don't know their surroundings, I couldn't let Dawn have those feelings while she was still alive. So the next day after I left work, I went to Jacksonville Memory Gardens and spoke to Joy. She was the lady I'd spoken to a couple months earlier. I asked her if she had two plots side by side and explained Dawn's wishes to her. We went out into the cemetery, and she showed me two spots, which I bought. Now you have to try and visualize this. The two plots were on a little slop under a big oak tree. It seemed to be a very nice location.

After leaving the cemetery, I phoned Dawn and told her I was on my way home and that I would bring us lunch. We went out on the lanai to eat, and I said, "Dawn, did you really mean what you said about wanting to be buried next to me?" She said she did, so I told her what I'd done. The look on her face, knowing she would not be alone was priceless. It seemed like a big burden was lifted off of her shoulders.

One day Dawn and I were out and about when she asked me to pull into the cemetery. I couldn't believe her request and asked her why. She told me she wanted to see where she was going to be laid to rest. My heart was breaking more. We pulled up alongside of the area and got out. I told her it was right in front of us.

As we stood in front of the plots, she said "Dad, I want the one on the right."

I looked at her and said, "You can have any one you want."

Then the Dawn humor came out. "You're not going to ask me why I want the one on the right?" she said.

"Okay, hon, why do you want the one on the right?" I asked her.

She said, "Well, if something ever happened, I don't want you to roll over and land on top of me." Can you believe her saying that? I couldn't help but laugh. She was such an amazing young lady.

After a few minutes standing there, Joy came up to us. Dawn told her what she'd said to me, and Joy just laughed. She then told Dawn that to the left of us about thirty feet were two spots on flat land. Dawn asked to see them, and when she showed us, Dawn asked if we could change them out. Joy changed them right there in front of us.

These questions—or should I say favors, as Dawn would refer to them—were done. The first was the arrangements, and the second was the plots. I told Dawn that I didn't want her to ask me for any more favors like that. Then I got to thinking how nothing worse could be asked of me to do. I just did the two hardest tasks any parent could ever have to do.

I couldn't find it in my heart to tell Dawn later that Friday night that they thought she should go back to the Hospice Center as an inpatient. I always knew I would not let her suffer in any way whatsoever. I didn't say anything to her that day or even the next day. I wanted to see if she would rebound or if her medication wasn't helping.

Then Sunday, July 12, came. Dawn was in a lot of pain. I called to see if the nurse could come earlier and explained why. They told me they would send the nurse right out. While we were waiting, Dawn said to me, "Dad, I think I better go in so they can get my medication regulated."

I told her we would do whatever she wanted and thought it was a very smart move. It wasn't long after that Sally arrived, and Dawn told her what she thought should be done. Sally was in full agreement and phoned the Northeast Community Hospice Center. So at six o'clock, I took Dawn back to the center. I packed a bag, because I knew I'd be staying with her.

For months on end I was warned by doctors and nurses about Delirium and Terminal Restlessness Syndrome. Because delirium is a fairly common symptom in many terminally ill patients, you may be the first one to notice that your loved one is experiencing some of its effects. Delirium can be terribly upsetting to both the patient and their loved ones.

Delirium is a sudden severe confusion and rapid changes in brain function that occur with physical or mental illness. It's like a sudden change in alertness and behavior that can fluctuate throughout the day.

The other stage that Dawn encountered was the Terminal Restlessness Syndrome. Terminal Restlessness may occur in some patients when it gets near the end of life. It is characterized by anguish, restlessness, agitation, and cognitive failure. It may also include delusions or hallucinations.

The doctors and nurses warned me about this stage. They told me that Dawn could lash out at me. I told them there was no way she would do that. They told me that was their way of breaking away from the one they love the most. Don't listen to it, let it go in one ear and out the other, they told me. Don't react to anything she says about you.

It was so sad to see my girl in that state. All I found myself doing was asking God why. If you're going to take her from me take her now and stop letting her suffer. During the time my mother was ill it was horrible seeing her like that. I thought at the time that there is nothing worse than seeing your parent ill. I loved my mother dearly but feelings you have when it's one of your children is horrific. There is nothing on this earth that you can compare it to. With your children, you have that bond between you. That bond isn't supposed to just go away.

CHAPTER NINETEEN

BY NOW, I knew all the nurses and doctors at the Hospice Center. They all came to accept Dawn. "Dawn was Dawn," as they always said. If something were to happen, the nurses had a standard operating procedure to follow. They used to joke around when it came to Dawn—well, just throw the procedures out the window. Dawn finally convinced them that if she wanted up, she was going to get up or have someone help her.

No one except God knew what we would be facing in the coming days and weeks at the center. Wednesday night, July 15, is a day I will never forget. Dawn went into the terminal restless stage.

Another thing that happens when a patient enters that stage is that she can start to see things and talk to people who aren't really there. The nurse taking care of Dawn that night was Liz. MaryAnn was the nurse at the station. Dawn really started in on me, and Liz stepped in and told me to get out of sight so Dawn wouldn't be so upset. I went to the corner of the room by the door. MaryAnn went in to help with Liz. Dawn wasn't making much sense, and we could hardly understand the things she was saying.

After a few minutes, Dawn looked Liz in the eyes and as clear as ever said, "You must hurry and finish up with what you are doing." Liz asked her why, and Dawn said, "Because I'm getting ready to go on a trip with my grandmom." Grandmom was what Dawn used to call my mother. I got chills over my entire body. After Dawn settled down, Liz came up to me and asked where my mother was. I told her my mother passed away in October, 1989. While Liz and I were talking, MaryAnn was in the room with Dawn.

I reentered Dawn's room, and MaryAnn was sitting on the edge of the bed holding Dawn's hand. I stayed out of sight again, because I didn't want Dawn to get upset. This time I sat in the chair that was in the corner, and Dawn couldn't see me unless she sat up and turned around. During this period of time, MaryAnn was talking to Dawn. Dawn was talking back, but we couldn't understand a word she was saying. MaryAnn agreed with Dawn on everything, because we couldn't make one word out.

The tumor on Dawn's brain stem had grown so large at this point that it kept her from holding her head up straight. About thirty minutes had passed since Dawn had first become so upset. Then I saw this with my on two eyes: Dawn wasn't making much sense with her vocabulary, and we could hardly understand her. Then all of a sudden Dawn's head and neck straightened up, and she looked over to the right side, which was opposite of where MaryAnn was, and said in clear English, "Is it as beautiful as they say it is?" There was a pause for a few seconds, and then Dawn said, "But I'm not ready to go there yet." Dawn's head went back to the side, and once again we couldn't understand a word she was saying. I truly believe she was talking to her grandmom, my mother.

What had I just witnessed? Was that my mother in the room with us? Those two were very close. These questions will only be answered when I meet my maker.

Cathy and the hospice staff finally talked me into going home for a night. After five weeks of staying with Dawn twenty-four/seven, I went home on a Friday night. I did tell Dawn the night before that I would be leaving for a while, and she opened her eyes and said, "It's about time." She had that little smirk on her face after saying that. I asked her what she meant by that, and she just laughed. She told me I needed to get out and that everything would be fine.

The next morning I was sitting next to her in bed, and she said to me, "Daddy, can we talk for a minute?"

"Dawn, we can talk anytime you want," I said.

"Daddy, I just wanted you to know how much I appreciate all you and Cathy have done for me. I can't thank you enough," she said. "You two have gone above and beyond of what anyone else could have done."

"Dawn, hon," I said, "we told you we would take care of you, and that is what we're doing."

"Daddy, I can never repay you for all you have done. However, I want you to know that I will come back and keep an eye out for you, and I'll take care of you." Hearing her talk like that broke my heart. No parent wants to hear one of his children talk as if they won't be around.

When I left that night, Dawn was sleeping, so I gave her a light kiss good-bye. All I kept thinking was *How can I just leave her?* Then I realized that she was in good hands with Cathy. I was home about forty-five minutes when my cell phone rang.

"Daddy, where are you?" said the voice on the other end.

I thought, *Oh no, Dawn is looking for me.*

"Why did you leave, Daddy?" Each time she said something I felt more guilty. Then I heard Dawn snicker a little followed by a whisper to Cathy. "I think I'm making him feel bad." Finally, Dawn said, "Daddy, I'm only kidding you. It's ladies' night out, and you needed to be home. Oh, by the way, when you come in tomorrow, please bring my nail polish. Cathy is going to give me a manicure and pedicure."

Later that night, after Dawn was a sleep, Cathy called me and told me that Dawn was going to pull that prank on me. I should have known, because Dawn was good about that. I do have to admit I was feeling guilty about leaving her when we talked. Deep down, I knew that Dawn was in wonderful hands with Cathy by her side and all of the nurses, but I still couldn't sleep that night.

I had my normal, everyday talk with God about all of this. I know we're not supposed to ask God why he does the things that he does, but I'm only human. I wanted to know why he was doing this to my baby girl.

I was back first thing in the morning. Dawn was really worrying me, because she hadn't been eating. The doctors told us that if Dawn could take some of her medication orally, then she could at least go home. Dawn wanted to die at home, and I didn't have a problem with that at all. There was one major factor that was preventing her from coming home—all her medication was being given by IV, and she wasn't able to take any orally. I had seen a major decline in her health during the past few days.

How could this be happening? How could I just sit back and watch this horrific cancer take my daughter away? God, please, she's so young. Please don't take her. The days and nights just ran alongside each other. Half the time I didn't know which part of the day it was.

Dawn wasn't coherent very much during the day. I realized the medication was keeping her heavily sedated. All the things about her were going through my mind every minute of the day. My goal that day was to try to get her to eat. I needed to tell her again that if she could eat for three consecutive days, then she could go home. I was sitting in the chair next to her bed reading the paper when she woke up Sunday morning. I asked her if she was hungry and wanted something to eat. She shook her head no. I then asked her if she wanted a cup of coffee. Again, she shook her head no.

The last thing I wanted to be was pushy, but I emphasized the importance of her eating if she wanted to go home. I was able to get her up out of bed and into her wheelchair. She loved me taking her for walks every chance we got. The hospice grounds had a pond in the back, and Dawn liked taking old bread out to feed the fish. So after feeding the fish, eating breakfast, and walking around the perimeter of the center, I took Dawn back to her room. Even though she was in a wheelchair, the ride wore her out.

Once we arrived back to Dawn's room, Cathy was waiting on us. She had a surprise for Dawn—a Starbucks coffee. That opened her eyes some when she heard that little bit of news. We sat and talked to Dawn briefly. She was so tired from our outing that she fell fast asleep.

It was getting close to lunch, and neither Cathy nor I had eaten breakfast. So we told the nurses that we would be back in about forty-five minutes to an hour. We ended up going right down the road to Steak 'n Shake. While we were there, Cathy and I were talking about our concerns. We had to get back to hospice, because I'd told the nurses we'd be back within the hour.

At this point, Dawn and I had been at hospice for five weeks. Every time I walked past the nurses' station someone would say something to me. In the past, I would hear "If you walk by us again, we're going to put you to work," or "Sorry we are short staffed today. We'll send in Mr. Hoffman."

When Cathy and I returned, the nurse at the station said, "Thought you would miss it all." I asked what she was talking about, and she said, "You will see in a minute."

As Cathy and I entered Dawn's room, there was Dawn sitting up and being fed mashed potatoes, finely cut up chicken, and banana pudding. Dawn saw us and said, "It's about time. I'm getting full." I was so excited I couldn't see straight.

I had a smile from ear to ear the rest of the afternoon. Dawn was so alert I couldn't believe it. We were able to hold some nice conversations. Once again, we took her out of her room for something different. I was just so ecstatic the rest of the day. I told Dawn that day one was being counted for our journey home. Dawn just looked at me and gave me that beautiful smirk of hers.

Dinnertime came, and Dawn asked Cathy and me to go get something to eat and bring it back. "We can all eat Sunday dinner together," she said. Dawn's food had to be bland and soft, but we were still able to bring her something back. She didn't always have to eat hospital food. We had a wonderful dinner. She was even up to going out on the lanai, and the three of us ate outside by the lake. It was like old times again. The nurses made positive comments, but the looks on their faces didn't match the positive comments.

That evening Cathy went home, and Dawn wanted to listen to her audio Bible. Dawn received another surprise from her church. Every Sunday evening anywhere from fifteen to twenty-five church members would come visit Dawn. They would read Bible verses, sing songs, and hand out communion to Dawn and me. Her church was so wonderful.

After they all left, Dawn said, "Daddy, I am so lucky to have friends like that."

"You sure are, hon, you sure are," I agreed.

Dawn got a fairly good night's rest that night. I was up early, so I thought I would surprise her with a Starbucks coffee. When I returned, she had just woken up. When she saw her coffee, that beautiful smile came over her face. Breakfast arrived a few minutes later, and Dawn just picked at it. I didn't say anything to her, but I sure wish she would have eaten more. I thought maybe the coffee had filled her up, and that's why she didn't want food.

Dawn was a little more tired than she'd been the day before. I'm sure the little energy she had went away quickly. Later that afternoon, Dawn said to me, "Daddy, would you go and get me a banana milkshake?" I told her I'd be right back, so off I went to Steak 'n Shake. Between the hours of two and four, they have happy hour—two for the price of one. I thought I would get four and could put them in the freezer back at hospice.

When I returned, I brought one of the milkshakes into Dawn's room, and there in front of me was a different person. She was back like she'd been the week before. *How could this be?* I thought. *God, what are you doing to her?*

I looked at the nurses, and they still had that look on their faces. That look they had when Dawn was eating. Why? What was wrong with them? I was able to get Dawn to drink some of her shake. The cold felt good in her mouth. It would take her maybe a couple of hours to finish one shake, but it was still protein for her. Before the day was totally over, she drank two and a half shakes. I told her that I'd go get more the next day.

Finally, while walking in the middle of the night, I saw that MaryAnn was on duty. I said, "MaryAnn, you have to be honest with me. You have always been honest with me, so I'm going to ask you a question. Please give me an honest answer. Why are the nurses saying positive comments, but the looks on their faces don't match what they're saying?"

"Mr. Hoffman, just enjoy the time you have with her," she said.

"MaryAnn, you didn't answer my question," I said.

"Maybe you should wait and ask the doctor that question tomorrow," MaryAnn said.

"I don't want to wait and ask the doctors. I'm asking you."

"Mr. Hoffman, please understand that all patients are different. Mainly, your daughter has defied all odds, and she does her own thing," she said to me.

"MaryAnn, what is going on?" I asked again.

"Mr. Hoffman, all patients, when they get near to death, get a spurt of energy," she finally said. "We honestly believe Dawn has hit that stage."

"No, MaryAnn, it can't be. You saw her yesterday."

"Yes, Mr. Hoffman, I did. I also see her today," MaryAnn said. "I'm sorry. I know that's not what you wanted to hear, but you insisted."

"No, MaryAnn, I thank you for being up-front. I really appreciate it," I told her.

I cried the whole night asking God to take me instead. I had lived my life, and I asked God to let Dawn live hers. That three-letter word kept crossing my lips—*why?* Then I got to thinking about how life was going to be without her. The pain was unbearable just thinking about it. What was it going to be like when I lost her?

In Isaiah 45:9-11, it says, "Will the pot contend with the potter or the earthenware with the hand that shapes it? Will the clay ask the potter what he is making? . . . Thus says the Lord, 'Would you dare question Me concerning My children or instruct Me in My handiwork? I alone, I made the earth and created man upon it.'"

This whole time the nurses and doctors and even Dawn's minister told me that I needed to go home. I told them I wouldn't, because if she was going to die, I was going to be with her. They all told me that she would not die with me present. *Well,* I thought, *I guess she's not going to die, because I'm not leaving.*

That entire week people around me started saying again that I should go home for a night. Cathy said she would stay with Dawn on Friday and then I could come back Saturday morning. This was Tuesday, and I told them I would think about it.

Dawn became weaker and weaker as the week went on. I was so blind at the time. I guess I just didn't want to accept the fact that I was getting ready to lose her. I continued to feed her milkshakes at her request. I would go to Steak 'n Shake every day and buy eight shakes. She started drinking four and a half to five milkshakes a day, and they all had to be banana.

Thursday, August 20, arrived, and I was asked to go home for the night. I finally told them I would go home Friday and come back Saturday morning. That Thursday night I whispered in Dawn's ear and told her I was going to spend Friday night at home but would be back anytime she wanted me back. She opened her eyes and gave me that smirk of hers. I said, "Okay, she is all right with it, so I'm going home Friday night." I told the nurses and the doctors my decision, and they all told me it was a smart idea.

Dawn's oldest and dearest friend, Lindsay, lived in the Orlando area. They had been friends since Dawn was four and Lindsay was three. After the school years, the two remained in contact with one another. When Dawn came down ill, Lindsay was right by Dawn's side. In April, when Dawn entered the hospice program, Lindsay would come up from Orlando every Friday on her day off from work. Lindsay would spend the entire day with Dawn and take her out of the house to their old stomping grounds. They would have lunch together every Friday. Dawn would remind me every Thursday that Lindsay would be over the next day.

Friday, August 21, came, and Dawn wasn't responding to much of anything. I didn't leave her side that day other than for a trip to the restroom. My breakfast and lunch were brought in to me. Around nine o'clock in the morning, I received a call from Lindsay telling me that she had to go into work that day and wouldn't be able to make it up. As the day was going forward, Dawn got to the point that she couldn't take her medication orally. It was around four o'clock when Cathy returned, and Dawn's son Tyler and his grandmother, GeGe, came by. Kristie Lynn was on her way, and we were all going out to dinner.

As time got closer, I went up to Dawn and told her I wasn't going home. I was going to stay with her. She opened her eyes and shook her head no. She whispered, "No, you go. I'll be okay."

The crew arrived, and Dawn was asleep, so we all left for dinner. I told the nurses we would be back in one hour. It wasn't a nice evening at all. We were getting one of those August evening thunderstorms. The rain was coming down sideways. We were only going a mile down the road to the Mexican restaurant. I didn't want to be gone long, so I ate pretty fast. I was back in Dawn's room within the hour, and she was still sleeping.

It was quarter after seven, and everyone was getting ready to leave. I decided that I might as well leave at the same time and walk out with everyone except Cathy, of course. She was staying with Dawn. I went over to Dawn and gave her a big hug and a kiss. I then walked over to the door and had the door half opened. I turned around to look at her, and she had turned her head and had her eyes open and was looking at me. I closed the door and went back over to her. I bent down and gave her another hug and a kiss. This time I whispered in her ear. "It's okay, hon. Everything is going to be okay." I then went back over to the door and turned around again. She was still looking at me. As I walked out that door, I didn't feel comfortable. I shouldn't be leaving, but I continued to walk out of the building.

My trip home only took twenty minutes; with better weather, I could make it in fifteen or less. When I arrived home, I noticed that it was 7:45. Not even five minutes after I walked into the house, the phone rang. It was Cathy. "Bren, you need to get back here. Dawn's running a fever of 104."

I took off, jumped in my truck, and headed back—it was now eight o'clock. I arrived back at hospice at 8:20. As I rushed to Dawn's room, there were three nurses at the station. Not one of them said a word to me. That right there should have been my first clue. In the past, I couldn't walk by without someone saying something to me. The closer to Dawn's room I got, the worse I felt. As I opened the door, there was Cathy sitting on the bed, crying and holding Dawn's hand.

"Honey, she's gone," Cathy said. "She died five minutes ago."

Please, God, don't take my girl, I thought. *Please let her come back. Take me please.*

On August 21, 2009, exactly ten months to the day after she was diagnosed, Dawn died, resting in Cathy's arms; she was asleep, so she went peacefully. I was told by many, including Dawn, that she would not pass away in front of me. On this particular day Dawn had asked Cathy to come and spend the evening and night with her. Dawn knew I was going home that night. Cathy was with her to the end, and that was the most important thing of all.

So the journey began—the new normal. When you lose a child, you lose your future. That path that Dawn and I traveled on came to a fork. I must now take another path, whether I liked it or not. The original path was closed, and I couldn't continue. This new path I was traveling what you would call the new *normal.* I can never put my old normal back together. The medical examiner should have written two death certificates that night, because a major part of me died right alongside Dawn.

The following section contains my thoughts and feelings that were written down starting with another promise I made—Dawn's eulogy. I made many promises to her, and I will fulfill each and every one of them. When I made this promise to her, she told me that my writings would help me and help others. I can honestly say they have helped me. I found it to be very therapeutic with every paper I finished.

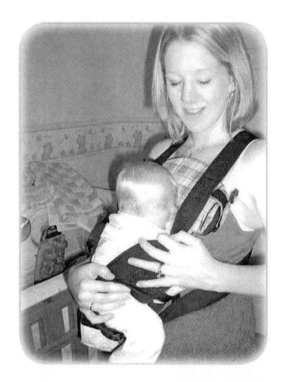

04.11.2009 18:07

SECTION 2

WHAT IS MELANOMA?

SEVERAL OF MY friends suggested that I tell my readers why I'm doing these writings about my daughter Dawn, who died from melanoma cancer at the age of twenty-eight. I honestly thought they knew the reason. My goal is to get as many people as I can to learn more about melanoma cancer. This is the silent cancer—the deadliest of all cancers if not detected right away. I also had people tell me that I was wasting my time and could be doing a hundred other things with my life. For those who think I'm wasting my time, I have news for you. If I can reach just one person and open his or her eyes and teach awareness, then it wasn't a waste of time. So, my apologies to all the negative people who think I'm wasting my time. One other thing—writing is the best therapy available, and I wouldn't change it for anything.

I in no way intend to try and make anyone feel unknowledgeable about melanoma cancer. This is often the easiest cancer to cure. However, if not detected, it is the fastest and deadliest of all cancers.

Melanoma is a kind of skin cancer. It is not as common as other types of skin cancer, but it is the most serious. Melanoma is the fastest spreading and most deadly cancer of all. It can spread to your organs and bones rapidly. Luckily, it can be cured if it's found and treated early.

You can get melanoma by spending too much time in the sun and in tanning beds from all of the ultraviolet (UV) rays. People need to be aware that tanning beds are like microwaves. The ultraviolet rays from a tanning bed can start from the inside and not just on the surface. Melanoma tends to run in families. Light skinned individuals are very much subjected to Melanoma. Other things in your family background can increase your chances of getting the disease. For example, you may have abnormal, or atypical, moles. Atypical moles may fade into the skin and have a flat part that is level with the skin. They may be smooth or slightly scaly, or they may look rough and pebbly. These moles don't cause cancer by themselves. But having many of them is a sign that melanoma may run in your family.

The main sign of melanoma is a change in a mole or other skin growth, such as a birthmark. Any change in the shape, size, or color of a mole may be a sign of melanoma.

Melanoma may grow in a mole or birthmark that you already have, but melanomas usually grow in unmarked skin. They can be found anywhere on your body. Most of the time, they are found a man's upper back and a woman's legs.

Melanoma looks like a flat, brown or black mole that has uneven edges. Melanomas usually have an irregular or asymmetrical shape. This means that one half of the mole doesn't match the other half. Melanoma moles or marks can be six millimeters or larger.

The best way to prevent all kinds of skin cancer, including melanoma, is to protect yourself whenever you are out in the sun. It's important to avoid exposure to the sun's ultraviolet (UV) rays.

- Try to stay out of the sun during the middle of the day (from 10:00 a.m. to 4:00 p.m.).
- Wear protective clothes when you are outside, such as a hat that shades your face, a long-sleeved shirt, and long pants.
- Get in the habit of using sunscreen every day. Your sunscreen should have an SPF of least 15. Look for a sunscreen that protects against both types of UV radiation in the sun's rays—UVA and UVB.
- Use a higher SPF when you are at higher elevations.
- Avoid sunbathing and tanning salons.

Check your skin every month for odd marks, moles, or sores that will not heal. Pay extra attention to areas that get a lot of sun, such as your hands, arms, and back. Ask your doctor to check your skin during regular physical exams or at least once a year. Even though the biggest cause of melanoma is spending too much time in the sun, it can be found on parts of your body that never see the sun.

Watching what melanoma cancer does to a patient is horrible. This cancer spread to nine locations in my daughter's body. Yes, nine—all within a six-month period. Like I said, it's the fastest and deadliest of all cancer. You can prevent a lot of this by protecting yourself with lotion or staying out of the sun during the peak hours.

Source: www.coxhealth.com, www.health.com,
www.melapp.net, www.webmd.com

Eulogy for
Dawn Cherie' Hoffman
September 2, 1980-
August 21, 2009
by
Brendan Hoffman (Father)
August 26, 2009

One of my all-time favorite quotes comes from Mother Teresa: "I know God will not give me anything I can't handle. I just wish He didn't trust me so much."

Driving back from the funeral home the other day seemed so odd to me. Businesses were open, and people were pumping gas and going on with their lives. For them, life goes on, but for me, it felt like life had stopped. It felt like life came to a sudden stop on Friday when you went home to God. It seemed that the world should have stopped because you left it

My Dearest Dawn,

How do I begin a farewell when I still can't believe you're gone? How do I say good-bye to a part of my soul? Where do you begin to describe the love we all had for you?

Our daughter, sister, mother, and friend, Dawn Cherie' Hoffman, was born on Tuesday, September 2, 1980, at the Naval Air Station Pensacola. The most beautiful little girl with a head full of blonde hair is now with God forever in eternity.

The day you were born I felt this indescribable love—a love I had felt only once before when your sister was born. I never knew I could have a love that was so strong. When you were an infant, you became very ill. The angels watched over you for three long months, a month and a half in ICU and the other month and a half in a private room. Well, it was supposed to be private, but the nurses always had you out by the nurses' station rocking you in a swing. Then a miracle happened, and you were able to come home with us. The nurses asked us if you could come home in a top they bought for you. It was a picture of Jesus walking on water and underneath it said, "A miracle just happened." You were our angel from the time you were an infant.

I then began to tell people how great you were, and they said, "Yeah, but wait until she is two!" When you were two, I told people how great you were, and they said, "Yeah, but wait until she is ten." When you were ten, I told people how great you were, and they said, "Yeah, but just wait until she is sixteen." And now you are twenty-eight, and I am still telling people how great you are and how proud I am of you.

You came into my life and changed me forever. Over the years, people have complimented me for being a good father, but I can't take credit for that. You were born good, and you were the one who was often teaching me. I believe you are an angel that God sent to teach me. You taught me love. You taught me honesty. You taught me how to forgive and how to be strong.

When you learned of your illness, I saw another side of you. I saw more strength and courage in you than in any other person that I've ever known. Your faith was so strong. You didn't know this, but I fed off of your strength, and you made me strong when I was weak. When times were sad and tough, I looked to you for courage. You taught me how to be myself. You taught family and friends the true meaning of strength, courage, and most of all faith.

You taught me about life and how to live. More importantly, you taught me to believe. You taught me to believe in the words of God. You brought God and his most holy name back into our household.

You brought God back into my heart. You knew I had drifted away from God and his church, and you put me back on course so that one day we will be together again. You did this, Dawn, and I can never thank you enough.

Losing you hurts so much, Dawn. I will miss you. I'll miss our walks and our talks in the morning and evening. I'll miss seeing your smiling face throughout the day. I'll miss going places with you and doing things with you. I'll miss your arms around me and your kisses. I'll miss you calling me. I'll miss everything about you.

When you got sick and the doctors told you that you had terminal brain cancer, my heart ripped open. We both held each other and cried. After only about two minutes from finding out this horrible news, you put your hands on each of my arms and stepped back. You looked me in the eyes and said, "Daddy, I am so sorry. I know how much you love me, and I know this will break your heart." Here was a person that was worried more about me and everyone else instead of herself! The pain you were in was excruciating, and yet, you never complained. You gave it everything you could. You fought to the very end.

Dawn, I miss you so much already, and I don't know if I can take this pain anymore. But then I think how can I be sad knowing you are no longer in pain and when I know you're in a better place? How can I be sad when you brought so many others and me so much happiness? How can I be sad when God is already working miracles through you and bringing family and friends closer together? How can I be sad when I feel like the luckiest person on earth to have been chosen to be your father? How can I be sad when God gave you to me for twenty-eight glorious years? I will thank God every day for the time we shared together.

I could never have asked for a more wonderful daughter. Everything you did made me proud. Dawn, you always had such a thirst for life. From your Brownie days with your long blonde pigtails to your cheerleading days, you lived your live to the fullest.

Dawn, you were always so active. I used to joke around with you when you were just knee-high. I used to ask you if you had ants in your pants, because you would never stay still. One day you came into the home, and you really did have ants in your pants! To this day, I don't know if it was an accident or if you wanted to find out what it was really like to have ants in your pants!

This thirst for life only grew. As you became an adult, you found yourself in the mortgage industry. You became very successful before the market crashed, and then your findings on your illness. Your whole life you hungered for knowledge.

You adored your family and your two children, Tyler and Jordan. You wanted to teach your children everything you had learned, and you hoped that they would have the same thirst for life as you did. Dawn, hon, you can count on all of us to pass on your name to your beautiful children.

During this sad time in our lives, I am trying my best to remain positive. Even death can be viewed in a positive manner. I found some comfort in the words of Henry Scott Holland, a professor of divinity at Oxford University. His outlook on death gave me a whole new perspective on death and what to look forward to. He said:

Death is nothing at all
I have only slipped away into the next room
I am I and you are you
Whatever we were to each other
That we are still
Call me by my old familiar name
Speak to me in the easy way you always used
Put no difference into your tone
Wear no forced air of solemnity or sorrow
Laugh as we always laughed
At the little jokes we always enjoyed together
Play, smile, think of me, pray for me
Let my name be ever the household word that it always was
Let it be spoken without effort
Without the ghost of a shadow in it
Life means all that it ever meant
It is the same as it ever was

There is absolute unbroken continuity
What is death but a negligible accident?
Why should I be out of mind
Because I am out of sight?
I am waiting for you for an interval
Somewhere very near
Just around the corner
All is well.
Nothing is past; nothing is lost
One brief moment and all will be as it was before
How we shall laugh at the trouble of parting when we meet again!

Dawn my love,

May the road rise up to meet you.
May the wind always be at your back.
May the sun shine warm upon your face, and rains fall soft upon your fields.
And until we meet again,
May God hold you in the palm of His hand.

I know that this is a Navy quote, but you use to tell me how proud you were of me. So, Dawn, fair winds and following seas. Until we meet in heaven (*big sister*), I will think of you daily and have you in my heart forever. It really is true that daughters are daddy's little girls forever.

September 2, 2009

My Dearest Dawn,

My beloved Dawn, today is the day I wish we could celebrate and cherish together. Twenty-nine years ago today, you came into my life. You were a ten-pound, three-ounce baby and strong as could be, with the amount of snow-white hair of a two-year-old. You don't remember it, but you made me so proud.

You don't remember this, but when you were five weeks old, you became gravely ill. For three long months, you were in ICU with a very rare illness. But God sent his angels down to watch over you and to give you strength every day of your young life. After three months, no one would have even imagined you had once been as ill as you were. You showed strength and courage even at three months old.

Your beautiful eyes were so blue and sparkly—always looking around to see who was there. My Dawn, you were beautiful, so beautiful. And you are beautiful now. More than anyone could ever imagine.

I know you didn't feel beautiful the last year of your life, but believe me when I tell you the beauty was in your heart. You went through such a horrible time when you were twenty-eight. You experienced real suffering. At times your pain was unbearable, but you never complained, not even once. I must say, I felt honored and loved that you turned to me during those difficult times.

I was always here for you. I promised to wipe away every one of your tears. I promised to never walk away from you. I promised never to stop loving you. I don't break my promises, Dawn. Believe me when I tell you this: you are always in my heart yesterday, today, and tomorrow.

Now if you were still with us, you would be twenty nine. How we talked about this day brings tears to my eyes. I can't tell you how helpless it makes me feel that I am here, and you are not. Dawn, I am so sorry you had to leave us behind. I really do know you had wonderful plans for your life. You and your favorite phrases "trust me" and "have I ever let you down?" Come on now. Be fair to your old man.

When you were just knee-high, I never let you out of my sight. I've always been there for you, even when you were busy. I've never changed my mind about you. I have been drawing you to me since that amazing day twenty-nine years ago today.

Girl, I will tell you this: whatever happens in my life—whether I live to be a hundred—you will not be disappointed. I will give hope that never disappoints. You aren't going to be disappointed. I am going to use your words. Trust me.

My beautiful girl, happy birthday, happy birthday to you! Today is your day.

I love you.

I miss you.

Dad

October 10, 2009

Many strong emotions are experienced when a parent loses a child. A father's grief is different than a mother's, as everyone grieves differently. Some experts claim that a mother has a stronger bond with her children than a father. These so-called experts should not make comments to that extreme. As bonds between people differ, everyone also grieves differently, and no one person should be compared to another. I know the way I experience grief, and how I deal with and express my feelings is greatly different from how other fathers grieve, or mothers for that matter. Normally, a father is never asked how he is doing. Fathers are expected to be the rock. Most of the time fathers don't show their emotions. From the start, I will tell you I'm not the "normal" father, because I show my emotions freely and shamelessly. As a bereaved father, it is not unusual to be asked, "And how is your wife?" Why don't people ever ask how I'm doing? I have feelings, and my girls are my life. This is probably a question that will never be answered.

There are many types or forms of grief. Some professionals will explain that there are five stages, and others tell you there are seven stages of grief. I believe there isn't a set number. I do know the stages that I have faced, and those are denial, anger, guilt, bargaining, and acceptance. There is no set order for these stages to hit you or when they are felt; sometimes one feeling dominates all others. At times, I may feel guilty because I have *not* thought of my grief for a while. I may even have laughed at something. Or, I may feel guilt simply because I am numb and seem to have lost all the expected emotions. I find myself getting more depressed in the evenings when the day's work is done, and I have my thoughts to myself.

Another situation I have to figure out is how to cope with those around me. I am bombarded with strange, thoughtless, and sometimes painful comments. Some of my friends, work colleagues, and even some family members (no neighbors of mine are included in this. I have the most understanding and loving neighbors in the world) avoid me, avoid any reference to my loss of Dawn, or try to give advice on how I should be conducting myself emotionally.

The comments I sometimes hear make me sick to my stomach. Comments like "Time heals," or "You must be strong for your family," or "You should be over it," or "You should be back to normal by now," and the worst one I've heard, "You at least have another daughter." Honestly, what does that mean? Does that mean I loved Kristie Lynn more than Dawn? Does that mean that the love I had for Dawn I should now transfer over to Kristie Lynn? Someone please, please tell me what that is supposed to mean. I have learned that I have to try to remain calm in such exchanges and hope that I am more careful with my words during this time of my life.

I have read that it is important to be aware that grief can be a wedge that may drive couples apart. Some marriages are broken by a child's death. I can honestly say I believe my marriage is stronger now than it was before. My wife Cathy treated Dawn as if she were her biological mother. The things Cathy did for Dawn were nothing less than remarkable and honorable. I can't thank Cathy enough for all she did for Dawn. I love her dearly for that. Not all stepmothers would have done what Cathy did. I better rephrase the above statement. Dawn didn't like the term *stepmother*. Instead, Dawn would say Cathy was her "mother by marriage." I loved it.

Kristie Lynn lost her only sister, and no matter her age, she still needs special care. She never said that or gave any indication; however, I do know. If she does need any, then she knows she can talk to me, and I know she will tell me. I need to support and guide her in any way I can, no matter how much time has passed. We do share our thoughts about how we feel about ways of remembering Dawn. It is also important to recognize that we can gain strength and companionship through just being with each other and without necessarily using words. Kristie Lynn has told me in the past that one of the things she misses most is how she used to vent to Dawn. I told Kristie Lynn she can vent with me; I will take Dawn's place. I realize it's totally different, but I want her to know I am always here for her.

Birthdays and holidays were very difficult this first year. After talking with several professionals such as counselors, a minister, and even during group sessions, I have been told the second year could be a lot worse, because it drives home the permanence of her being deceased. I'm certainly not looking forward to that. The first year was bad enough.

Grief such as I'm facing can bring lethargy, tiredness, sleeplessness, and illness. This is my deepest downfall at this time. I know I must do some physical exercise. I know it will do me well both physically and mentally. At times, I may feel that I have no energy to participate in such activity, but I need to force myself to do so. I know I can find relief from stress and feel better afterward. Having the willpower to get started and to stay with it is where my problem lies. I have never in my life had a problem with willpower until now. I just cannot find it, and yet, I know deep down I must. I feel that I need someone or something to push me, to motivate me. I have never failed at anything I set my mind to; however, this is one goal that I am having trouble meeting.

I try not to have any feelings of guilt about resuming my old interest in some enjoyable leisure activities, like getting back into my woodworking or playing darts with the neighbors. In the past, I made little knickknack items out of wood. Doing these activities relaxes me and keeps my mind clear. I am also contemplating getting back into umpiring. I find umpiring to be very relaxing. This is something I must sit down and discuss with Cathy.

Counselors and ministers have told me that I could find relief in writing my thoughts and feelings down. As you can see, I have been doing that, and yes, I do find comfort in it. It truly is therapeutic. Family and friends have mentioned about writing a book. I am doing that; however, I plan on keeping it for family and friends only. Even though I would love to help others in the same situation I'm in, these are my personal thoughts. I will one day pass everything I have written down over to Dawn's children. I will continue to write my thoughts and feelings whenever I feel I need to, and I am also aware there will still be occasions when I become choked up with emotions and have eyes filled with tears. Dawn, my love, I miss you so very much.

Dad/Brendan

November 2, 2009

It is perfectly normal and expected of me to have intense feelings of anger and bitterness and a feeling that life is just not fair. It is also normal and natural to feel singled out, like I am being picked on or punished because I lost Dawn. After my shock wore off, I went through a denial and isolation stage. I made statements like, "This really isn't real. This is just a bad dream. I am going to wake up, and Dawn will be here still." Day after day I said that to myself. Night after night I would pray this was nothing more than a horrible nightmare. Each morning I would awaken, and nothing had changed.

I cannot count how many times I came across the anger, along with the sadness. As I mentioned before, there can be many stages or steps of grief. I mentioned five in my previous thoughts; however, you can't limit it to just those five. And believe me when I say they don't come in any order. You might think you have passed a stage and are moving on to the next, but then you find yourself experiencing that same stage all over again. Although I personally feel I can never fully accept Dawn's loss, I must learn to live with it. I now live with a new normal. My life of the past is no longer. There is a new normal whether I like it or not.

It is important to acknowledge the whole range of feelings and even my attempt to try and run away from this problem. Trying to hide from feelings, or run away, only causes more depression in the long run. I, to this day, catch myself at times isolating myself from others. I honestly don't mean to do it, but I do. On the other hand, there are times when I need to be alone. These two are totally different situations from one another.

When it comes to anger, I was told it is okay to be angry. Life is not fair, and I don't really know why. In another story, I explained how I was very angry with God. I was told that was normal also. God understands and will listen to me. God wants to know my feelings; he wants me to express myself. Most of all, he will forgive me. I truly believe he gives me strength after I express myself to him. There are times I feel that an injustice was served. I have a tendency to ask God why.

A very good friend of mine pointed out this scripture passage, which helps me rectify it, in Isaiah 45:9-11. "Will the pot contend with the potter or the earthenware with the hand that shapes it? Will the clay ask the potter what he is making? . . . Thus says the Lord, 'Would you dare question Me concerning My children or instruct Me in My handiwork? I alone, I made the earth and created man upon it.'"

"Now is it a sin to ask God why? It's always best to go first for our answers to Jesus Himself. He cried out on the cross, 'My God, My God, why have You forsaken Me?' (Mark 15:34) It was a human cry; a cry of desperation springing from His heart's agony at the prospect of being put into the hands of wicked men and actually becoming sin for you and me. We can never suffer anything like that, yet we do at times feel forsaken, don't we? It's quite natural for us to cry, 'Why, Lord?'"

There were times I wanted to avoid social functions. It took time, but I learned not to beat myself up over it. I have to decide on my own when to get involved with things again. Time will tell me when I'm ready. I found out the worst thing I can do is push myself into going somewhere that I'm not ready for and then be miserable the whole time.

I must always remember to have compassion for my feelings and myself. I just lost my daughter, my heart, the love of my life, and the feelings that come along with such a great and sad loss are natural, normal, and expected. I know this is hard to believe, but I have learned this in the beginning stages of my loss—time is on my side. I learned I have to be patient with myself and remember that there is no timetable for grief, and its stages do not necessarily run in order as I listed above.

I have found myself going back and forth through each of the stages, although in time the anger and pain does get softer. It will never go completely away but is now at a point where I feel a little more at ease. There was this one day I woke up glad to be alive. After awhile, I came to realize that I want to live on for my loved ones who are still in my life, those who still love and need me. I always want to carry on my beautiful Dawn's memory and grace for the rest of my life. I must always remember that now I am a survivor.

I have found out during my trials and tribulations that bereavement doesn't go away overnight. I have found if I find a quiet place in my home with no distractions, I can make myself comfortable and start typing on the computer. I jot down a few phrases of good memories I can think of when relating to Dawn. I am even writing a book in Dawn's honor, so one day her two children will know their beautiful mother. I have found this to be very therapeutic in helping me get though this time.

At first I found it very difficult to think of stories or memories of times with Dawn, because I was so consumed by her death. As time moved forward, many of the memories returned, and my mind began to focus once again.

I have noticed that family, friends, and even coworkers would be afraid to bring up Dawn's name for fear it would hurt me and make me sad. Maybe for some it might, but I am the opposite. When someone brings up Dawn's name and asks a question, I am so happy to talk about her. In turn, that shows others they do not have to be afraid that I will be upset. What makes me upset is when others ignore the fact that I had even lost a child and try to avoid me. I could talk about Dawn twenty-four/seven.

Something else I started doing after reading about it on a website is that I start writing down memories as soon as I think of them. If not, I would forget them by the time I found the time to sit down. I am keeping these memories in a file, so I don't lose them. Then, when I have the time, I add them to her book. Putting all these memories in a book will be fun to look back on years later when the pain is less severe and the memories begin to fade. Such memories are those that I always want to reinforce in my heart and mind, because I will never, nor do I want to ever, forget them.

The beautiful queen palms, crape myrtle, and flowers planted in Dawn's memory in the corner of the backyard are beautiful. Every day I walk out to pay the site a visit and tell Dawn I hope she likes her little garden. Thank God for purple and lavender flowers. I can find them year-round, and I know she would love them.

I have found myself being repetitious on a few thoughts and comments. I do apologize for that, but I type down whatever crosses my mind at that time.

Dad/Brendan

December 2, 2009

Does an individual's story end when they pass away? Until Dawn passed, I thought it did, but I now have a different opinion and belief. When I pick up a book off the shelf, I normally look at the title, the cover, maybe the author to see if it is a book that I want to read. I start at chapter one and move through the book chapter by chapter. Usually, I wait until I get to the last chapter to find out how the story ends. Occasionally, if I just can't stand the suspense, I will skip to the back just to see if my favorite character made it through to the end. I can't count the times I did that with my Tom Clancy novels to see if Jack Ryan survived another conflict. I know it ruins the whole story, but maybe one day I'll learn not to do that.

The story of our lives is waiting to be told. I don't have the power to look to the end and see what awaits us. Instead, I have to be content to go through it, chapter by chapter, day by day, until the end. When I lost Dawn, I thought I knew the end of the story: "Life is over. The End." I am left only with sadness and despair. But the truth is that the story is not over. There will be sadness in the coming days, weeks, months, and yes, even years, but there can also be joy and happiness. In truth, I can write the end of the story myself, so I can write in happy events and good times with family and friends. I can write in sweet memories of Dawn, who doesn't live in our world anymore. The story is not over when our cherished one dies, and I should not live as if it is! My story still has the opportunity for a happy ending. The final chapter of Dawn's story will come straight from my heart!

Am I being a negative person during this time? I continue to hear comments from those around me. I am a firm believer that people should speak what's on their minds; however, they should think before they speak. How many of my family members, friends, coworkers, or even mutual acquaintances (No neighbors of mine are included. As I said before I have the most understanding loving neighbors in the world.) have hinted or been so bold as to say such a thing to me after I have suffered the death of Dawn? Unfortunately, the death of Dawn is a negative event! I don't think anyone can find one thing positive to say about the death of a child, although many have tried by using common and irritating comments. "When are you going to move on and stop looking in the past?" "You need to stop thinking about her. She is in a better place." "You need to stop being depressed; it makes others uncomfortable."

I truly don't understand people. Losing a child—what do they think? Do they think it's like losing a pet hamster? I know they don't understand, because they can't come close to knowing how it feels. But even after I have grieved and felt sorrow and tears for a while, still my outlook on life is negative, because I find it hard to see anything positive at the moment.

What I really want to tell the world is this: Just surviving the death of Dawn is the first *positive* step I am taking to get through this tragedy. Living through one second, one minute, one hour, one day, one week, one month, one year are all *positive* steps toward recovery. Finding a moment of laughter or having loving, warm, and happier memories are other *positive* steps I am making. Coexisting with the death of Dawn is not something that any of us are given the choice of making. However, living and accepting this tragedy is another *positive* step toward learning to live some type of life again. I yearn to let the pain go. Sharing my grief, my sorrow, and my pain with other grieving parents is positive, because not only does it help to comfort the other grieving parents, but it also helps me to heal as well. We all benefit from one another in our pain and sorrow, in our comfort and hugs, in the ability to lean upon each other.

Yes, the death of a child is tragic, negative, painful, and whatever other adjectives one may use. But for the idea of me being negative—*no,* I'm not. The next time you hear that word, *negative,* say instead *realistic,* because that is what I really am. I was given a crash course of reality when Dawn died. I know now how precious life is, how important it is to savor every moment given to me. I have to take pride in the *positive* accomplishments I have made since the death of Dawn, because not only have I worked so hard to obtain them, but I have earned them.

Dad/Brendan

December 14, 2009

Surviving the death of my daughter has taken quite a toll on my life. I am not a coward or someone who usually doesn't finish something once it is started. I am just tired. I am not a whiner. I am more a private person, and most of my emotions I deal with myself; however, I'm not afraid to show them in public. I have good coping skills and the ability to shake myself off and move forward in most situations. I just do not have the will to fight like I used to. I have always taken pride in myself for being a strong person. I am the type who stands up for what I believe in, and I give 100 percent. I am level-headed, set goals, and work hard to achieve them. I have had a steady job since I was fourteen years old. My career consists of twenty-one years with the United States Navy, eight years with Humana, and now more than ten years with the State of Florida. For the past year, I have struggled daily and sometimes hourly to maintain and just live my life. I try to look at things from the perspective of the glass being half full instead of half empty, but today I feel the emptiness.

From the time Dawn was born, she was the center of my world. I rocked her to sleep at night, played games with her, put Band-Aids on her knees, and loved her with all my heart. We did homework together when I was home from the Navy. I went to her cheerleading practices and all of her games. I tried to set the very best example I knew to teach her how to be honest and truthful, have good morals and ethics, and stand up for what she believed was right. I reprimanded her when she disobeyed, I set curfews, and I was interested and aware of where she went and who she hung out with.

We laughed and cried together and had our share of disagreements and struggles that go along with father-daughter relationships during teenage years. I talked to her about boys and the importance in being treated with kindness, love, and respect, and to be able to return the same love and respect. I taught her about God and tried to set a good example in our home with church and prayer. Then one day, I looked up and saw this young woman where there used to be this little girl whom I had pushed for hours on the swing, taught to ride a bicycle, and tucked into bed at night. Her face was still so familiar to me—her kind blue eyes, big bright smile, and that head full blonde hair. Dawn was a soft-spoken person. She had this funny laugh that everyone just loved to hear. She loved to give me hugs, and she never wanted to let go. She loved me and was respectful to me, and I was so proud of my little girl.

I saw the tears rolling down Dawn's cheeks when her first child was born and she looked into his eyes for the first time when they were just minutes old. I watched her carry that tiny baby in her arms, learn to change his diapers, feed him, and deal with the joys, demands, and responsibilities of motherhood.

I held back my tears and stood in disbelief as I looked at my baby girl in her casket. I touched her face and kissed her for the last time. On August 21, 2009, at 8:15 p.m., the center of my world crashed and disappeared forever.

As a twenty-one-year retired Navy man, I know firsthand that there are things much worse than death. It was a very long road she encountered, and she fought every step of the way. The battle with cancer took her from us at a young age of twenty-eight. She fought for ten months with cancer being in nine locations and never once complained. The strength and will to live was so powerfully strong. I have never seen such strength and courage in any one human being like the strength and courage we saw in Dawn. My heart goes out to any parent who has had to deal with those types of situations regarding their children.

Counting my blessings is how I survive and continue to function and live with the loss of Dawn. I had a very beautiful daughter that blessed my life for twenty-eight years. The death of a child, no matter how it comes about, is the worst fear and most horrible ache of a father's heart. Learning to live again afterward is equally as difficult. You think that you will never to able to smile or laugh again or watch someone else hold and hug their child.

The memories of my daughter's life are the most precious and important things I own. My grandchildren will not have these memories of their own. Tyler was eight and Jordan was three when she died. She will not be at their ball games or school functions. She will not be there to watch them graduate or be present when they get married—or anywhere else in between, for that matter. What they will have is other people's memories and a few pictures of the lady they called Mommy. She was not a perfect person, as none of us are, and I am not trying to make her some kind of saint in death, but I hope I can capture some of those memories and preserve them in my writings for my grandchildren.

I still think about that little blonde-headed girl I used to push on the swings. I pray to God and ask for him to allow Dawn to watch over us. I also thank God for the wonderful years he gave her to me to be her father on earth. The memories will always be in my heart, and she will never be forgotten.

Dad/Brendan

December 13, 2009

In our house at Christmastime, we have six Christmas trees. We have two seven-footers and four six-footers. Each tree has a different theme. We have a fifties tree with nothing but ornaments from the fifties that were our parents. Then there's the traditional tree with every kind of ornament out there. I have a white tree with blue and red lights, and that's our military tree. As much as I love sports, I couldn't go without a sports tree. Everyone says it's my Ohio State tree, but I have ornaments on it that represent every sport played. Last year I even put on a Gator ornament. That's another story. Then for our grandchildren, we have one with little people ornaments on it.

Cathy and I have had multiple trees for years. Dawn has always loved the different themes. One night Dawn said to me, "Daddy, why don't you have an angel tree?" I looked at her and told her it was because I didn't need seven trees. We both laughed and changed the subject. About forty-five minutes later while sitting on the lanai, Dawn said out of the blue, "Daddy, make it a purple one."

"Make what a purple one?" I asked.

"The angel tree," she said. After telling Dawn that they don't even make purple Christmas trees, she looked me in the eyes and said, "Trust me. You will find one." I didn't give it any more thought, and Dawn never brought it up again.

The above paragraphs were in my story. I am going to pick it up here on Monday, November 2, 2009. I was sitting at work this Monday morning, and I kept looking at the clock, because the day was going slow. Then, out of the blue, I heard this whisper in my ear. At the time, no one was in my office but me. I couldn't recognize the voice, but I heard this whisper a couple of times. This voice was telling me to go up to The Regency area and go to Garden Ridge. Now, I haven't been to Garden Ridge since Thanksgiving 2008.

If someone or something told me to go, then I'm going to go and see if I can figure out why. I only work three miles from the store, so it didn't take me long to get there. I parked my truck and started inside the store. When I entered, I was mainly looking down. I was in the store about fifteen to twenty feet when I looked straight ahead. What I saw was unbelievable. There standing in front of me, about thirty feet away, was a seven-foot, four hundred-bulb, purple Christmas tree. My heart started pounding; I couldn't believe what I was seeing.

Now, they had several different colors of trees, but the difference was that all the others were on another row around the corner. This purple was the only colored tree in sight. I couldn't buy it fast enough. I went and got a cart and put the tree in it. I then started looking at all of the different angel ornaments. I picked out six different ones and went to the checkout counter.

That night at dinner I said to Cathy, "You will never guess what I bought at lunch today. Come on, guess." But she didn't have a clue. I told her I bought a seven-foot purple tree.

At first I don't think she believed me. Then, after just a few minutes, she said, "Why are we surprised? Dawn did say you would find one."

That evening I said to Cathy, "We only have a dozen angels. How are we going to fill this tree?" We both laughed. A short time later, I told Cathy I was going to send out an email to my family, Cathy's family, Dawn's friends, and Kristie Lynn's friends and explain about the tree. I then told them if they would like to donate an angel ornament, I would really appreciate it. I then told them that when Dawn's kids got old enough, I would give all the angels to them.

In the email I mentioned that if they were interested in donating an angel to have them to me before December 5. I invited Dawn's friends over to help decorate the tree if they wanted. It only took about ten days after my email went out for the angels to start coming in. A day didn't go by without a couple of packages in the mail.

On Saturday, December 5, the seven-foot purple tree was set up and decorated with 157 angels that had been sent to us. Only four of the 157 angels were duplicates. That just goes to show you how many angel ornaments are out there. The tree is so beautiful. I know Dawn can see it, but I sure wish I would have done one sooner when she was still with us.

A purple Christmas tree—who would have ever known?

Dad/Brendan

January 6, 2010

As I stated in a previous story, most of the time fathers are neglected grievers. I realize a half a year of being a griever doesn't make me an expert; however, I've experienced a lot this past year. People still aren't sure how to respond to a man's feelings. They continue to believe it's safer to ask how my wife is doing than to ask how I'm feeling. And as a man, I have a lot of thoughts and feelings now. I will never understand why people think that a father cares less. Fathers are told that they have more anger to deal with than grief. I find that to be so ignorant. Why do these so-called experts think that all females are the same and all males are the same? I guess that is why I always thought the book, *Men Are from Mars, Women Are from Venus"* was really asinine. Don't compare me to others. I am my own self, and no one knows my grief better than I do.

Since Dawn's death, I have felt angry, depressed, lonely, hopeless, disappointed, confused, hurt, sad, afraid, out of control, empty, guilty, helpless, like a failure, and frustrated. Sometimes I feel all of the above. The sad part is that sometimes I feel all at the same time. Having to deal with this type of grieving is second to none. For the life of me, I can't figure out what could be worse. Nothing on this earth could bring worse grief than losing a child. It leaves you feeling completely empty inside. Just knowing you will never be whole again is very difficult.

I have asked myself over and over if am I dealing with Dawn's loss well enough to still be able to help the rest of my family. Remember, like they say, I'm supposed to be the "rock" and be there for the rest of the family. I don't want to lose my confidence of being a father to Kristie Lynn or a grandfather to my grandkids. Yet, I continue to spend a lot of time asking myself "why?"

This is the toughest time in my life, and it's important to take care of myself, as well as the hurt that I'm feeling. Each human being is touched by tragedy at some point in their lives. I found out early during this crisis that I needed to step up, be strong, and take control. Reflecting back to when Dawn passed away, I had a lot of anger inside me because Kristie Lynn, Cathy, and I had to finish making all the arrangements and doing all the work. This was especially true as we made funeral arrangements and greeted family and friends. It also amazes me how people think everything is "over" after the funeral. Believe it or not, there are people out there who expect you to act as if nothing happened. It's over, and now it's the past. Leave it in the past. How can people think that way? After thinking about this subject for a year now and looking into these individuals' lives, I have found they can say that because they've never lost anyone they loved. They've never lost anyone close to them. Because of that, it's easy it is for them to say that, don't you think?

Here is a subject I have yet to touch on but I need to. I honestly believe it's a joke how businesses treat death with their guidelines on bereavement leave. Some companies give you two days of bereavement leave, while others give you three days. Please, I don't expect a month, but think about it—Dawn passed away Friday night. My bereavement leave started Monday, and I received two days. Dawn's funeral was Wednesday, which means I didn't even have the bereavement leave through her funeral. What about people who don't have the time to take off? This is very sad.

I have always been the type who likes to make my own opinion on different situations, but I can truly understand when I'm told you never get over it. To this day, I still try and compare the loss of Dawn to the loss of my mother—my God, there's no comparison whatsoever. I loved my mother dearly, but it's like comparing apples to oranges.

I honestly believe I will never get over the loss of Dawn. I sometimes feel like I'm going through the motions of living. I sometimes feel distant from other people, and I may find myself unusually angry. I have been told that this is part of the grieving process, so these people need to step back and give me my breathing space. They must remember one very important tidbit—I'm not the average father. I grieve my own way, not the way these counselors tell me I'm supposed to grieve.

As I mentioned previously, men and women grieve differently. Women have more permission to cry and talk. Men have more permission to be angry. Is that stupid? Yes, I had been and sometimes still am angry. It's okay to be angry when you lose a child. Hello, are we supposed to jump for joy? It's unfair, unjust, and an angry situation. The biggest problem with anger is where to direct it. My problem is that I continue to be angry with God.

I can hear everyone now. *What? God?* Yes, God. I'm not saying it's right, but it is normal. There are many statements out there that people say and that you just can't grasp. Well, this is one I try to understand but have not yet. God let his son die for us, but God saw his son three days later. I know I shouldn't think that way, but it's those apples to oranges again. To me, there are so many things people shouldn't try to compare. I can honestly say that I am getting better with my anger. Even after the statement I said above, I know that God understands. I know he will forgive me. I'm sure I'm not the only one who has ever been angry with Him.

One of the many things I have learned is that people don't want to talk to you about your loss. They feel you will get upset about it. I'm not like everyone else. I truly feel better when I can sit and talk about Dawn. I might get sad at times, but it's not because someone brought her name up. When a person does bring her name up and we're finished talking about her, I thank them for thinking of her and also for letting me talk about her.

One of the healing processes is talking about your loss. Individuals should know whom they can talk to about their loss. Friends should know that they won't upset you when talking about your loss. People can help your hurt by talking about it. You have strong, cherished memories, and they should be shared. I have memories of bad times, good times, and the actual experience of her death. I will be honest when I say I try to forget the bad memories. Why would I want to remember them and talk about the bad when I have so many good to remember? I also have found talking about Dawn does lighten my pain and anger for a while. I guess that's better than none at all.

After Dawn's death, I was fortunate enough to be able to take a month off from work. I felt I would not be productive if I went back right away or even a week or two later. I do take tremendous pride in my work, so I knew I would not be able to perform to the best of my abilities. I have found even now that I'm at the year mark of her passing, I do have moments at work. They are getting further apart; however, I do have them. There are a couple of different ways I get through these times. I might get up from my desk and go for a little walk. Other times I get up and close my door for a few minutes. Both seem to help me, and the wonderful thing about it is that my coworkers know not to bother me when my door is closed.

Some articles I have read say that a child's death makes couples closer. However, the opposite is more often the case. Losing a child can break up a family faster than one may think. Even though I don't have any children at home, I feel that Cathy and I are closer than we were before. The care that Cathy gave to Dawn was remarkable. She was there for Dawn whenever Dawn needed her, and Cathy wasn't even her biological mother. That just goes to show how much love Cathy had for Dawn. That is why I feel our marriage is stronger. I can never thank Cathy enough for all she did for Dawn.

January 17, 2010

All loss is hard. All loss is lonely. But there is something about the loss of a child that puts it in a unique category.

I have experienced other types of loss. When my very much-loved mother died in October 1989, I was devastated. My mother was a wonderful, kind lady, a devoted wife, and a mother of nine. I grieved for her. I helped bury her on my birthday. I will forever miss having her in my life. I will treasure my wonderful memories of her forever.

Then, in August 2009, my twenty-eight-year-old daughter died of melanoma cancer. In a single night, my life as I knew it came to a complete halt. I lost all hope and joy, and the worst was yet to come. The life that I once had was totally upside down. Indeed, in the early days and weeks, being able to survive the death of Dawn was seriously in question.

That is why, six months after her death, I thought I must have a problem. I read an article on this very subject. I thought I must have something wrong with my mental health, because I was still obsessing over the loss of Dawn. What I felt was a lot of anger, because the loss of a child is not fair, and anger is an immense part of it. How dare someone tell me I should be over her death within six months? What gives these people the right to even publish such trash? Losing a child is a forever life-changing event, and anger is the biggest part of trying to cope with the loss.

I tried to put into words what the pain, heartache, anger, and loss of hope and joy does to you when you lose a child. Even my words cannot fully come close to the way my life was shattered after Dawn's death.

It is my hope that one day more people will understand what I, as a grieving father, am going through and how losing a child is the worst loss of all. Please remember that this is about me. I'm not trying to write about or speak of others. I have mentioned numerous times that everyone grieves differently. I, in no way, intend to be disrespectful toward anyone's loss. God knows how hard it is to deal with it.

I want you to try to imagine, if you can, never seeing your child again, never hearing her laugh, never hearing the sound of her voice, never smelling the scent you have come to recognize as your child's, never hearing her say, "I love you." *Nothing*—just silence and emptiness. Now imagine never seeing your child's smile, never seeing her upset or happy, never being able to watch her sleep.

Imagine missing her so much that you are twisted up inside, and the pain stays with you every minute of every day. You smell your child's pillow and clothes; you look at her pictures and can only cry. You have never felt longing like this in your life—longing to hear her voice, to see her face again—and you know deep in your soul you cannot fix it. Now imagine every single thing that used to give you joy and pleasure turns into *hurt* and *despair* overnight. Not a gradual thing, but going from pleasure to hurt, from happiness to sadness, from peace to no peace overnight. Everything you loved now hurts like hell.

For example, I used to love music. It gave me pleasure. I didn't realize how much music was a part of my life and how it is everywhere. Now I cannot listen to it; it sears me like a red-hot knife. Every song reminds me of the void in my life without Dawn. I am not unique in that pain—if you lost a child, you would know.

That is just one little example of how your life is affected by the loss of your child. You also feel the loss with your other children. You still love your other children just as much as always, but as hard as it is, even they hurt you now. When you see them, you *feel* the loss of the child who died not being with her sibling. There is a piece missing, a person missing; your whole life doesn't fit anymore. Things that felt right now feel wrong. There is always the missing—the horrible, gut-wrenching, out-of-your-control missing.

As good parents, we were always able to fix things or make things better for our children. This we cannot fix, cannot make better. So on top of everything else you are feeling, you also feel helpless, out-of-control, and hopeless.

Are you starting to imagine now how it feels?

Day after day, month after month, no matter what you are doing or whom you are talking to, a tape of your child plays over and over in your mind. The life of your child when she was a baby, a laughing happy little girl, a cute young teen, and a wonderful young woman plays in your head, and you do not want to forget even a single second of your beautiful child's life. That is a fear you have—that as time passes, you will start to forget.

This is what it really feels like: A part of me has died—a real, beautiful, living part of me has died, and I am still living, left behind to try to pick up the pieces of my shattered life without a clue where to even begin. No wonder a high percentage of marriages break up and parents have breakdowns and turn to alcohol, drugs, or a destructive way of life. A part of me does not exist anymore, and it is scary as hell.

When people say to me "I want the old you back," "It's been six months. Don't you feel better yet?," "You are making it harder on yourself," or "Grief can become a selfish thing, you know" I can only shake my head and feel sadness and hopelessness, because there is no way my life will ever be like it was when Dawn was alive.

I wish very much that you could somehow understand my loss and my grief, my silence and my tears, my void and my pain. I pray that you will never understand.

Now go on, put on your favorite CD, and enjoy the music. Go home and hug your children, listen to them laugh, watch them smile, and smell their scent. And please do not tell me how I should feel.

A grieving father,
Dad/Brendan

February 16, 2010

I have not had a normal night's sleep in well over a year and a half. Before, I was able to get five hours and function without any problems. Since November 2008, I have been averaging two and a half to three hours of sleep a night. Well, this one particular night was no different. Northeast Florida had one of the coldest winters on record. Now I know if the people in the northern states heard that, they would pray for a winter like ours. Well, we do live in Florida, so we expect warm weather.

Tuesday, February 16, 2010, will be a day that will stick with me for the rest of my life. As I have mentioned in some of my other writings, anger is one of the five categories of the grieving process. The strange thing about these five steps of grieving is that when you approach one and then it passes you, you think you are through with that stage. But they can reoccur over and over. One stage that I have found often finds its way back to me is anger, but this time my anger was directed toward something different. This time my anger was directed toward God. I was so mad at him. I was even at the point to where I thought I hated him.

It was three o'clock in the morning, and I went for my walk. It was very windy that morning and 28 degrees. I found out later that with the windchill, it was only 12 degrees. Come on, people, this is Florida! My morning walk normally lasted anywhere from thirty to forty-five minutes. I would just walk the streets in my development. During a normal morning walk, I would talk to Dawn. That was my daily one-on-one with her. Not that morning. That particular morning my conversation was directed toward God. The sailor in me came out that morning.

As I was talking to God, I cursed him out. I called him every name in the book and pretty much told him he wasn't worth a damn. "Why did you take my daughter at an early age?" I demanded. I told him, "The hell with being nice to others. You don't care, so why should I?" I told him I didn't care about him or any of his beliefs. "If you are supposed to be so loving, how could you take someone so young with two beautiful young kids?" I asked. Normally, when a person vents, he feels better after he is through. Not me—I didn't feel better at all.

After my walk, I went home and took a shower. I left for work and arrived at 4:50 a.m. No one starts getting to the office until 6:30, so I turned off the alarm and went to my office. When I got there, I realized I'd forgotten something in my truck. I thought, *What's wrong with me? I never forget bringing my things in.*

As I was walking up to the door to go back out to my truck, I noticed a man going through the trash can right outside the door. He pulled this old McDonald's bag out and started to go through it. I knocked on the window and told him he had to leave. The man had on a zipped up blue hooded jacket. Not one time did he look up. He turned, walked down the steps, and made a left down the sidewalk. When he made his turn, I went out the door and down the steps to my truck. When I arrived at my truck, I turned to see where he was. He was at the corner of the building about seventy to eighty feet from me.

I don't know why I did what I did, because I have never done anything like this. I said, "Hey, buddy." The man turned to face me with his head still down. "Come here for a minute," I said.

As he was walking to me, still with his head down, I reached in my pocket and pulled out five dollars. When he reached me, I said, "Here, take this and go across the street to McDonald's and get something to eat. Get yourself a hot cup of coffee."

The man put his hand out with his head still down. When the money was in his hand, he finally lifted his head and looked me square in the eye. "Thank you, my son," he said. "Thank you very much."

I still didn't think much of it. He turned and started to walk back the same way he came. I turned, opened my truck door, and reached onto the seat to get my checkbook, which took a whole six seconds. I turned back around, and there was no sight of this man. Knowing the approximate distance from where I was and where this stranger was, there was no way he could have gone seventy or eighty feet in six seconds or less. My vehicle was the only vehicle in the parking lot. I went around the side of the building to see him but had no luck. I waited about ten minutes and then got in my truck and drove to McDonald's. I wanted to see this man, but he was a no-show.

What in the world had just happened? Who was that man, or should I say, what was that? Where did he go? So many things were going through my head. I was so confused about so many things. I keep asking myself how this could be. What just happened to me? Was he God? No, he doesn't appear to people like that. Was he Jesus? Was he an angel God sent to me? Either way, that man was not a normal man, and he wasn't from the earth.

The rest of the day I kept having flashbacks from that morning. I kept trying to see if I could remember any distinguishing markings on the man. I couldn't think of anything, because when he raised his head, his eyes and my eyes immediately locked with each other. I can tell you that the man did have blue eyes. I have always been told that things happen for a reason, and sometimes you're not supposed to ask why. Well, this did happen, and there is nothing I can do about it. I will tell you one thing, though; my opinion and attitude has changed, because I know that what I had witnessed was not just an encounter with a normal man.

Dad/Brendan

March 1, 2010

Did you every play the game tug-of-war when you were a little kid? Kids were divided into two teams, and each side took hold of different ends of a long piece of rope. The object of the game was to see which team could pull the other side over a line on the ground that marked the middle of the rope. If the teams were evenly matched, the tugging could go on for some time. Eventually, one side would get the better of the other, and the losing team would fall over in a heap.

This game is very much like the struggle I've experienced since I lost Dawn. As I try to let go of the life I once knew and begin to live a different life, it's a struggle that goes back and forth, many times over. On one hand, I know that I need to actively build a new life for myself. On the other hand, I don't want to, because that means letting go of the life I had before. I am not against change; however, there are some things you don't want to change even if you know you should or have to.

Given this particular situation, changing to me is giving up the past. I just can't seem to give up my past. I feel if I do that, then I'm giving up on Dawn. I know and realize that the object of this tug-of-war game is for the winner to move on to a new life, but I just can't change. It's not like a light where you just flip a switch. People make it sound like it's that easy to do.

I must try and find away to incorporate my memories of Dawn into this so-called new life. There has to be some kind of a compromise. I cannot and will not give up or forget the wonderful memories of my baby girl. If it means I hang in limbo, then so be it. My girl will always be with me in my heart and in my thoughts. You don't realize it until it happens to you, but a person is forever changed when a child is lost. The death of a child leaves a scar that will always be with you, always reminding you of your loss. Sometimes I kind of compare it to a sore thumb that always seems to hit something and reminds you that you need to be more careful with it. This hurt is like that—it's always in the way and hard to heal. Does that make sense?

I have heard many times that life is referred to as a journey down a curvy path. If you think in these terms, then before Dawn died, we were traveling together on one path. Most people have a sense of where they are heading on their paths. Unfortunately, with the death of Dawn, I have now come to a fork in my path. At the fork, I'm forced onto a different path that heads off in another direction. This new path is not one of my choosing, and I'm not sure of what lies ahead. The path I was originally on is now closed and is no longer an option. The challenge I now face is finding out how to make the new path as rewarding as possible, given that I wished I were still on my original path. Before I can do this, I need to pay attention to my feelings, work out what I have to do to express my loss, and figure out how to help myself adjust to living without Dawn.

What does it mean to have hope about something? Hope is an emotion characterized by the expectation that one will have positive experience or that a potentially threatening or negative situation will not materialize or will ultimately result in a favorable state of affairs and by the belief that one can influence one's experiences in a positive way. That is a mouthful for someone to handle after losing a child.

Here is how I feel about hope. When I am grieving the death of Dawn and I'm trying to imagine a new life for myself, I must try to have hope for the future. I hope that eventually my pain will ease, that I will find a renewed sense of purpose in my life, and that one day I will again find some kind of happiness. I know I am not the only person in this world who has lost a child. I also know that others have moved on with their lives. I think one of the worst statements I've heard is "If I can do it, anyone can do it." I find that statement to be very ignorant. Like I said before, everyone grieves differently. Again, please don't compare me to someone else.

Dad/Brendan

March 3, 2010

I was standing out front this morning, sipping coffee and watching the hummingbirds put on a show. We planted three bottlebrush trees in the front and side yards almost three years ago. We've seen hummingbirds flying around the trees and have enjoyed watching them. This year they were different.

There are a lot of them. They come in bunches. Sometimes one will fly over and hover a few feet away, just watching me. And the chirping—I didn't know they could do that. I've never heard them before. But this year, they're making a ruckus as they chirp and chatter.

I have read many books about losing a child and how the parents survive, or try to, for that matter. Many of the authors claim they receive signs from their departed loved ones via nature. These signs usually come from animals or butterflies.

So, is that possible? It does seem we've had more flying critters in the past year.

As I mow the grass, I have butterflies hovering around me. Not the little moths I'm used to seeing, but big, beautiful ones that I haven't noticed in our yard in previous summers. And there was one day last fall when the entire bottlebrush tree in the front yard was full of them. I've never seen that many butterflies around those trees in the past.

When I'm mowing down the slope behind the house, I now have a beautiful white crane diving around me. I've never seen them do that before when someone is nearby.

During our visit with family in Ohio this past July, things like that seemed to happen everywhere we went. We'd had the prettiest red cardinal flying around us as soon as we got out of the car. At times, it would be sitting on a sign or shopping cart or tree nearby, waiting for us or watching us in some way.

So could these be signs from Dawn? Or has the idea been planted in my brain from the stories I've read? Or is it that now I'm just more observant of the nature that's been around me all along, and I've never noticed before? And if Dawn can manipulate the animals, why can't she just come down and talk to me directly?

As usual, these are questions I have no way to answer.

Dad/Brendan

April 11, 2010

I mentioned my neighbors briefly in previous thoughts and feelings. I would like to talk about them for a bit and explain some things about them. Prior to Cathy and me moving to Nocatee, we lived in a very nice neighborhood in East Arlington. We had a beautiful home, but I believe what makes a neighborhood are your neighbors. People in East Arlington just seemed to keep to themselves and went their own ways. I don't expect everyone to be buddy-buddy, but they should at least acknowledge one in passing. Living on that cul-de-sac in East Arlington, we were one of twelve homes. Within those twelve homes, we could only count on one family. The others just minded their own business.

Cathy and I had a home built in Nocatee in St. John's County. We moved into our dream home in October 2007. At the time we moved in, only two families lived on our new cul-de-sac. We had met them prior to moving in, so when we did move, we weren't strangers with one another.

The neighborhood started to grow, and we got more new neighbors. The fun we started to have was unbelievable. Block parties or gatherings at each other's homes once a month for theme dinners weren't uncommon, and the closeness of everyone was wonderful. It seemed like we had known each other all our lives. Word got out in the neighborhood about how much fun our street always had. Other neighbors would be out walking and wander back into our cul-de-sac to talk with us. That's how we began to meet neighbors from other streets.

Then the street behind our house started to fill up. The families we met on that street were just as fun-loving and caring. There were five families we got to know, but one moved back to Texas. I sure do miss them, but I do understand why they returned home. That left the other four families. They fell right in with the rest of us. It seemed we'd known each other for years.

Now I have to explain a little more about all of these wonderful neighbors. I believe every neighborhood has good people; however,

I cannot imagine a neighborhood like mine. In October 2008, on the twenty-first, to be exact, my daughter was diagnosed with stage-three melanoma cancer. Then on November 6, she was told she had eight tumors on her brain and her cancer was terminal. She was given six months to a year to live. What a devastating blow to Dawn and to us.

Then it was like a miracle. I saw something I never thought would or even could happen. The families in our neighborhood all came together and helped out in every way possible. From cleaning the house, to preparing meals, to doing the landscaping, they were always there. That was the physical part, but they were also there for the mental part.

The neighbors on our cul-de-sac all got to meet Dawn. They would come over and sit with her and watch movies and do all kinds of things together. The neighbors on the back street didn't get the opportunity to meet her. The majority of the families on that street had moved in about the time Dawn was in hospice or after she had passed away.

It was amazing to witness how the new neighbors stepped up and joined in to give us the support we needed. I have said many times that it was a godsend that we moved there. If this tragedy had happened while we were in our old neighborhood, we probably would have been basket cases. To this day, these families are so remarkable. I honestly wish I could do something for each and every one of them. I know I could go up to any one of them and ask them for a favor, and they would not hesitate in doing it. God brought these families into our lives for a reason, and I couldn't ask for any better ones.

Dad/Brendan

June 20, 2010

My first Father's Day in twenty-nine years without Dawn has arrived. I've wondered for months what this day will be like without her. It isn't going to be what I am used to. Being a military man, I did miss two Father's Days with my girls due to deployments. It isn't going to be as it was before, relaxing on Sunday morning, reading the newspaper, while sitting on the lanai and drinking coffee. It isn't going to be a gathering of my two girls for a cookout. It isn't going to be a typical or normal Father's Day I am used to having.

Honestly, I don't know what it's going to be—confusing, probably. I often wonder how Kristie Lynn feels about not having her sister. I can only imagine how this must affect her too. I know I will enjoy spending time with Kristie Lynn on Father's Day as always. I also know she will feel a little uncomfortable about not having her little sister around. These are times when we must support one another to make it through. We must remember past Father's Days and reminisce and include Dawn in the stories.

My days always start out very early, and this Sunday was no different. There were so many thoughts going through my head about Dawn and how this day was going to be. If only I could see her one more time. If only I could talk to her face-to-face. It was early morning, around six thirty, and I was out sitting on the glider and looking out at the lake and her corner of the yard with her palm trees and flowers. I was trying to read from Psalms but couldn't concentrate on the words. I was looking around at the beauty of Dawn's queen palms and thinking, *If only Dawn were this easy to see.* I stared into the palm tree fronds swaying from side to side. Beforehand, everything was so still. "Then shall all the trees of the woods rejoice," says Psalm 96. I closed my Bible. *Dawn, you were easy to see,* I thought. *You were in the breeze swaying the fronds, and you were in the wind on my cheek.*

Cathy and I made arrangements with Kristie Lynn to meet at the cemetery at ten o'clock in the morning. We stood at Dawn's gravesite and talked for about an hour. While we were there, my phone rang, and it was Tyler calling to wish me a happy Father's Day. I thought that was so special and appropriate. He didn't know where I was, and it was like he was wishing me a Happy Father's Day for Dawn.

After leaving the cemetery, we all went to Applebee's for lunch. Oh how different that was without Dawn. We did make the best of it. We laughed, and we cried as we reminisced about the past and how she used to tell stories to get us all laughing. It was priceless.

So, I guess, future Father's Days will be what I make them to be. A more proactive approach seems needed here. I could sulk, which is valid, or I could celebrate, which is preferred. I could spend the day thankful for the twenty-eight other Father's Days I had with her, how she made me a father, how she is making me a stronger man and a better husband. I could spend the day making the memory of Dawn a time of enjoying the legacy rather than fixating on the loss.

Thank you, Kristie Lynn, for a wonderful Father's Day. I enjoyed our time together. Dawn, I knew at six thirty that this Father's Day was going to be different; however, I know you were with me during those early morning hours. My love, I miss you so much. You are always on my mind and in my heart.

With all my love girls,

Dad/Brendan

July 3, 2010

Nearly a year has passed since the death of my dear Dawn. As the anniversary of her death approaches, I find myself going over the details of the weeks leading up to that fateful day. At times, it seems like forever since I last saw Dawn, talked to, or touched that special girl. Oh how I miss that beautiful smile. On the other hand, it sometimes seems like only yesterday when I lost her.

I may dread the first anniversary, or I may be anxious for it to arrive and know that I was able to make it this far. Whatever the anticipation, the day will certainly be one with a flood of memories. It is important to be aware that some friends and family will *not* acknowledge this date. Some think if they don't bring the date up, you won't remember it. For those who do remember, I give you my thanks and appreciation in advance. In this past year, I have faced many changes in my life.

My loss has caused me to look at myself and my life differently. I have new hopes and goals for my future. This is a good time to look over my past year and see how far I have come, where I am now, and where I would like to go from here.

There are people around me who would expect life to be "back to normal" after the first year. I *cannot* and *will not* be discouraged, because I am not "over it" or "back to normal." I must keep in mind that grief is a *process* with no particular timetable. Each and every one of us goes through this process at his or her own pace. Thinking back over the past year, I have come a long way but still have a long way to go.

My circle of friends is still giving support like they have from the beginning. I can't forget to mention the new friends who have come into my life and have been giving me their love and support. These new friends got to know me and accepted me the way I am now, not what I was in the past. Like I said, my life and the lives of all of Dawn's loved ones have changed.

There are many times the road ahead looks frightening and lonely, but as I look around, I can now see others who are on the same road. Truly, I am not alone. It is time to reach out to others. They may need a hand to hold. I will stand by them and give them my love and support.

Even though grief does not end with the first anniversary, hopefully I can say that I have learned many lessons this past year.

I have learned to receive and accept the love and support of those around me.

I have learned that my tears and memories are healing.

I have learned to think of only the good memories.

I have learned that although my life is changed, there is still a joy in living.

I have learned that the memories that hurt so much can become a healing bridge from the past to the future.

I have learned that the pain of my loss will never go away; however, the meaning in my life is growing stronger because of Dawn.

I have learned to treasure each day, to show love to others, and to try to help others in any way I possibly can. This was a wish of Dawn's, and I will carry on her wish. I also know I will continue to gather strength from Dawn each and every day.

I have learned to never, never take for granted the gift of life. The first anniversary is an important milestone—looking back at my progress, looking at today and congratulating myself for the major achievements of coming this far, and looking ahead to the opportunities that are yet to come to be there for others.

I have learned to appreciate the people around me more. I want to thank each and every one of you. I would not have made it this far without your love and support.

And most importantly, I am keeping my promise to Dawn in studying and learning more of the Bible. This is the best promise I made to you, Dawn. Thank you for opening my eyes.

Here are some plans / ideas for commemorating the "first anniversary":

Maybe the death anniversary is a time for some special care and activities. I would like to set aside Saturday, August 21, (the one-year anniversary) as a get-together at my home to honor Dawn's life. You all know how Dawn liked to throw parties, so let's throw one for her. The party will start at 3:00 p.m. and has no time limit. For those who will be coming, please bring a covered dish of some sort. If you are interested in coming, please RSVP to me no later than August 10. Being lavender and purple were her favorite colors, we are going to make it a purple day, so wear something lavender or purple.

- Visit the cemetery on Saturday, August 21, at 9:00 a.m. Meet at the gravesite. Take along a flower, a note, or a balloon bouquet (lavender or purple). I hope there will be a large turnout.
- Plant a tree or flowers and watch them grow year after year. I have already done this, and it honestly makes me feel good.
- Spend some time with family or friends talking about the good things you remember, the funny things, the jokes played, the special moments.
- Do something you enjoy—a walk on the beach (don't forget your sunscreen) or a visit to a museum or art gallery.
- Write a letter to Dawn, sharing the year's happenings, the accomplishments you've made, and what you have missed about her being gone. If you would like to share, you can read it at the gravesite or the party. I know I will have one to read at both locations.
- Go through old photo albums or videos and recall the special memories. Share these photos with others. Please make copies and bring them to the party. If you can't attend, please mail them to me. I would truly appreciate it.
- Start a cancer awareness charity or foundation to help others suffering from the same kind of cancer. Starting a support group for people like you who are grieving can be quite fulfilling.

And with every entry I made on Dawn's CaringBridge page, I left with a prayer. So this is to all of you.

Father, I ask You to bless my family, friends, and email friends reading this right now. Show them a new revelation of Your love and power. Father, I ask You to minister to their spirits at this very moment. Where there is pain, give them Your peace and mercy. Where there is self-doubt, release a renewed confidence through Your grace. Bless their homes, families, finances, their goings, and their comings.

Blessed are You, loving Father, for all Your gifts to us. Blessed are You for giving us family and friends to be with us in times of joy and sorrow, to help us in days of need, and to rejoice with us in moments of celebration. Father, we praise You for Your Son Jesus, Who knew the happiness of family and friends, and in the love of Your Holy Spirit. Blessed are You. In Jesus's precious name, amen.

Dad/Brendan

Dear God,

I thought I would write you a letter instead of talking to you on a walk. You are well aware of how things are going for me right now. I am having a rough time. I read in books and everyone tells me I have to adjust. I need to know how to adjust; this isn't something that can happen overnight. This is something that's going to take time.

I can't say it's been awhile since I've talked with you. It seems like I say something to you at least daily. It might not be much, but I do. I do remember very vividly about one conversation we had together. Well it really wasn't together. I had mine, and then I honestly believe you had yours two hours later. I need your help, God. I honestly thought what happened February 16, 2010, explained things to me. I truly believed after that day, things would be different and clearer to me—so I thought. God, why am I back to where I was six months ago? Why am I back to the anger stage? God, why am I angry with you? I am angry at another person, but I will explain that later on in this letter.

Six months ago, God, I had a question for you. So I think I better ask it. I will never know the answer if I don't ask. But will I ever get the answer?

Why do I have so much anger, and who is this anger directed toward from losing Dawn?

A. Dawn
B. God
C. Myself
D. All of the above

I don't know why I'm asking you this, because you already know the answer. God, no one knows me better than you, so you already know my answer and why. You know the answer. Yes, I was at one time at the A stage. I was mad at Dawn because she left me; she left her family. It was wrong of me. I know it was totally out of her hands. I really should have never been angry with her in the first place. She didn't ask to die. Now I need to explain the B. You know I was angry with you for taking her from me. She was so young, had so much to accomplish. And you just took her away. You know, God, I thought I was passed that that point in my life where I would not be angry with you.

During a person's grieving period, anger is one of the several stages you must overcome. These stages really don't come in any order, and I have found out once you arrive at one of them, it can return several times. I am finding out you could possibly never get rid of them. You sometimes have to learn to adjust or learn to manage them. They become one of your challenges in normal life. Where my problem is, God, is that anger arrived back into my life, and it's geared back on you. I thought I could move ahead, but instead I am taking those steps back again. When you take those two steps forward and three steps back, you know you can't catch up when you have those types of setbacks. You know a person can never get ahead. What is a person to do, God? How can a person stay optimistic when you know that each day you are losing a step, knowing you can't catch up?

The day I have been dreading for a year now has arrived. That horrible day I lost my girl. Once again, God, I pointed my finger at you and wondered why. What was so important that you had to take her? I'm sure, God, you get that question thrown at you on a daily basis. I am aware I'm not the only one who lost a child.

There is so much a person needs to learn. I don't know how many times I have told people in my life that God has a reason why he does the things he does. I told them that we're not supposed to ask why, because you have your own reasons and we're not to question you. I would continue to tell them you must have faith. Faith will get you through your hard times. God will not give you more than you can handle. *Wow!* I guess I can't practice what I have preached in the past. I hate to put a label on me as being a hypocrite, but I'm the one now asking the "whys."

God, when I say there is still much for me to learn, it's the truth. There are several things I just don't understand. Why can I not think this out for myself? Others have and can move on. I have always been told and taught, for that matter, that if you have faith, you can make it through anything. God, I honestly believe I have the faith in you, so why can't I move on? Why am I stagnating at this point in my life?

I'm confused, God. I know deep in my heart I have faith in you and your son Jesus Christ. I read the definition of faith, and I don't want to believe that I fall in that category. I truly do believe in everything about you and your son. What is my hold? What am I not seeing?

Faith: to believe in someone, something, or some cause is to have faith in that person, thing, or movement—to believe it is true, just, and worthy of one's support and involvement. In the same way, to have faith as it is defined in the Bible is to fully believe in someone (God), to believe in and act on the truth of His Word (the Bible), and to live for the greatest of causes: salvation for all who believe in the coming Kingdom of God (Mark 1:14-15).

Faith is belief. But let's not make the age-old mistake of thinking that if we believe in God—that is, that He exists—we therefore have faith. Many hold to this mistaken idea. They say they believe in God; therefore, they think they have faith.

To believe in God is only the starting point of faith. But believing in God does not necessarily involve conviction or commitment to Jesus Christ and God the Father. Belief in God is profitable but incomplete. As the apostle James noted, "You believe that there is one God. You do well. Even the demons [fallen angels] believe—and tremble!" (James 2:19). We must go beyond the level of the faith exhibited by demons.

If we want to better our lives, our model for living faith should be Jesus Christ. His life is the perfect model of faith. Throughout His human years, Jesus displayed perfect, living faith and motivated others not only to believe in God but to go a step beyond by believing what He says.

I mentioned to you earlier that I was angry with someone else. That someone else is me. In the ten months I took care of Dawn, I have no regrets. I did everything humanly possible for her. It's the time before we found out she was sick. I knew there was something wrong with Dawn. There isn't anyone on this earth who knew her better than me. I should have been more persistent in finding out from Dawn what was wrong. I knew she was keeping something from me, and I should have gotten it out of her.

God, all these year she talked to me about everything and anything. Why didn't she tell me about this? Why did she keep it from me? She told me later on that she knew something was wrong. She told me she could feel her body change. That is where I have 99.9 percent of my anger. Could I have prevented this terrible situation? Could we have caught it in time? Would you still have taken her? Why was I not supposed to find out? Why wasn't I supposed to stop this? See, God, all these whys—they never seem to end. God, even your own Son Jesus Christ asked you why when he was on the cross.

"And at the ninth hour Jesus cried with a loud voice, saying My God, My God, *why* hast thou forsaken me." (Mark 15:34 So you see, God, we humans are just persistent, don't you think?

I wish you could give me answers to all my whys, but I know you can't. I also realize that I must come to terms and accept it as it is. This happened for a reason—a reason you set forth. I am just a loving father who cares so much for his daughter.

I realize, God, you have a plan for us all. However, when something like this happens, it is only human nature for us to question You. I'm not saying it is right, but it is only human nature. I did find a scripture from Isaiah 45:9-11 that could be an answer to the whys. Is this what you are talking about, God? Is this what I'm supposed to accept as my why answer?

Dawn and I had several one-on-one conversations during the last ten months of her life. I do want to thank you for that time. As Dawn's minister once stated to me, "If Dawn had lived another forty years, would the two of us had the same amount of quality time like we did the last ten months?" God, even though Dawn and I were very close and we talked every day, I can honestly say we probably would not have had the quality time like we did. So I do thank you from the bottom of my heart.

I, on the other hand, need to apologize to you for being selfish. I am just a loving father who misses his baby girl so much. What is wrong with that? I was raised to love my family, love my children. This is what was taught to us from the time I was a child.

So, God, thank you for your time. I didn't mean to blabber on this long. And I will promise to you that I will continue to try harder and will also try to do what is right. You take good care of my girl up there. I sure would appreciate it if you let her come see me and give me some kind of a sign from you. I know I'm probably asking too much there, but what do I have to lose?

Love with all my heart, Your son,
Brendan

July 12, 2010

1. I **wish** my girl hadn't died. I wish I had her back.

2. I **wish** you wouldn't be afraid to speak Dawn's name. My girl lived and was very important to me. I need to hear that she was important to you also.

3. If I cry and get emotional when you talk about Dawn, I **wish** you knew it isn't because you have hurt me. My girl's death is the cause of my tears. You have talked about my girl, and you have allowed me to share my grief. I thank you for both.

4. Being a bereaved father is not contagious, so I **wish** you wouldn't shy away from me. I need you now more than ever.

5. I need diversions, so I do want to hear about you, but I also want you to hear about me. I might be sad and I might cry, but I **wish** you would let me talk about Dawn, my favorite topic of the day.

6. I know you think of and pray for me often. I also know that Dawn's death pains you too. I **wish** you would let me know those things through a phone call, a card or note, or a really big hug.

7. I **wish** you wouldn't expect my grief to be over in six months. These first months are traumatic for me, but I **wish** you could understand that my grief will never be over. I will suffer the death of Dawn until the day I die.

8. I am working very hard on my recovery, but I **wish** you could understand that I will never fully recover. I will always miss Dawn, and I will always grieve that she is dead.

9. I **wish** you wouldn't expect me "not to think about it" or to "be happy." Neither will happen for a very long time, so don't frustrate yourself.

10. I don't want to have a "pity party," but I do **wish** you would let me grieve. I must hurt before I can heal.

11. I **wish** you understood how my life has shattered. I know it is miserable for you to be around me when I am feeling miserable. Please be as patient with me as I am with you.

12. When I say "I'm doing okay," I **wish** you could understand that I don't "feel" okay and that I struggle daily.

13. I **wish** you knew that all of the reactions to grief that I am experiencing are very normal. Depression, anger, frustration, hopelessness, and overwhelming sadness are all to be expected. So, please excuse me when I'm quiet and withdrawn or irritable and cranky.

14. Your advice to "take one day at a time" is excellent advice. However, a day is too much and too fast for me right now. I **wish** you could understand that I'm doing good to handle an hour at a time.

15. Please excuse me if I seem rude; certainly it is not my intent. Sometimes the world around me goes too fast, and I need to get off. When I walk away, I **wish** you would let me find a quiet place to spend time alone.

16. I **wish** you understood that grief changes people. When Dawn died, a big part of me died with her. I am not the same person I was before she died and will never be that person again.

17. I **wish** very much that you could understand—understand my loss and my grief, my silence and my tears, my void and my pain. *But,* I pray that you will never understand.

Dad/Brendan

First Anniversary of your passing
Saturday August 21, 2010
Dawn Cherie' Hoffman
You are always in our hearts.

You are truly missed by all.

Dawn Cherie' Hoffman
September 2, 1980 - August 21, 2009
Beloved Daughter, Sister, Mother, and Friend

Order of Service:

Opening Prayer: Cathy

First Scripture Reading, John: 11:25: Kristie Lynn

Second Scripture Reading, John: 14:1-6: Kristie Lynn

The Gathering: Dad

Spirit of Life: Dad

Letter from Father to Daughter: Dad

Open to Family and Friends: Anyone

Closing prayer: Cathy

Opening Prayer

Dear God, Our Heavenly Father, the maker and giver of every good and perfect gift.

Thank you for the gift of love, life, family, and friends and all the things in life that we sometimes take for granted. God, we all thank you for this special service today held in memory of our dear daughter, sister, mother, and friend—Dawn Hoffman.

She was a special servant. Dawn was a faithful servant toward you, a loyal friend, and a true servant who cannot be separated from your love, not even by life or death. Thank you, God, for creating her in your own image. May her spirit find rest and peace in your loving care.

Lord God, I ask you watch over her family and friends. Strengthen them and help them to understand that death is not the period that ends this great sentence of life, but it is an exclamation point that punctuates it to a loftier significance.

Keep us all now and help us to remember—we stand in life and look at death and wonder, why? But, who knows. In death, Dawn may stand and look at life and wonder, why not?

Scriptures

John 11:25-27

"Jesus said to her, 'I am the resurrection and the life. He who believes in me will live, even though he dies; and whoever lives and believes in me will never die. Do you believe this?' 'Yes, LORD,' she told him, 'I believe that you are the Christ, the Son of God, who was to come into the world.'"

John 14:1-6

"'Do not let your hearts be troubled. Trust in God; trust also in me. In my Father's house are many rooms; if it were not so, I would have told you. I am going there to prepare a place for you. And if I go and prepare a place for you, I will come back and take you to be with me that you also may be where I am. You know the way to the place where I am going.' Thomas said to him, 'LORD, we don't know where you are going, so how can we know the way?' Jesus answered, 'I am the way and the truth and the life. No one comes to the Father except through me.'"

The Gathering

For months leading up to this day, I didn't know what I was going to do when this day arrived. A part of me didn't want this day to come at all, but I knew I couldn't prevent it. Then one night about a month and a half ago I had the most vivid dream of my life. In this dream it was you, Dawn, telling me to throw a party to celebrate your life. We are gathered here this morning to do just that—celebrate her life. I want to thank you all for coming out and sharing this day with me, Cathy, and family. I am so blessed to have you all a part of our lives. The love and support you have given us this past eighteen months are second to none.

On the first anniversary of Dawn's death, I wanted to do something significant. I decided on meeting here at her resting place and talk a little about our special girl. We wanted to bring you some flowers. We also wanted to bring balloons to send to you in heaven. Dawn, my love, the four balloons we have represents daughter, sister, mother, and friend. You, my love, were more than just a daughter; you were also my friend. I was so proud because of the trust you had in me. You talked to me about everything under the sun. Not too many fathers can say that, but I can. Thank you, Dawn, for being that wonderful daughter and friend. I truly miss you.

Dawn, even during your worse days with your illness, you wanted to throw a party. You are the strongest person I have ever known. So, young lady, this afternoon we are having a party in your honor. And, yes, it starts at 3:00 p.m. I remember you telling Cathy and I that parties need to start at 3:00. This party is going to be a gathering to reminisce. We will listen to different stories of your life. Oh, girl, I know I will find out some new stories of you. We are going to play your music. That I think will be easy, because you actually liked most music. You, my love, will never be forgotten.

Spirit of Life

Let us join now in the Spirit of Thought, Spirit of Life, and also our Companion at the end of life are with us.

We are all here now because of our love for Dawn. Today we celebrate her life and her spirit.

Not only who she was, but what her life has meant and will always mean. Grant that each of us may hold on to a shining moment of memory, that we may carry it in our hearts as a candle, a companion in our darkness.

We have come to remember Dawn as she was long ago and as she was just a year ago. I hope you will share in my belief that even in times of sadness, there is room for laughter.

Some people try to tie themselves to joy and in doing so bind it more tightly than a rubber band. But as William Blake once said, "She was one who lightly kissed joy as it flew and lived in eternity's sunrise."

May we all remember that the joy, which comes from loving and friendship, remains with us. For it is through each of us that her memory stays alive, that what she stood for will be carried forth.

May we all remember well her smiles, her companionship, her conversations, her life.

Letter from Father to Daughter

August 21, 2010

My Dear Dawn,

I know that everything I type here you are already are aware of. You told me that I need to write my thoughts and feelings down and that it will help me. Girl, I haven't been writing them down, but I sure have been typing them. I never knew I would have calluses on the tips of my fingers. It seems that is all I do now is type my feelings and memories down. And yes, girl, it does seem to help, just like you said it would.

It has been a year to the day since your passing. At times it seems like forever since I last saw you, talked to or touched you, or looked at that beautiful smile. On the other hand, it sometimes seems like only yesterday when I lost you. Life is not the same without you. I don't feel whole anymore.

I guess you could say I'm from the old school or just don't understand certain things like what a person does after a loved one passes on. In the past, I used to hear people say that they are going to have a celebration of life gathering for a loved one that passed. I would think to myself, *How could someone do that and enjoy it? This is a day of mourning. This is the day you lost a loved one. How could you have a gathering or a party to celebrate their life?* I could never for the life of me figure that one out.

Before I knew it, I was approaching that dreadful day—the day I lost you. I asked Cathy what we could do that day, because I knew it would be rough. I knew we had to go somewhere. I knew if we didn't, I would just sit at home and look at the walls. Then this Wednesday night in mid-July I was sitting upstairs talking to you. I asked for your help in guiding me to this day. Please tell me what I need to do. Please tell me how to make it through this day. That night I had the most vivid dream of my life. In that dream, you, Dawn, told me to have a party. You told me to have a gathering and have a celebration of life for you.

You told me, "Daddy, you know I like parties, so throw me a party."

My love, there weren't too many things I didn't do for you when you asked. A party you shall have. That next evening I sat down with Cathy and told her about my dream. Before I even said anything about a party, she looked at me and said, "Looks like we're having a party."

Some people around me think like I did in the past. They think I am wrong in doing what I'm doing. Dawn, I know my dream, and

I know what you told me. I have to go with what is in my heart. You mean the world to me, and I wouldn't hurt you for anything. So this is what I have decided. I am doing what I feel is right. If others don't agree, then they can stay away. Life is too short to worry about what others think.

It is very true that life is not the same. No one can ever imagine how I wish I could go back to the old normal, but I know I can't because I cannot return to what I once was, because all of the parts are no longer there. There is now a new normal, and it is something I will have to adjust to.

There still are many rough days I encounter, but my friends are still giving support like they did from the beginning. And now there are so many other new families and friends in the neighborhood. I wish you could have met them. These new friends and neighbors stepped right in and are giving Cathy and me their love and support. The feeling that it gives us is wonderful. This was another conversation we had. You told me that others would come into our lives and stand by our side—you and your famous "trust me" words.

In May of 2009, you set me up on Facebook. You emphasized to me that Facebook would help me out. I remember telling you that I wasn't interested in it, but you once again told me to "trust me." You told me that Facebook would help me make it through the hard times. You told me to open my mind and to let outsiders in to help me. Dawn, it was like you could see into the future. How right you were. The friends that have come together because of you are unbelievable.

I want you to know that my grief will not end here on this first anniversary; you will always have that special place in my heart. You will always be thought of, and you will never be forgotten. Not you, young lady.

I will continue to shed many tears; however, I will try and make them happy tears. It will definitely take some work, because I do get very lonely with you gone.

With all that has transpired this past year, I will never, never take for granted the gift of life. This first anniversary is an important milestone. I compare it to a year ago; I realize I still have a ways to go, but with you by my side, I will get there.

You told me that I must carry out good deeds; I must move on and help others. But mostly you told me to keep the faith and to learn more of what the Bible says. Hon, I have been doing all of this. Dawn, hon, I made several promises on many different subjects to you, and I am going to keep every one of them. As you know, some will take time, and others I have already accomplished. My sweet girl, I will never let you down. I cannot put into words how much I miss you. You are truly on my mind every minute of every day.

Love you with all my heart,
Dad

Closing Prayer

O Lord, you are the Good Shepherd. Yet we roam in fear like sheep without a shepherd. We seek your gift of deliverance. And, God, that's why we're here today at Dawn's resting place.

We come together so we can taste again the wonders of your grace, another sweet taste of your bread of eternal life. Lord of life, we are hungry.

O Lord. You are here with us, in us, surrounding us in your loving embrace—your presence with us in and through the presence of our brothers and sisters, as the Holy Spirit binds us together with love, the love of Jesus. We are here, God, this morning so we can celebrate the life of Dawn who is in heaven with you. You, Lord, are the gift of our salvation, the gift of Jesus Christ, our rock, our savior.

God, as we prepare to leave and to celebrate Dawn's life with your grace, we can't help but ask that you would pour out your love and peace and justice, your forgiveness and reconciliation, on all that will join us this afternoon. Lord, I ask that you guide us; protect us during our travels. I ask that you bless each and everyone here and their families.

God, thank you for opening our eyes and ears this morning so that we may learn new words, new ways of proclaiming the gospel of your Son, the good news of your kingdom. And, God, give us eyes to see and ears to hear the manifold work of your Holy Spirit as we leave this place and return to our daily lives. Water our souls today with your living waters. Satisfy our hunger with your bread of life. Lord God, I ask you this in your most holy name.

August 21, 2010

My Dearest Dawn,

How I wish you were here with me right now. Although days, months, and now a year have arrived, the pain is still so fresh, feels so strong. There are times that it seems like years since we talked, but it sometimes feels like just yesterday that I lost you.

I spend so much of my life thinking of you. There are so many things I think of, so many things I miss. Like how you would put your arms around me and hug and kiss me whenever I was having a bad day. Your bright eyes, the sound of your voice calling me "Daddy," and those oh-so-big bear hugs meant the world to me. You always cheered me up. I could use one from you right now!

I miss your ever-smiling face and the way I held your little hand when you were first born. As you got older, you still wanted to hold my hand.

I miss when you crawled into bed next to me after you had a disturbing dream and then cuddled up close and fell right back to sleep.

I miss kissing you good-bye every time I left the house. If I ever missed a day, you would remind me when I returned home.

I miss your messy room. What I wouldn't give to be able to sit down in the middle of that mess right now and help you clean it.

I miss seeing you brush your beautiful, long blonde hair and put it in a ponytail.

I miss watching you become a cheerleader from the Pop Warner age up to your high school years.

I miss how you were able to come to me and tell me the most intimate secrets. How you had so much trust in me.

I miss your singing and dancing in the house. You loved to karaoke and pretend you were some famous singer. Girl, you did that from the time you could walk until your couldn't do it any longer due to your illness.

I miss our clowning around at the dinner table and how Cathy used to get onto us for playing "see food."

I miss meeting up with you and having a father-daughter lunch.

I miss our one-on-one conversations, how we talked about everything under the sun.

I miss hearing you tell people that we are a father-daughter moment. I was also so proud of my baby girl.

I miss our walks and talks in the morning and evenings, the quality time we spent together.

I miss the fact that I will not see you raise your two beautiful children, Tyler and Jordan.

Dawn, like I have said in the past, you were a gift from God.

I knew the moment you were born that you were my little girl. And when I held you and looked at that beautiful face and a head full of blonde hair, I never would have guessed what a joy and honor it would be to have such a precious and sweet girl for a daughter.

You have no idea how your sister and you changed my life. With all that love in my heart, there is something to be said about daddies and their little girls. Daughters affect their fathers profoundly. God only knows the true impact you had on my life. You definitely had a major impact on me.

I know you're in heaven right now with Grandmom. And I know I'm supposed to be happy about that. But it still hurts. I'll never forget those big hugs you always had for me. I love you very much and look forward to the day that I get to see you and Grandmom once again. When that day arrives, I'll be able to turn these tears of grief and sorrow into tears of joy.

Daddy

September 2, 2010

It seems like every time I turn around, another day that I dread facing has arrived. I took August 26 and 27 off of work, because August 26 was the day we buried Dawn. I knew that day would be rough, but I should have taken into consideration that this day, Dawn's birthday, would be rough—maybe even worse. Today would have been her thirtieth birthday.

Today also opens up the college football season, and Ohio State plays for the first time ever on a Thursday night. I wear my team colors on every game day, so today was no exception. Dawn would make comments when she saw me dressed in my scarlet and gray colors. She would make comments like, "I like you in those colors," "I like those colors together," or "You look good in those colors." So, of course, I dressed in my colors, and off to work I went.

The day has not gone well, even from the very beginning. At about nine o'clock this morning, I went to my supervisor Mike to see if I could take the afternoon off. He informed me that we already had one employee that had taken the day off and that he would be leaving at noon. That meant I had to stick around. I went back to my office and told myself that I needed to suck it up. This was a statement that Dawn and I would say to each other.

Since Mike was leaving early, I decided to take an earlier-than-usual lunch break to drive to Orange Park and visit Dawn at the cemetery. I left work at 10:15. I have an hour lunch break every day, so I told a coworker that I would probably be fifteen minutes late and explained why.

I arrived at the Jacksonville Memory Gardens, went to Dawn's gravesite, and began talking to her. Of course, I was crying. I miss my girl very much. I said to Dawn, "I have your favorite colors on today." I told her I was having a very rough time and that I didn't know if I could make it through this day. "Please show me or tell me it will be okay and that I will make it through." After a few minutes at her site, I left to go back to work.

As I was leaving the cemetery, I thought I would stop at the Home Depot off of Wells Road. I needed to pick up some cleaning compound for a project at home. I walked up front to check out, and there were only two registers open. Number 1 and 7 were the only checkout lines open except for the self-check out. There were about five people in checkout line 1. I looked at 7, and no one was in line. As soon as I got to the register, I realized I had two different items. I told the lady I had a wrong item and that I had to go back and retrieve the correct item. I went back and exchanged it off the shelf and returned up front. This took about thirty seconds for me to return. This time, checkout 7 had several people in line, and checkout 1 had only one customer, and he was just finishing up.

So, of course, I go to checkout 1. I know it was very obvious to anyone that I had recently been crying. Being of such a light complexion, after crying, my eyes are always red. I get to the lady to scan my items, and she said to me, "I like those colors together." Then she said, "It will be okay today. You will be just fine."

I looked at her and said, "What did you say?"

She looked at me again and said, "You will be fine today. God is good, and he is with you always." She then touched my hand.

As I was walking out into the parking lot, I realized that lady told me everything I asked Dawn for at the cemetery. She said everything word for word. It did make my day a little brighter than it was before. In the past, I used to believe in coincidences, but since Dawn's passing, I stopped believing in them. This was not a coincidence, what happened in Home Depot. What she said to me was word for word, and that's no coincidence. I truly believe that Dawn was with me, watching over me, and saw that I needed help. My girl kept her word to me, and I am so very grateful.

Happy birthday, my girl. Oh what I would give to have you back. I love and miss you with all my heart.

Dad/Brendan

September 2, 2010

When I arrived home from work today, I was so relieved to be in my own home. The day was very rough for me, as it was Dawn's birthday. When Cathy got home, she came up to me and gave me a hug. She knew the day was hard on me, and she was giving me all her love and support. I told her I had something for her to read. I had to let her know what happened to me at Home Depot. Cathy read it and then looked at me and said, "I'm not surprised."

I remember so vividly a conversation Dawn and I had. She said, "Daddy, I can't thank you enough for all you are doing for me. There is nobody on this earth that could've taken better care of me. One day I will come back and take care of you. You can believe that."

I told her, "Don't you forget, because I am going to need you."

After Cathy and I ate dinner, I went upstairs on the computer to check my emails. Nothing but the computer was on—no TV, no stereo, nothing. I was sitting on the computer checking my emails when the TV came on. The time was 6:30 in the evening. I was going to wait until 7:00 to turn on the football game. The game was on the Big Ten Network, which was channel 610 on DirecTV. I had not turned on that channel in weeks. The remote was about eight feet from me just sitting on the coffee table. How did that TV turn on, and how did it tune itself to the Big Ten Network? Those were two questions I could not answer.

Grant, my neighbor, told me earlier in the week he would try and come over and watch the game with me. He was trying to get caught up with work, so he didn't make it over until the end of the first quarter. When he arrived, he asked me about my day. I told him it didn't start off well. I then told him it was Dawn's birthday, and I felt down in the dumps. I gave him my story of what happened earlier in the day at Home Depot, and he read it.

"You know, Grant," I said to him. "There are people out there who don't believe in things like this. I honestly don't know what you think about stuff like this, but this really is hard not to believe."

In the upstairs room, I have a bottle opener that plays the Ohio State fight song when you open a bottle. Grant and I had an adult beverage; however, we had the twist-off caps and didn't need an opener. We did not need an opener the whole time we were upstairs.

Grant was just getting ready to throw darts, and I was standing next to him. We were about ten feet from the bar where the opener was sitting. All of a sudden, the fight song started to play. Grant looked at me and asked me how I'd done that. I told him I didn't do a thing. He went over and picked up the opener and tried to get it to play but could not. I then told him the story about the TV.

About thirty minutes later, Cathy came up to see how we were doing. I told her I let Grant read what I wrote about Home Depot. Grant then told Cathy about the bottle opener and how it just started playing out of the blue. Cathy looked at us like we were crazy and told us we must have had too many adult beverages. About that time, the fight song played again. This time the three of us walked over to it and just looked at it sitting on the bar. When it finished, Cathy picked it up and tried to get it to play again. Once again, I believe it was some kind of sign to let me know Dawn was okay, just like I asked her.

As I stated before, I used to believe in coincidences, but since Dawn's passing, too many unexplained things have happened. Could these be signs from Dawn or someone else that God sent? I'm sure I could find individuals who would argue with me by telling me that there is some logical explanation for all the unexplained incidents. I look at it this way: I honestly believe things like this happen, and as long as I believe, then I believe it was either Dawn or someone God sent. So the last thing I will say on this is: prove me wrong, and if you can't, then keep it closed.

Dad/Brendan

September 15, 2010

The phone rang at 7:40 p.m. on Friday, August 21, 2009. As I looked at the caller ID and quickly picked it up, a feeling of foreboding came over me, a usual feeling since Dawn had been an inpatient with hospice. It was Cathy. "You need to get back here right away . . . . Dawn's running a fever of 104 . . . . It doesn't look good, Bren. Hurry, you need to get back here now." And so the journey began.

Dawn was only twenty-eight years young. She was getting her life back from a messy divorce and was heading back to college. She told me she wanted to be a counselor so she could help others like they had helped her. I honestly believe she would have been an outstanding one, at that. She had the determination to do whatever she wanted to do.

For one year, I searched for answers, as many do when they lose someone they love. For one year, I was sad with a pit of emptiness in my stomach. On the outside, I would appear to be okay, but inside, the pit was always there. My heart actually hurt every day; it was like half of it was gone.

Then on Tuesday, February 16, 2010, God opened my eyes, and I realized I was on a journey. When you lose someone you love, your soul moves to another place. Only others who have also lost someone they love share this place. You know by the look in their eyes when they tell you how sorry they are for your loss. They have traveled the journey I was about to travel and know the emptiness I feel. This place is where my life seems to stand still for a while. I am still physically here, and yet, I sense I'm just not here right now.

To the observer, my life is carrying on. Inside, however, those who have been there know I'm still on a journey for quite some time. I think it must be time for me to come back now, and for short periods I do. Then something, some place, some song sends me on that journey again.

Those who have been there can journey with me for a time if I let them. Company on a journey is sometimes helpful, and sometimes I must journey alone.

The road on my journey has been much traveled. There are hills to climb, corners to go around, and roadblocks to get through. There are flat tires to repair and tanks gone empty that need refilling. Most welcomed on the journey are the straight stretches. They allow me to coast easily and build up strength again to approach the next hill with a bit more ease.

As time goes on, I am told the hills become smaller and the road on my journey does lead home again. At first, it's only for short periods of time, then eventually for much longer times. It is a different home now and a different me now. I will travel far and experience much, and my eyes, my eyes will speak of my journey. I'll be ready then to guide another, look in his eyes and say, "I am so sorry for your loss."

Death has taught me many things. Things that, if listed, would fill pages upon pages, and time wouldn't permit me to read them all. For today, it's taught me:

To hold onto my wife Cathy a little longer and a little tighter when we hug.

To hold onto my daughter Kristie Lynn a little longer and tighter when we hug.

To hold onto my grandchildren a little longer and tighter when we hug.

That I'm not being silly telling all who I love that I love them each day.

That I'll not wait to do things, and I'll not wait to say things.

To be happy today while in this journey.

That life is short, and it's meant to be experienced and celebrated every day that we're here.

That we have a choice following the death of those we love to honor their death with anger or to honor it with our life and living it to the fullest. That is what we are doing today.

Most importantly, death has taught me to love and live.

Dad/Brendan

October 14, 2010

When Dawn was informed that her cancer was terminal, we sat down to discuss what needed to take place. Cathy and I asked Dawn to move in with us so we could take care of her. We wanted to make her as comfortable as we possibly could. Dawn accepted the offer with open arms. From that day on, Cathy and I gave Dawn our undivided attention and our unconditional love.

I must emphasize the devoted care Cathy administered. The time and dedication Cathy spent caring and helping Dawn was nothing less than outstanding. All friends, family, and even the medical staff noticed Cathy's compassion. By succeeding as a caregiver, I must give most of the credit to Cathy for being by my side. Cathy and I both learned from the situations that we found ourselves in and also found ways that helped us do our best in order to help Dawn. We found that if we went with what our hearts told us, then we knew Dawn would be comfortable and stress free as much as possible.

- We had to realize, because we chose to become caregivers, even with the assistance of a hospice program, that this would not be merely an important job, not merely the most important job, but instead, the one and only job that we had for as long as we had it.
- We had to be totally honest with ourselves. We had to ask ourselves deep down if we could accept the job on those terms. If not, then we need not accept it at all.
- Once we were in the hospice program, then we could call for help and be assured of regular visitation, advice, encouragement, and understanding.
- We had to learn all we could from the hospice nurses about current conditions, but we did not expect a detailed or guaranteed prognosis.
- We watched and learned from the hospice aids on how to do things, but we did not expect them to do everything that was needed.

- We had to adapt techniques of care so that we could learn from aids to care for Dawn, because we knew her and loved her more than even dedicated hospice helpers, aids, volunteers, and nurses possibly could.
- We had to let Dawn, if possible, express her desires and use them as a guide to what we could do and how we could do it.
- We could not be afraid to ask questions. Do not let a question linger: ask for an answer from hospice personnel or medical personnel. There is no such thing as a dumb, foolish, or stupid question, except for the question that goes unasked. We were dealing with a life. Don't be afraid to ask that question.
- We learned to sleep in short sessions. It was not easy or good for us, but long sleep periods weren't good, because Dawn wasn't sleeping through the night. Many nights Dawn needed medical attention or just companion time. When our term of service was over, I spent a considerable amount of time trying to reestablish my normal sleep cycle. After one year, I still have not been able to regain my normal schedule.
- We prepared ourselves to do jobs that we normally didn't do. Changing diapers and cleaning up messes that we were accustomed to think of as private and often foul became routine. Washing private areas of your loved one is both necessary and routine. In all such matters, we reassured Dawn, because her privacy, dignity, and self-respect were at stake.
- We had to be able to accept the sight of unbearable things, such as blood, stool, urine, unhealing sores, and vomit. We must not react negatively to them. We learned to take them in stride.
- We could not chastise Dawn for what she could not control. She already felt humiliated enough. Likewise, we did not present her with a falsely cheerful face. We took the serious, seriously. We took the unpleasant in stride (and cursed the walls of another room, if necessary), made the situation

pleasant, and even told a funny story whenever she was prepared to hear such things.

- We made special occasions, like parties, for Dawn and her closest friends. But, we made sure we let her make the plans or be a major part of it. We tried to make her feel needed.
- We allowed the visitors to be alone with her, especially if the visitor was a special friend. We instructed the guest to call us at the earliest sign of a need. We did not overly restrict the duration of the visit. Dawn would get tired out from the visit, but we would discover that she also strengthened after a little rest. She would be cheered if the visitors were sensitive enough to focus on their mutual interests and not on her condition.
- We informed family members and her closest friends of any changes of her condition. We found it very helpful in asking a family member who would act as the relay to the rest of the family. Depending on the type of change of condition, we would notify family and friends of her change.
- We always had either a cordless telephone or a cell phone available to her. It was wonderful for letting her stay in touch with family and friends as long as possible.
- Having a hospital bed or Dawn's own bed became a serious matter for decision. Dawn loved her bed. She also had a hospital bed. If she could move or roll, then a full-size or larger bed was preferable. A hospital bed is narrow but has head and leg adjustments for when she could no longer effectively roll from side to side. She knew she would have to eventually switch beds.
- For me, this was the most important lesson to learn. It was imperative that we learned to administer medications accurately, effectively, and on time. It wasn't our pain, so we had to care for hers.
- We learned to assist with feeding, but we did not force food, not even water. She stopped eating altogether; at one time, all she ate were milkshakes. If we feared dehydration, we asked for advice and assistance.

- We monitored her breathing, and if we were worried, we asked for assistance.
- We insisted on effective and prompt pain management. Dawn's pain fluctuated so often that the staff was constantly adjusting her pump. There is no reason for a cancer patient to be in pain. We had to be persistent and firm with the medical staff and accept no delays.
- Do not try to reform the person you're caring for; we did at first. If they smoke, this is no time to change that, unless smoking hinders necessary medications. Instead, think about safety. When it came to the point where Dawn could no longer light or hold her cigarette, then Cathy and I would light it and hold it for her. That was one of Dawn's stress releases; we couldn't deny her of it.
- We learned not sit and stare at her. Instead, we engaged in conversation with her, even if the conversation was somewhat one-way.
- We held hands—a lot! The comfort that brought to her was amazing. She felt so at peace.
- The hardest about being a caregiver was preparing for the nearing of the end. Expect delirium, short attention spans that grow increasingly shorter, nonresponsiveness, noneating, refusal of water despite a growing amount of dried bile in the mouth, and labored breathing that you wish you could ease.
- We found that nearing the end is a time of growing caregiver fatigue and aversion. We had experienced heartbreak every time that we looked in on her, almost to the point of not being able to bear to see her in that condition. It hurt so much seeing her like that. We had to find the extra strength to look in more often, even if it meant feeling helpless at not being able to do anything at all. We had to always be there for her for strength. We always learned that this was the time to talk with trusted friends or family members to share those feelings. That helped us muster the strength to carry on until the end arrived.

- Do not expect to be present or feel guilty if you are not present in the room at the exact moment of passing. That moment is beyond your control. But call for help if you sense that moment is near. At first, I was determined that I was going to be with her when she passed no matter what. As Dawn's minister used to tell me, "it's God's will" if you are to be present at the time of passing.

- We had several questions for a considerable time after Dawn's passing. Did we do all that could and should have been done? Did we do things right? Did we do something wrong that made things worse? We must not and cannot dwell on these questions, because there are no answers except this one: if we did all that we could in the best way that we knew how, then we did very well, indeed.

- As much as we hated to leave, we had to let the professionals care for Dawn after she had passed away.

- You will feel empty once the end has come. Tears are natural at this time; believe me, they will flow. We had to find time among the necessary chores and phone calls to simply sit and grieve, although, for many, a family member or friend nearby is also a good aid for such grieving.

- I learned a valuable lesson during all of this. Every sense of loss has two sides. We may be much less than we were now that we are without Dawn, but we are much more than we could have been had we not loved her.

- There is nothing harder than caring for a terminally ill loved one, especially when it's your daughter.

There may be a lot to try and comprehend, but believe me, when it's one of your loved ones, everything will come naturally. The last thing on this earth you want to do is have your loved one uncomfortable when they don't have to be.

Dad/Brendan

January 2011

Dawn's Comments about Death

Dawn's minister, Acie Sanders once told me that I should be grateful for the quantity of time I got to spend with Dawn. The last ten months of her life I was with her twenty-four hours a day, seven days a week. The conversations we had were priceless. Dawn definitely made me a stronger person. She taught me so many things about life, about myself but also about others. Some of our talks were on a personal level and I will eventually share some of those in her book.

A conversation between us took place one day in June 2009 while sitting on the Lanai at home. Dawn asked me to make sure that I let people know what her thoughts were because she knew they had questions—questions on how does a terminally ill patient makes it through each day. She also provided me written notes, in order to help me convey her thoughts. The following are excerpts from those notes.

People ask and wonder how I handle the fact I'm going to die so well. Or they will praise me on how well I'm coping with my cancer and the fact its terminal. I get these types of questions from family and friends, to Dr's and social workers. You name it, and I get praise for handling my demise so well and not being afraid of it. Well here is the TRUTH. I am afraid to die. I sure don't want to die, do you? I have panic attacks and bouts of depression. I lie in bed some nights and cry over the people I'll hurt when I do pass. I cry over my entire family and all my friends. How I will miss all those that I love so very much. They know who they are.

I pray and read the bible every day. I was away from the church for several years. I started going back after my divorce from Erik because I knew I needed spiritual help and the only way to get that was to return to God. When I returned I started going with some friends of mine. We went to the All Denominational Church that was on the campus at the University of North Florida. I liked that because it was more of a younger crowd and I could relate better. I know I was raised catholic but I wanted something different. I talked about it with my dad because I didn't want him upset. He then told me that a church is a church; you go and worship God wherever you feel comfortable. He told me that he goes to the United Methodist Church. Then one day I met a friend that went to Arlington Church of Christ. This is where I met Acie. Praying each day somehow and someway gave me the piece I needed. I don't question it. I don't feel guilty or hypercritical for being out of the church for so many years. I just deep down feel such calm and peace come over me when I pray. It's kind of like something coming over me and saying, "It's going to be OK". So again, prayer gets me through a lot.

I do try not to dwell on the fact that I'm terminal and the prognosis is that there is nothing more they can do for me treatment wise to save my life or prolong it. Not sure what prolonging my life means. Prolong from what? A certain date or time? None of us really have a set date or time anyway. I honestly believe that talking openly about my cancer and it being terminal etc. to be very therapeutic for me. I use the words dying and death in my everyday normal conversations with people. Sometimes that freaks them out, you can see it. They try to act like it didn't bother them, but you could see it really did bother them. They knew my cancer is killing me at a rapid rate. Why should I act like I have to not talk about death or all the words that go with terminal cancer? I'm not trying to shock people or anything. Although for me, it helps to be open. If I was to never use words like dying, death, terminal or cancer does that make it all go away? Does my cancer get swept under the rug? No it doesn't and with me when I'm having a really bad day, it's twice as bad mentally if I'm living in a fantasy world that I'm 100% healthy and cancer is not going to hurt me. When I'm having a bad day, I know why I'm having a bad day. It's because the damn CANCER is making me have a bad day! With me knowing that I can do what it takes to help me feel better. If its medication, or rest and prayer, then I will do what I need to do. I'm not going to sit there in pain and say oh its OK this will pass I'm just having a bad day. I cuss cancer out every single day. I hate cancer.

I hate what it does to people's bodies and minds and their families. You know cancer may be what ends my life. I can tell you right now as God and my family is my witness. Cancer will not win. It won't beat me. It won't control how I think every second of the day. It won't scare me into silence.

Yes it's going to end my life here on earth several years sooner than if I didn't have it. Though it won't take away what I have. I have a loving father and best friend. I have Cathy, my wonderful mother by marriage. I have my mother and Kristie who I love so very much. I have the two most beautiful children in the world in Tyler and Jordan. To my lovely children, you will know your mommy, you will honestly know that I loved you and I will miss you. PapPap promises me that you will know the truth. Jordan my love, I continue to pray every day that I get to see you before I leave this earth.

I have peace with God and myself. I also have which is so important to me, I have love from all those I just mentioned. They love me. So you see cancer didn't win. It can never take what I have. Just because I talk about my cancer and what it does to me physically and mentally and that the outcome is probably my death. Please understand I haven't given up on a miracle nor have I given up on life here on earth. I won't live my life waiting on a miracle. I'm going to live my life as if I don't need a miracle. I won't live my life in fear of death. I'm going to live my life as if I have nothing to fear. Yes, I will do whatever it takes to LIVE. I'm going to do my best to do what it takes in being happy not depressed. So yes, I hate that I have cancer. Although I LOVE my life and those who are in it, and make it what it is.

Love You All!
Dawn

January 2011

"I have my peace now; Daddy"

Dawn was twenty-eight and beautiful. Had a brilliant mind, and was a wonderful entertainer with a magnificent sense of humor. She was coming off a very ugly and nasty divorce from Erik, and she also had two beautiful children, Tyler 8 and Jordan 3. On October 21, 2008 malignant melanoma was the diagnosis. Stage three was the word, not good, not very good news at all. Two weeks later a MRI and CAT scan were performed which revealed eight tumors on her brain. Dawn was diagnosed as terminal and given six months to a year to live. She had very little time left. This Metastatic disease spread to nine locations very rapidly throughout her body. It all seemed surreal; surely it could not possibly be happening. Dawn was just so young, and she was beginning to love life at its fullest. Rebounding after the horrible divorce she was determined to make a name for herself. She wanted to return to school and become a counselor to help others that were going through what she did with her divorce. After her diagnosis, Dawn saw things as they were and not as she wished them to be, and slowly but surely, she began putting things in order.

As her disease progressed, Dawn was less able to do things for herself. You can imagine how hard that would be for a woman so young and independent and who was accustomed to calling all the shots. Everyone around her was so sensitive and patient in allowing her to do as much as she could on her own, not wanting to take away any of her dignity. This was not easy. As her balance became a bigger challenge for her to deal with, Cathy suggested a walker, which would make walking easier. At first Dawn railed at the thought of something so large and unwieldy and "out there." When she did not want to do something, she did not make it a secret. Finally, and with great reluctance she agreed to try one, on her terms, when no one was looking—and she sheepishly admitted she liked it! Dawn was so independent by nature and remained that way until the last day of her life, accomplishing a list of things she wanted to get done.

Humor had always been a major part of Dawn's life, and this did not change now. One day she asked me to take her to the cemetery. She wanted to see the two plots I picked out. Dawn had asked me if I would make all of her arrangements, which believe me, was the hardest thing I have ever had to do. We arrived at the area of the cemetery where the plots were, and Jay, an employee of Jacksonville Memory Garden was nearby. Jay is the individual I purchased the plots from. She happened to be in the area and saw us and she came to see us. Now if this isn't humor I don't know what is. The two plots were on a little slope. As the three of us were standing in front, Dawn said to me, "Daddy, I want this one and pointed to the one on the right." I told her she could have whatever one she wanted. Once again, she made that same statement. I said, "OK hon." She then said, "Daddy, you're not going to ask me why I want the one on the right." "OK hon, why do you want the one on the right?" She said, "Because Daddy, if you were on the right and you happen to turn over, you would roll down and end up on top of me and you're too heavy!" I should have known she would have said something like that. She even had a joke about her final resting place. The look on Jay's face was priceless. Jay then said, "Ms Dawn, I do have two that are available just fifty feet from these and they are on level ground." Dawn asked to see them. Once again, the three of us are standing in front and Dawn said again, "Daddy, I want the one on the right." "OK Dawn, why do you want the one on the right?" "Well can't you see daddy, I have (as she read the name of the gravestone next to the available plot) Mr. Looney next to me and there is no one next to the one on the left. At least I will be next to a Looney!" We laughed and joked about it all the way home because we think Jay was in shock after being around the two of us. I think Dawn just blew the poor woman away.

In early January of 2009, our pastor from Beaches United Methodist Church dropped by the house on a Sunday afternoon. Both Dawn and Pastor Jimmy John hit it off right away. Everyday Dawn would read and take notes of the bible for hours on end. Once she couldn't read any longer I went out and purchased the audio version of the bible. The two of them spent an hour on the Lanai discussing the bible. Pastor Jimmy came inside the house and looked at Cathy and me and said, "I sure wish I could have her teach my Sunday school class." Dawn did not attend our church. She attended Arlington Church of Christ. Several months before Dawn found out her illness she would say to me, "Daddy, I want you to meet my new minister." He is so wonderful. I never got around meeting him until February 2009. I returned home from work one day and I came inside the house. As I walked into the family room I noticed we had company. I overheard Dawn say, "Great, my daddy's home." About that time this man stood up from the sofa, and I thought 'oh my how tall this man was'. This man put his hand out and said my name is Acie, Acie Sanders. Acie will be mentioned several times from this point on in Dawn's story. Acie would stop by at least once a week. Each time Dawn would ask to have private time with him. After each visit Dawn would tell me what transpired. I told her that she didn't have to but she insisted I know what was going on. Dawn talked to me about everything under the sun. The two of them were making her funeral arrangements so that her service would be a meaningful memory for us. She wanted it to be upbeat, not sad, with happy songs. She wanted it to reflect all that was most important to her in life. She wanted the memory of it to be a good one for all of us and to give us comfort knowing she loved us all so very much. She could not have chosen a more compassionate man than Minister Acie to discuss the important things in life, and together they planned the service that would celebrate her young and very full life. Minister Acie told us later that as they chose the readings and songs for the day she had never been more aware of the presence of Christ.

Dawn remained as busy as her illness would allow, trying hard to put as many things in good order as she could, and not wanting to concentrate too much on what was really happening to her. Although she was a realist at heart, the pain she knew her family would suffer in losing her was matched only by the heartache she felt in leaving us. One day out of the blue, Dawn said to me, "I really don't want to die, you know, daddy, but I wouldn't give anything in the world for these past six months. I have never loved so much, and I have never known how to accept love like I do now. This is the happiest I have ever been in my life daddy, can you understand that?" I could not answer her right away. Here was a young lady who knew she was terminal, but was telling me this is the happiest she has ever been. She really was at peace with God.

One day in early July, Dawn and I were sitting on the Lanai, she said, "Daddy, you and I have to talk privately, really talk. I'm losing control. Please help me, I'm afraid I'm going to get angry with everyone one day, like I did when I dropped the soap in the shower this morning. I just lost it and I couldn't help myself. I couldn't bend down to pick it up. I didn't want to ask anyone for help." She spoke with as much anguish and sadness in her eyes; I thought my heart was going to break right there in front of her. "What can you do to help me daddy?" she asked. "Baby girl I have nothing to give you that will change the physical things that are happening to you," I said to her. "But I think if we talk to God about them, He will help you in ways that I cannot. He knows everything that's happening to you, and only He understands what will make this time easier for you." Dawn, sitting next to me on the Lanai, simply nodded her head in agreement. "Do you want to pray together and ask God for his help?" I asked.

"Yes, please," she responded.

Dawn said to me, "So, can we hold hands?"

Reaching out, she simply took both my hands in hers, wordlessly, and bowed her head.

"Heavenly Father, You promise when two or more people are gathered together in your name, that Your divine Son is always present with us. Lord, we take you at your word. Lord Jesus, we ask you to be present here in this very room with Dawn now. Please put Your loving arms around her and hold her close to your heart and give her the peace that only You have to give. Above everything else, help her to see how much you love her, how close you are to her now, and how safe she is in your care." We sat together quietly for a few minutes, then Dawn asked me if she could be alone for a few minutes. So I got up and went inside the house. Dawn's favorite part of the house was the Lanai. Cathy and I quietly talked in the kitchen for the next half hour. Cathy and Dawn were like two peas in a pod. Dawn was so appreciative of Cathy for all she did for her. I know words are cheap but I told God to please take that cancer out of her and give it to me. I would have given anything for this not to be happening to her now. But I knew I couldn't change any of it for her. She was unbelievably brave.

Later that evening Dawn asked me if we could go for a walk. By this time Dawn is pretty much getting around in a wheel chair. As we were out walking she asked me to push her into the park at the end of our street. As I did she said push me up by the swings. When I did she asked me to help her get onto one. "Push me daddy, push me just like you did when I was little." After a few minutes of pushing her she asked me to stop her and to come stand in front of her. When I got in front my baby girl said to me, "Daddy, you don't have to worry about me. I have my peace now," she said it quietly, looking me straight in the eye, "and nothing can take it away from me." From that day forward until the day she died, Dawn reminded me in very comforting tones that she had her peace. God had put a gentle and quieting hand on her soul now, and she knew it.

Dawn had to return to Hospice on July 12th. We asked Hospice if I could bring her in and they told me that would be all right. Normally, you have to be brought in by ambulance. As we were leaving the house Dawn asked me which way we were going. I told her and she asked me if we could go a different way. She wanted to stop at Starbucks. The girl loved Starbucks. We arrived and she said she wanted to get out and order and then sit outside, I had no problem with any of her wishes. Then she said to me, "Can we come back here in a couple of days?" "Make it Saturday, OK?" I promised her I would, and if she couldn't leave Hospice I would go pick one up for her. She was in total agreement with that. Deep down, I honestly believe she knew once she entered Hospice this time she was not coming out.

The brave front of being "daddy" and being around Dawn this whole time; watching what she was going through was so painful. It's lasting and powerful to see and caused an ache in my heart too deep for words. When someone who is so close to dying looks at you with the complete knowledge that you know and they know they are dying, souls touch and are never the same again. Now, we would have our quiet time together, just Dawn and me. After our time together I would let her rest. I would put a CD of her bible into the CD player and hit play. She loved listening to them.

Dawn died the evening of August 21, 2009, resting in Cathy's arms; she was asleep so she did go peacefully. I was told by many including Dawn that she would not pass away in front of me. On this particularly day, Dawn asked Cathy to come and spend the evening and night with her. Dawn knew I was going home that night. Cathy was with her to the end, and that was the most important thing of all.

Dad / Brendan

February 21, 2011

That rainy August night in 2009 will forever be etched in my mind. It was the night Dawn lost her life at the young age of twenty-eight. The death of a child at any age seems to go against the natural order of life itself. Everyone always expects that our children will outlive us. When I lost Dawn to this horrific cancer, it was like I lost a part of myself. I don't think I will ever be whole or complete again. There will always be that void, and it will never go away.

In most of my previous writings, I have stated that everyone grieves differently and in his or her own time. Some things that have helped me might not help the next person. However, I will share with you some of the things that I have found still help me, even eighteen months later.

The thoughts that would come and go were like a merry-go-round. You think you have passed one of the steps of grieving and are moving on when that very same step would come right back around and hit you as hard, if not harder, than it did the first time. Did I do everything humanly possible for Dawn? Was I always there for her when she needed something? Any time you second-guess yourself, you have doubt.

During my grieving time, and still to this day, I had to start a new journey, which was like riding a roller coaster. So many twists and turns and upside downs. At times, I felt guilty, or I'd ask myself if I did enough for her. The one step of grieving that would constantly return was anger. The first thing that would cross my mine when I was angry was the unfairness of her untimely death. Anything could set me off and change my whole personality for the day. Believe me; expect to have emotional ups and downs. These are a normal part of the grieving process.

I have learned that you must do the best you can in taking care of your own health. I didn't do that during my caregiver days and even up to eighteen months after her passing. I now, at the eighteen-month mark, finally realize that I must get back to taking care of my health. It is important to maintain your health and strength as you cope with such a traumatic loss. You must ensure you eat properly, get enough rest, and take any medicines your doctor has prescribed to you. You are doing more harm to yourself if you continue to ignore your health.

You must plan on how you are going to spend upcoming special days, like those anniversary days, birthdays, holidays, etc., and how to best cope with those types of days, as they can be difficult to manage. Two months before the one-year anniversary of Dawn's death, I discussed with my family and friends what I wanted to do to honor Dawn on that day. I had individuals who were against me holding a celebration of life party in her honor; however, I did it anyway. During the gathering, we reminisced about Dawn. There were tears, but they were happy tears—tears of joy. From those who attended, I received wonderful feedback on this gathering and how it helped them also.

It took me awhile, but I gathered all of Dawn's photos. I then arraigned them by age group and put them in photo albums. I already had some albums, but I left those alone. You may already have photos in albums or books; just leave them as they are. If you find some photos that have a special meaning, get copies made and frame them. You don't have to put photos throughout your home or office, but having a couple here and there is nice. Another thing people find helpful is to create a special remembrance of their loved one—a tribute to honor his or her memory. For example, you might light a special candle or plant a tree or garden. A couple of my sisters and brothers-in-law had a landscaping company come to our house and plant a tree in memory of Dawn. Cathy and I made a memory garden in one section of our yard.

Some individuals seek comfort from their spiritual beliefs. You must believe that faith has ways of offering comfort during times of grief. I have found that support and practical help from people who share their faith also makes a difference. Numerous times I felt I received comfort from prayer and meditation. You may find it helpful to discuss your feelings about the loss of your loved one with your minister or priest who has experience working with grieving parents.

As you can see, there are so many ways that you can get help. There are so many resources out there to help you with your grief. Use it; you'll feel better that you did.

Some articles and books I have read suggest keeping a journal. Dawn had told me numerous times that putting my thoughts and feelings on paper would help me feel more in control. I found writing down my memories of Dawn was, and still is, comforting. When I fall into a depressed mode, I often go back and reread them, and it actually helps me get through the rough times. I find I can help myself more through my own writings. It is very therapeutic to me.

Utilize the professional help that is available for you and your family. Counseling exists to help you manage your feelings, understand the grief process, and refocus on the day-to-day tasks that need to be done. Hospice offered free counseling for up to one year after Dawn's death. One of the goals of bereavement counseling is to help you find a way to cherish your memories of your loved one while remaining open to new experiences in your life. At Cancer*Care*, you can receive free counseling from oncology social workers that specialize in helping people affected by cancer. Join a support group. Talking to other parents who have lost an adult child to cancer can help you feel less alone in your grief. Bereavement support groups led by trained counselors, such as those offered by Cancer*Care*, offer a chance to share and learn from others.

Is there a difference between a young child's death and the death of an adult child? Even during a parent's darkest hour, I have come across individuals who think losing their own young child is worse than you losing an adult child. I have always said that no matter the age, the pain is the same. Are there parents out there who have it worse than others? Have you ever heard the saying that there is someone, somewhere who has it worse than you? Even in my darkest time of grieving, I found someone who did have it worse than me and everyone else.

In our The Compassionate Friends group, I met a wonderful couple. At the beginning of our session, you state your name, the name of your loved one you lost, and their age. This couple told the story of their thirty-five-year-old daughter who had been murdered by her estranged husband along with their three children, ages ten, seven, and four. The pain and sorrow for one is insurmountable. I couldn't imagine grieving over four loved ones.

I have encountered the most difficult and most painful situation a parent will ever have to face. There is nothing on this earth you can relate to losing a child. As I wrote in a previous paper, "A wife who loses a husband is called a widow. A husband who loses a wife is called a widower. A child who loses his parents is called an orphan. But . . . there is no word for a parent who loses a child. That's how awful the loss is!" The death of a child, regardless of age, is overwhelming. You can never be fully prepared for your child to die. The grief is intense, long-lasting, and complex. My heart actually hurts. The day Dawn died it was like I just found out. Maybe it was because I blocked it out or didn't want to believe I was going to lose my girl.

The grief and the healing process contain similar elements for all grieving parents, but for those whose adult children have died, there are additional factors that may affect their grief. Others often assume that when the child who died was an adult, the parents' pain is less than if the child had been young. Parents whose adult child has died often find their grief discounted or disallowed.

I know that my relationship with Dawn was more than just a father-daughter relationship. Dawn and I were the best of friends. This might sound strange to some, but we had a trust and bond better than any mother-daughter relationship. You see, I not only lost my daughter; I lost my best friend as well.

Over time, it is normal for a relationship between a father and daughter to develop from a parent-child relationship to that of a more mature relationship. I had loved, reared, and encouraged Dawn's development into maturity and a full life of her own, and I felt a sense of pride and accomplishment as she completed her education, established a career, and gave me two beautiful grandchildren. Then we developed that best friend relationship. I often question my own purpose in life, because everything I did to raise Dawn now seems for naught.

Throughout my grieving period, I felt guilty at times for having outlived Dawn. I often wonder what I could have done differently to prevent her situation from taking place. She would tell me everything, and I can't help wonder why she never told me about this until it was too late. The many what-ifs are constantly going through my head. What if I had know something ten months earlier? I knew Dawn like a book. Why didn't I ask her what was wrong? These types of thoughts and questions can and will eat at you. Guilt will literally make you sick. There are so many different things guilt can do to the human body.

On Thanksgiving Day 2009, just three months after Dawn's passing, I thought I was having a stroke. Cathy took me to the emergency room, and I was told later it wasn't a stroke but Bell's palsy. I asked the doctor what in the world it was and what caused it. He commented that99 percent of the time it's due to stress. Then in September 2010, I was hospitalized for six days for internal bleeding. After some tests, it was explained to me that my entire colon was inflamed and that I had a serious colon disease. Stress is also the cause of this medical problem. I guess it was a sign telling me my health was deteriorating right before my eyes.

Do not be surprised by the guilty feelings that cross your mind when you're alone. You must not let these feelings stay inside you. It's done and passed; you couldn't change it from happening. If you do seem to have that guilt inside and are unable to let it go, talk to someone. Talk to a close friend or family member. Don't be afraid or ashamed of not being able to cope with your emotions alone. I always seemed a little more relieved when I had a meltdown. I have friends who I know will sit and listen to me vent. I guess that's why I call them friends.

After Dawn's passing, many thoughts went through my head. Some thoughts were stronger than others, and some were very brief thoughts. One thought that came across my mind was the feeling that I didn't have anything to live for and thus thought about a release from the intense pain. Nine out of ten people have this same thought and feeling. It's a normal process of grieving. You are throwing the blame on yourself.

One thing that comes to mind is shortly after Dawn died, I had individuals tell me "it does get easier." I would just look at them and tell them it will never get easier. What I have noticed—and if this is what they mean, then things do get easier—is that I find it easier to talk about Dawn's death without having a meltdown. I believe I will never get totally over her death, and I will continue to have meltdowns periodically. So if this is what they were talking about, then I suppose I have hit that milestone.

I have felt this way for quite some time, but be assured that a sense of purpose and meaning does return. The pain does lesson, but your heart continues to ache. One of the most demanding challenges I have faced at the eighteen-month mark is trying to refocus my life. Trying to reestablish my life seems so far out that I often cannot see any light at the end of the tunnel. The loss and the thought of living the rest of my life without Dawn are very frightening.

Reexamining priorities and even questioning belief structures is not abnormal. If you are working outside the home, concentrate on arranging additional time off from work and plan ahead how you will handle those special days, such as anniversary dates and holidays. Often the day is easier than the dread that usually leads up to it. I should have planned better on Dawn's birthday. It was a horrible day; I honestly didn't think I would make it through the entire day. However, I had some help from above, and I did make it through it.

I have noticed that talking about Dawn's death, my loss, and my pain seems to help me. I know some who can't or don't want to talk about the loss of their loved ones. I love talking about Dawn, because I know I will feel better. Find a friend or family member you can talk to. Not everyone wants to hear about death. I constantly revisit the good memories of Dawn and not just the immediate memories of her death. I do try to block out the bad memories, but sometimes I just can't. I only want to remember the good ones. You must also try to understand that every person within the family will be grieving in his or her own manner. I have found it better to express my feelings than to internalize them; crying has been proven to be healthy and therapeutic.

You should never have regrets, but I do think about one thing I would change I could, and that is to allow friends to help. When they ask what they can do for you, don't be afraid to tell them your needs. This would have helped tremendously if I had let them. You don't always have to let them do things, but occasionally, the amount of time it saves is so helpful. Those who ask you if you need help, really mean it. They want to help, so don't be afraid to utilize their generosity and kindness.

There is so much assistance out there, whether it's a one-on-one with a counselor or a group session. I personally found the group counseling more helpful. Some others might like the private setting with a one-on-one meeting. I did come across a counseling group that is internationally known called the Compassionate Friends. I attended several meetings. They meet once a month on the second Monday of each month. There is plenty of support surrounding you; you truly do find hope and comfort by sharing your story with others. In this way, I have gained insight and learned ways to cope. Sharing also eased the loneliness and allowed me to express my grief in an atmosphere of acceptance and understanding.

I can't emphasize enough that everyone grieves differently and at a different rate. The things that may be good for me and helped me might not help you. You have to find your own comfort zone. You must find a release to help you. You cannot let all of your stress and anger build up inside; if you do, then you might as well plan your departure to join your loved one.

I will continue to do my writings as I promised my dear Dawn; however, I am going to try and make my future writing about helpful information for others who are going through the same nightmare I went through. If I can help one person, then I will feel I have accomplished something. I will also continue to write my feelings and thoughts down, as I do find relief in rereading my papers.

Previously, I talked about keeping up your health. I have no room to really tell someone that they need to so, because I never kept mine up. I can sit with the best and tell them what they need to do, but I could never practice what I preached. I guess you could say I would make a good politician. Back in September when I was hospitalized for internal bleeding, Dr. Reid, my specialist doctor, asked me several questions about the stress in my life. She asked me about my job and marriage, and I told her there was no stress from either. The next day she started asking me more questions, and finally, she got to the part about Dawn. Most individuals who find out that you lost a loved one would normally say, "I am so sorry to hear that." Not Dr. Reid. She looked me dead in the eyes and said, "Are you trying to join her?" To most people, that would have been an eye-opening moment and motivation to change their lifestyle, but not me—no, it just didn't register for me.

Remember the paragraph above when I talked about having friends help you? This wasn't something just from the time period when Dawn was ill or right after her passing. This is for however long it takes you to find that new route and be able to function on your own. That's why we call these people friends. Most individuals (mainly me) don't like asking for help because of pride. It's wonderful to have pride in yourself; however, asking for someone's help doesn't make you less of a person. Put your pride aside and ask for help if you need it.

Because I have been preaching about taking care of your health and I haven't practiced it, I am telling you all right now. I am finally admitting to myself and the whole world that I can't do it alone. I need help, or I will be joining Dawn. As much as I miss her and would love to be with her, it's not my time. There are still things here in my life that I have not completed. I, on the other hand, am facing the fact I cannot do this alone, so this is what I did. I emailed a close friend of my girls. This young lady, Danielle, whom I love dearly, is a personal trainer. Danielle is going to get my life back to where it should be.

On Monday, February 21, 2011, exactly eighteen months after the day I lost Dawn, my training begins. What a perfect day to start that journey—a journey for better health and a journey to begin practicing what I preach.

Danielle, I love you dearly, and I have the upmost respect for you. For you to take your time and help me is admirable. You are putting life back into me. You are sharing your strength and willpower with me. I remember something you told me eighteen months ago. You said, "Brendan, I am and always will be here for you. If you need me, just let me know." I am telling you here and now, I will not let her down.

Dad/Brendan

March 1, 2011

No matter how long ago my daughter died, I continue to have meltdowns. There are moments when, out of the blue, something is said or done to bring my focus back to Dawn, who I have so carefully placed in a special section of my heart. In those moments, I remember everything. My reaction may be to smile and simply go on as though nothing has happened, I may get an excruciating pain, and/or I might have a meltdown.

Of the last two just mentioned, I at times get a pain in my heart when something reminds me of her. Other times, I have a meltdown. Just the other day, I walked into the Navy Exchange and passed a lady spraying on perfume. It was Dawn's perfume. There are so many things that can trigger your emotions. Things such as restaurants, certain coffee shops, and even a song can set off a reaction. Sometimes my heart will beat fast, and I may have to stop what I am doing and take deep breaths until I'm able to breathe normally again. The memories linger—sometimes pleasant, sometimes not so pleasant. Days, months, years that I love to think about, but I know that those memories are no longer part of my reality, even though they will always remain a part of my heart and soul.

The anniversary of Dawn's death on August 21 and her birthday on September 2 are not easy days for me. I try to keep busy, and I honor those days by reflecting on her life, looking at pictures, and reminiscing about the wonderful memories I have of her. However, those special days always seem to stay in the front of my mind. I do know I have to learn a way to deal with it a little better than I am now.

Holidays when families get together, such as Christmas, Thanksgiving, or Father's Day, are particularly difficult. These three holidays are for families to be together, whether it is to celebrate the birth of Jesus, to give thanks, or to honor fathers. I feel very lost on Father's Day; I feel that a part of me is missing. There is an empty feeling within my heart just knowing these holidays are not complete.

Sometimes I will hear a song that Dawn used to like. She loved music and would sing with every song that came on the radio. She should have been a singer; her voice was so beautiful and clear. I smile when I think of her picking up something, pretending it was a microphone, and singing and dancing around the room. These are wonderful memories—memories I will cherish the rest of my life.

When I am traveling to places I know she had been with either me or a friend, I become sad, knowing she loved that area as much as I do. At times, I am not only sad but also mad that she will never be able to enjoy new places, new experiences, new friends. So I travel now not only for my own enjoyment but also for Dawn's.

All these triggers are dealt with as best as I can. I try to be good to myself and to others. I treasure my good friends and my wonderful wife. Whether it's one, two, five, ten, or twenty years, you will never forget. Try to work through those meltdowns that will always come when you least expect them and make them a positive experience. Think of the good times and memories.

So, yes, meltdowns continue to be part of my life now. Maybe they're not as often as they once were, but I continue to have them. I truly believe they are now a part of my new life—a life I have to learn to adjust to.

Dad/Brendan

March 6, 2011

I am continually working on recovering from the death of Dawn. What do I do? How do I move on? How do I cope? Here are my honest answers.

I constantly think of the wonderful times we had together talking, going for walks, playing games, going out for coffee, and going to the Redbox to rent movies and then watching them together. She would ask my opinion on many topics that were on her mind and even followed my suggestions on some of them. Even if she did her own thing, I was honored to know she thought enough of my opinion to ask.

I talk about Dawn whenever possible to whoever will listen. Talking about her is very therapeutic for me. At times, I will test individuals. Will they ignore my comments, or will they pick up the conversation and continue to talk about Dawn until the end of our conversation? Good friends feel more comfortable doing that. I believe I can eventually make everyone comfortable and let him or her know I want my daughter to always be a part of the conversation. The real joy comes when a spontaneous question is asked about her— "Didn't she have two beautiful children, a boy and a girl?"—and I can respond with joy in my heart. Best of all, they will listen with interest in what I have to say, and suddenly, she is alive in all our hearts again.

Crying is triggered at very unusual times. I talked to Dawn every day either by phone or in person. That is something you just don't forget or get used to not having. It's like a habit; you are so accustom to it that you continue to expect it to happen. My phone could ring while I was out running errands, and for a split second or two, I would think it was Dawn. I could just be driving from one area to another, and it would hit me. "She is gone. I can't talk to her. I can't call her and ask her how her day is going or what is happening today." I can't count the number of times that a song, an anniversary, or a beautiful sunset have set me off. Fortunately, most times don't last long, but they're long enough to get me thinking about her again. I don't let the memories consume me; however, I will think of them often, because I do feel better afterward. Strangely enough, I feel better after a little cry. It does my heart and soul good.

I try and help other bereaved parents when I can. I am in contact with four different parents in three states. I have been dealing with mainly mothers who have lost a child. In one of my papers, I stated that fathers seem to keep things bottled up or don't want to show outward emotions.

Just the other day, we were having our air-conditioning unit serviced. The technician made a comment about a picture of my daughters. He asked me some questions about them, and I told him one had passed away. He turned to me, and I could see the tears in his eyes. Just five months prior, he'd lost his son to cancer. He began to open up. He felt so much relief after talking about his son. I try to give back when I can, and it is so rewarding to know I just might be helping a parent going through what I went through. To this day, I still struggle at times to make it to the next day. Only those who have gone through it know the feelings involved.

One of the biggest promises I made to myself and to Dawn was that I would continue to write. I am still working on the book about my daughter but hope to be finished soon. I continue to write my thoughts and feelings down. More of my writings now are geared to try and help others, although, in turn, my writing continues to help me.

The last time I saw my daughter she was in her hospice bed. After spending six weeks with her twenty-four/seven, I was told I should go home and spend the night. I didn't feel comfortable in doing it, but I did. Before I left that Friday evening, I went to her and gave her a long, big hug. I held her tight for a few seconds, almost as though I sensed the future. I couldn't remember the last time I had held her like that, but my mind lingered on how wonderful she felt in my arms, a grown-up child who had just gone through a horrible divorce and was putting her life back together. With her death that evening, there was never a chance to say good-bye, but I did tell her I loved her right before I left to go home.

Dealing with the death of my daughter is the greatest challenge I face and will continue to face for the rest of my life. After talking with several parents, I hear them say the same thing—coping with the loss of their child is the most difficult challenge they have ever faced. I cannot speak for others, but from the time Dawn died, I began to live day to day.

Dad/Brendan

March 10, 2011

Less than two years ago I couldn't tell you what it would be like losing one of my two children. I can tell you now that losing a child is the most devastating of all deaths. Other deaths are difficult, but they are not unexpected. In the back of your mind, you've thought about the possibility of your mother and father dying. You know your grandparents are going to die before you. A child's death is unnatural. It's unexpected even if the child has been sick for some time. It's impossible to psychologically prepare for it. When it happens, you feel all hope is lost. Your heart feels like someone is literally squeezing it. You have nothing left to live for. Your life is over. Nothing anyone says can make it any easier. Nothing can ease the pain.

I have heard so many comments from people who I had, at one time, thought were intelligent. People really should think before making comments to a parent who just lost a child. There are so many things that could be said but aren't. People want to help, but they don't know how. What you say may be more discouraging than encouraging. The last thing you want to do is hurt a friend even more. So, what do you say? More importantly, what shouldn't you say?

The Do *Not* Say List

- "You have another child, don't you? You should be thankful for that." That may be true, but does that mean I don't care anymore about my loss? Or that I don't care period? Now that I lost one, does that mean I take the love I had for the one I lost and put it with the one I still have?
- "Well, you should be thankful; you at least had your child for X number of years." There is no time that this is an appropriate statement, because there is never a good time for your child to die. Parents are supposed to die first. Period!
- "I know how you feel," or "I can imagine what you are going through." Unless you have been through the death of a child, you cannot imagine what we're going through. Even if you

were close to the child, the parent you're saying this to may be hurt by such a comment.

- "The child is in heaven now." When a parent is grieving, it doesn't matter where that child is. All that matters is that the child is not *here!*

- "It was God's time." Please understand that parents will, in turn, blame God for taking their child from them. They will not be able to comprehend how God could "time" the death of their child so poorly. They will not be able to understand why God would want them to go through so much pain.

- "This will all work out for the better." There is nothing more painful than the death of your child. When parents are grieving, they don't comprehend "better." Instead, parents feel that nothing is good anymore, because their children aren't here.

- "You can do this, because God won't give you more than you can bear." We can't bear it. We are devastated beyond words, and we do not see an end to this pain and suffering. All we know is that we can't take this much longer. There is no way to cope with the pain. We take life one day at a time. This too can lead us to blame God.

- "When are you going to clean out her room?" We will clean the room out when we are ready. Is there a timetable for this? *No.*

- "When are you going to put pictures away," or "When are you going to bring them back out?" I personally want pictures out. I want to see her beautiful face. However, there are other parents who don't want them out. Just like everything else, time will heal, and they may change their feelings and put them back out.

So, what can a person say? Say nothing. Be there for us. Support us. Listen to us. If we talk about our children and memories, then feel free to reminisce with us. If we don't talk about our children, remain silent.

How can you help? Learn to read our moods. Some days, conversations about our children will come easily. Other days, talking about it will be torturous. We may be fine one day, and the next day we may be a basket case. In some cases, our moods may change from one minute to the next. Be aware of our body language. Our friends may be going through life, and then, all of a sudden, we see something that reminds us of our children and have a meltdown right then and there. It can happen, so don't be surprised when it does.

Stick around! That may sound strange, but so many people come to the funeral and offer support for the first week or two and then disappear. What some people don't understand is we're going to need you the most once everything else is gone. During the first week or two, friends are pretty much oblivious to your surroundings. Reality is going to hit and hit hard. We're going to need you then more than ever. Be there for us.

Now, there are always two sides to everything. Above I mentioned "The Don't Say List." Believe it or not, there is a "Can Say List," and here are a few.

The Can Say List

While you can't take away the pain of the loss, you *can* provide much-needed comfort and support. There are many ways to help a grieving friend or family member, starting with letting the person know you care. Now here are some comments that can help you.

- Acknowledge the situation. "I heard that your daughter/son died." Use the word *died*. That will show you are more open to talk about how the person really feels.
- Express your concern. "I'm sorry to hear that this happened to you."
- Be genuine in your communication and don't hide your feelings. "I'm not sure what to say, but I want you to know I care."
- Offer your support. "Tell me what I can do for you."

- Ask how he or she feels, and don't assume you know how the bereaved person feels on any given day.

These are my feelings about comments people often make. I am sure there are many more. I guess the best rule to follow is if you don't know what to say, then don't say anything. Just make your presence known and let it be known that you will always be there for the parent.

Only a father's opinion.
Dad/Brendan

March 18, 2011

Although you grieve when you lose a loved one, most people understand that death is a natural part of life. You feel the void left when a grandparent or parent dies, but you know that death is part of the cycle of life and accept it as such. Although you mourn the loss, you still smile, reminisce, and even laugh with the memories of the way that person touched your life. Although you'll always miss that person, you'll accept his or her absence as the natural order of life.

When you lose a child, it's much more difficult to reconcile that death with the cycle of life. The death of a child seems to violate the natural order of life, and the ensuing confusion leaves us ill equipped to deal with the loss. How do you deal with the loss of a child? How can you find that place of reconciliation between life and your child's death? Every parent grieves differently, of course, and comes to acceptance at different times in the grieving process. Through my own grieving experience, after my daughter died from melanoma cancer at the age of twenty-eight, I've learned that there are several things that can help ease the pain of that journey toward inner peace.

Some families find it comforting to set up a memorial corner, either in the house or outside. Some plant a memorial garden and decorate it with some of the child's favorite things. Family members can gather in the garden, acknowledging their loss, yet reaffirming their family unit through shared memories and future visions. My wife and I made a memorial garden in the corner of our yard. We planted a couple of queen palms, a couple pigmy palms, and flowers in Dawn's favorite colors and added a bench. Also, before her death, Dawn said she wanted me to get a purple Christmas tree. Yes, purple, and yes, I found one. So every Christmas this purple tree is put up and decorated with nothing but angels.

Sometimes after the loss of a child, it may seem that you are also losing friends. That may be true, to an extent. After all, you change deep inside when you lose a child. Your friends love you, but they simply can't understand what you're going through unless they've lost a child themselves. Unable to imagine your pain, they don't know how to comfort and encourage you, and it seems like they just walk away. They really haven't left you; they just don't know how to reach you. Just remember that as you come to terms with the changes in your life and learn how to deal with them, you will find the friends that you thought you had once lost. You'll get to know each other all over again. The relationships will never be exactly the same, but the love that brought you together will still be there to build a new friendship.

How do you deal with the loss of a child? You deal with it slowly, often painfully, but always with the love and support of those who love you. You lean on the light of your memories of the child whom you lost. But most of all, you learn to lean on the love of the hearts that still beat around you. Together you walk that journey of grief toward the peace that you will reach along the way. Looking back and then moving on, love enables you to deal with the loss of a child.

Dad/Brendan

March 30, 2011

Cancer is a horrifying disease no matter what part of the body it attacks. When a loved one is diagnosed, life seems to come to a standstill. Helping her cope becomes a top priority, but to do this, you will also have to find a way to cope.

I was involved with Dawn's illness from the first day she learned her test results to her last day on earth. Can you try to put yourself, just for a brief moment, in the cancer patient's life? What would go through your head after finding out you are terminal? How do you cope? How do you handle life in general? How do you sleep or wake up each day not knowing how much longer you're going to be here? Dawn lived the last ten months of her life not knowing how much time was left, and she kept a positive attitude.

The caregiver's responsibilities are endless. I say endless because Cathy and I did everything we possibly could to make Dawn comfortable. No one can ever be prepared for the horrible news that a loved one has cancer. The first thing that came to my mind was I am going to take care of her. She is my baby girl, and I will give every ounce of energy that I have to care for her. Several things go through your head. Things like, I'll worry about myself later, I'm not the priority here, and many more similar comments.

I don't know if I would have done anything differently on my part as far as caring for myself; however, if I were aware of some of the things I'm going to soon mention, then maybe things might have been different after Dawn's death. I have zero regrets about my care for Dawn. I honestly believe Cathy and I did everything humanly possible for her. Some individuals believe I let my own daughter die. They feel I didn't do enough to have her cured. They feel I should have taken her overseas for treatment. What they don't realize is that I did contact Munich, Germany, and was told they couldn't do any more than what had already been done.

If there was any chance at all of knowing what I was going to face, then maybe, just maybe, things would be different today. I am going to mention a few suggestions that I find to be helpful for anyone that encounters such a horrible situation.

Difficulty: Challenging

1. Learn as much as you can about your loved one's cancer. Knowing what to expect will help you be better prepared even if the diagnosis is bleak. This was one area I did learn about. I never knew when Dawn would have questions I could answer for her. Ask questions; never think it's too stupid to ask. Write your questions down if you're not going to see the doctor for a couple of days. You won't remember unless you write them down. Be very careful if you try to find the answer on the Internet. You could very well find something that you think is the correct answer, but it isn't. It's always best to hold off and ask the doctor.

2. See the doctor with your loved one. Be there to hold her hand and help her remember exactly what the doctor said. Cancer can be overwhelming, and the details sometimes get overlooked. Make it a priority that you go to all of the appointments. Don't ever let your loved one be alone; he will not hear everything being told to him. Ask your loved one if you can ask the doctor questions. As I mentioned above, take notes.

3. Take care of yourself. This sounds impossible, but you'll do a better job handling the stress and coping if you're well rested and get some exercise. This is a very important statement here. I didn't take care of myself; I didn't get the proper daily exercising. I didn't take care of myself at all, and now I find myself trying to get back into at least a decent condition. It has been very difficult.

4. Accept help from friends and family. Housework doesn't seem so important when you're coping with cancer. So lean

on your friends to help you out around the house, so you can spend time with your loved one. Most of the time I was guilty of this. I never asked for help. I didn't want to burden anyone. People would always ask if they could do something, and I would always say, "Well, there really isn't anything you can do right now." How very wrong that was. There were always things friends and family could do. Put your pride aside and let them help you.

5. Don't be ashamed of your feelings. Cancer affects everyone, not just the person diagnosed. Talking about your feelings with friends and family will help you cope. This is a very difficult one. I personally didn't have any problems showing my feelings. I know many individuals who wouldn't show feelings, thinking that makes them less of a person. I always thought, *Who cares what others think.* Find someone you can talk to. It doesn't matter if it's a close friend or a family member, but talk about it. If you don't, it will just eat at you and cause your health to decline.

6. Seek professional help. If you can't seem to handle everything on your own, there is no shame in contacting a professional to help you cope when a loved one has cancer. I was not much of a believer in counselors or therapists. I always felt that it was my opinion compared to theirs. Do they really know what it is like, or are they just telling me things I'm supposed to do? I did put my pride aside and talk to professionals, and yes, it did make me feel better.

A Few Tips and Suggestions

1. While you may want to spend every moment with your loved one, always ask if she wants visitors. Don't be offended if she says no. Your loved one will need times of quiet contemplation to help her cope.

2. Always give your loved one space. As much as you want to be with him every minute of the day, he needs space. There will be times he wants to be alone. Grant him that wish.

3. Let your loved one do things for herself for as long as she can. We all know they are going to lose their ability soon, so don't take it from them early.

4. Let your loved one have as much freedom as she can. Taking everything away from her at one time could be devastating.

Dad/Brendan

April 21, 2011

Did you ever get punched in the stomach so hard that you could not breathe? You grab your stomach and clutch it for dear life. It's like the wind was knocked out of you, and you can't get your breath. You grasp for air, but it doesn't seem to come back to you.

Receiving the horrific news about my daughter having terminal brain cancer and having her given six months to a year to live was devastating. It can feel like a surreal punch in the gut multiplied by a thousand, but the sensation, unlike that, doesn't seem to fade. Instead, it seems to intensify in the days and weeks after and then lingers about. Then the day comes when you lose your child. The feeling is unlike anything I could ever explain in words, and that is saying a lot, as I'm pretty good about putting feelings into words. It's an indescribable ache that no parent should ever be made to feel. It's a loss that leaves you feeling like you have lost a chunk of yourself and have died too. You feel empty inside. You have a huge hole in your heart, and you know it will never close.

I felt compelled to write articles about losing a child, because not only have I been there, but I am living through the nightmare for myself. The main reason I'm writing these articles is to try and reach out to others, to try and take away a little of their pain. For me, I know to talk and write about it, because it's therapeutic—that I do know for certain. So, it's good for me as well, and I know there are plenty of moms and dads out there who are hurting and need some advice and guidance. I will tell you that I am only approaching the second anniversary of the death of my daughter. No, I am not an expert or a professional about this subject; however, knowing what I know and the possibility of helping others just inspires me more. I would hope to be able to help others who are still "fresh" in their pain in any way I can. No, it never does go away. It will always linger and affect you, but does it get better?

Yes, it gets better, as long as you're getting yourself out of bed. You will learn to crack a smile again, brush your teeth, and laugh at a funny joke. You will go out to dinners. You will be able to pick up old hobbies and continue to watch your children and or grandchildren grow. You'll enjoy every second of that and love your children and/or grandchildren maybe even a little more than other parents do because of what you endured. Life will go on, and you will have gained something very special out of your enormous ordeal—strength you never knew you could posses and a forever-by-your-side guardian angel.

I honestly believe I have a couple of those angels myself. There are times I can just feel them around me. Being aware of them and knowing that they are real helps get me through my everyday life. I have zero doubt that there is life after death, and when my time comes, I no longer fear it, because I know I'll be greeted by the ones I have lost. That gives me immense peace to think about. Trust me, I had feared death since childhood, but since losing my daughter, I no longer do because I know I'll be with her one day.

Losing a child is the worst thing any human being could ever possibly endure. Losing a child, well it's unfathomable, it's unimaginable, and yet, it sadly happens to someone out there each and every day.

How do you get through it? Those early days and weeks that turn into months seem to just slip right through your fingers. Every day seems connected, and life becomes one long, seemingly endless day. How do you get through the pain and face the day again? I know I have said in the past that if I ever lost a child, I'd just die on the spot or would have to be locked away in a sanitarium somewhere, because I just couldn't go on after that. Yet, here I am. I live and breathe, I find joy in loved ones, but I never forget my loss. My biggest problem was anger, and to this day, that anger shows up.

I try to be strong; however, I do allow myself the proper course of grieving. There are people out there who put on fronts of being unbreakable, which works in most of life's hardships. But with this one, eventually even the best will break down. If you don't allow yourself time to grieve, and I mean really grieve, you truly kill yourself slowly from the inside out. You can't survive a loss without dealing with that loss.

Here is some advice that was given to me after I lost Dawn:

Don't numb your feelings by shutting out the world and denying your pain. Accept your pain, embrace it, feel it, and work through it.

Know this isn't the end. Always keep in your mind and believe that your child is always among you. Even though you may not be able to see or hear him, he is always there, and in your darkest hours, you will feel him near you. If you don't shut them out, your angels will give you signs, little things to let you know they are near and haven't left you. You will see your loved one again one day. Hope, faith, and love are boundless and important in life and in death. This is so important, because you really will get signs from your love done, and oh how it makes you feel.

Don't get yourself into any negative behaviors. Don't start a bad habit like smoking, drinking, and/or drugs. If you thought you had a problem before, you just gave yourself another one.

Cry! Allow yourself to cry. Fathers must realize and understand that it is okay to cry. You're not less of a man because you show your emotions. You must have that release to be able to accept and move on. I guess I'm not your average father, because I am not ashamed to show my emotions. There are times when I do have a good cry, and I feel better both mentally and physically. If you don't want to be seen, then go behind closed doors and let those tears out. You need to get your feelings out. No one can be that strong.

Reach out to others. This is and can be a touchy one. Before my daughter's passing she always told me, "Daddy, never sugarcoat anything. Be totally honest with everything you say or write." A death in the family most often brings family together; in my case, it didn't. Only two members out of eight actually helped during my daughter's illness and even after her death. I learned a valuable lesson during this time. You will truly find out who your friends are. What a remarkable group of neighbors and friends Cathy and I have. God watched out for us knowing we would need that support, and he gave it to us another way.

If you have to, seek professional help. There are so many different types of people in this world. With a tragic loss of this magnitude, some people just cannot get past it, lose the will to live, and become secluded from society. You can't hide from this; it's real, and you must sooner or later face it head on. You need professional help, and there are so many different ways to receive it. Two types of help that I went through were one-on-one and group counseling. I preferred the group, because I wanted to hear others. I wanted to hear what happened to them and how they were coping. You can pick up so much information and ideas that you can use for yourself. Never forget that your story could help another grieving parent who may be sitting right next to you. Another reason you may need to seek professional help is that you may need a short-term medication to help with the depression aspect of things. Never be ashamed if you need to take something. You must learn to swallow your pride, if only for a short while. It won't be forever.

Feel important because you *are*! Know you still have people here in this world who love you and need you. If you have other children, you especially have to keep yourself going for their sakes. They rely on you. Put your focus on the positive things you have and put your heart and soul into those things, even if it's a hobby. Just be sure that in the process you are dealing with, not suppressing, your pain. There must be times of grief; there is no quick fix or roundabout way to avoid it. Grief, in all honesty, is something that keeps you connected to your child when he or she is gone. Remembering your child is important and a good thing. Even though it can hurt an awful lot, it can also make you smile.

Create a way to remember your lost child. Plant a tree or a little garden in his name. A tree will grow and grow long after you yourself have left this world, and it's an absolutely great way to pay tribute to your lost loved one. I have done both, and watching that tree grow and having a place to grieve in my own backyard while watching the beautiful flowers around the palm trees brings me an amazing amount of peace in my heart. I often feel as if Dawn's spirit lives on through the fronds of those queen palms. Do memorialize your loved one. It's not strange at all; it's therapeutic.

Write! My daughter made me promise her that I would write my feelings and thoughts down. I thank her every day for the wonderful advice. You don't have to be a poet or a writer. Just write from your heart and write it however you feel. It doesn't have to be perfect English or spelling. I can't tell you how much relief I get from doing this. Just write, even if it's to help your soul and not sell a book. No need for talent here. Poetry and journal writing had never been a part of my life until my daughter's death. I now find myself doing it all the time. I guess you can say it's the new me.

Every remembrance day, like Father's Day, the anniversary of Dawn's death, her birthday, etc., I write a letter to my daughter. I then put it in my notebook and reread them throughout the year. On the anniversary of her death, we released balloons at her gravesite. I do this because I know she would want us to celebrate her life.

Forgive. No matter how your child dies, you place some blame on yourself. Even when there is nothing you could have done, it makes no difference. We are predisposed to feel guilt when anything bad happens to our kids; it's just the parental way. But it is *not* your fault, and there is nothing that you could have ever done to change the situation at hand. You have to learn to not beat yourself up and instead forgive yourself and forgive God. There were times when I just got so angry with God that I stopped praying. This was my hardest—I blamed myself for the longest time until I listened to two very wise people who pointed out that I couldn't have saved her. They opened my eyes.

Join support groups and/or message boards where you will find others who are going through the same thing. I know when horrible things like this happen, we tend to feel like we are the only ones in the world going through this. In all honesty, there are millions out there just like us who are feeling the exact same pain and going through the exact same emotions. Being able to reach out to others and in turn provide help and comfort to others is always beneficial to your own self-esteem. We have a huge, huge advantage nowadays

253

with the Internet. Use it to your advantage and go through your pain with people who do truly "get it" and understand.

It's going to be a long, long process that may seem endless and even impossible at times, but you will see the sun again. Even if it's never going to shine quite as brightly, it will shine; you will see. Don't shut out help, and don't beat yourself up with guilt. Do feel your pain, do mourn, do celebrate your lost loved one, do reach out to others, do get your feelings down in ink, and do seek professional help if you think you can't handle it and all else has failed you. There is zero shame in it. We all need help at some point in our lives.

There is no greater pain that losing a child, but there is also nothing else in the world that will ever make you stronger. Know that if you can get through this, you can get through absolutely anything. You are a true warrior, and if you ever need a friend to confide in and feel like you don't have that anywhere else in life—well, we are all here for you!

Thanks for reading. My heart goes out to every parent who has lost a child. However, you all must remember that you need to keep your heads held up so your loved ones can see you as they look down on you from heaven. Things will get better; it's just a matter of time.

Dad/Brendan

April 30, 2011

I can recall clearly the day I took Dawn for her first bicycle ride. It was a warm autumn day, and the sun was shining on her brand-new Huffy. I remember my hand gently guiding her bike along the road that ran by our housing development on the Naval Air Station. I even recall her smile as she began steering the bike on her own. The memory lingers with me as I begin to make preparations for my daughter's funeral. She battled melanoma cancer for ten months. She was given only six months to a year to live. Nothing could have prepared me for the day she actually died.

While I anticipated a period of mourning, I failed to realize that I would encounter a great deal of stress as a result of her death. I was surprised, even shocked, by the amount of stress I felt. We seldom associate death with stress, yet the death of a loved one is one of the most stressful events that can happen in our lives. Whether it is the death of a parent, a spouse, a child, a sibling, or a beloved friend, death makes us anxious not only about our loss but about our own mortality.

The most stressful aspect of death may be the fear of the unknown. You may not know what to expect next, and you may wonder how you will handle the next obstacle that comes your way. The most important thing you can do to deal with death-related stress is to recognize it and work toward getting through it. Realize that it is perfectly natural for you to feel worried and anxious during this difficult time.

Try to give yourself some time to pause and reflect. Don't feel as if you have to hurry up and get over the death. Allowing yourself an opportunity to grieve should help reduce your stress level and make you a healthier person, emotionally speaking. You must remember there is *no* time frame on grieving. Never compare your grieving to someone else's. We all grieve differently.

One way to help yourself deal with the stress is to do something positive to remember your loved one. In other words, consider planting a tree or a flower garden or creating some other project he or she might have liked. Discovering that life still offers pleasant possibilities can give you hope and help you deal with your stress more effectively.

Give considerable thought to how your loved one would want you to carry on after her death. Chances are great she wouldn't want you sulking in the corner for the rest of your life. In your own time, give yourself permission to go on with life. As a result, you should feel less stress and enjoy life more. It took me two years, but I returned to doing something I loved doing very much. I found having a hobby to be a stress release for me. I feel so much better now that I'm doing it.

Another effective stress-reducing technique is to commit your thoughts to paper. Writing can be quite therapeutic and can help you gain perspective on your situation. The process of writing can improve your problem-solving skills and, thus, allow yourself to become able to cope with your situation. Also, give yourself time to reread your journal entries. You might be amazed at how much you've grown over a short period of time.

If the stress of death becomes overwhelming, by all means seek the advice of a professional. A counselor can help you to sort out your feelings and recommend coping techniques. You might find it quite liberating to talk to another individual about everything you're feeling inside. In some cases, you might also want to consult with a psychiatrist to see if there may be a medication that will help you deal with death-related anxiety.

Not everyone will experience the death of a child, but most people will experience the death of someone close to them at some point in their lives. However, it's good to know that there are positive things we can do to help us deal more effectively with the stress related to death. While, in a certain sense, we may never get over a loved one's death, we can learn to cope with the loss. We may even learn to smile again. As always, keep your head held up so your loved one can see your face as he looks down from heaven.

Dad/Brendan

May 3, 2011

I've talked with a few grieving dads during our group sessions about their thoughts and feelings since the loss of their children. It seems that we had many of the same traits—the same feelings of emptiness and loneness. We are experiencing many of the same impacts after the death of our children, and it scares the hell out of us.

Not long after Dawn's passing, I noticed that I had lost my drive, focus, confidence, and hope. I also started to feel things that I had never experienced before, including despair, fear, and depression. Things that used to be important in my life became unimportant.

I used to love setting goals and achieving them. I did this to prove to myself and to others that nothing could get in my way. For most of my career, my work was pretty much independent. My counterparts weren't in the same area as me, but we competed with one another. I always took pride in my work, whether it was the U.S. Navy or my jobs after my Navy career. I was my worst critic. I always ensured that my reports were done well before the deadline. It wasn't to make others look bad; it was because I wanted it done and off my desk.

The death of my daughter brought all of this insanity to a screeching halt. I fought it as hard as I could, but the reality was that my daughter had died and I was left standing with no one around me except for my wife, my other daughter, and a few family members and dear friends. I came to the realization, like many of the men I have met through this group session, that my life has been changed forever. The old me died when Dawn died, and the new me was going through some major growing pains.

The transition from the old me to the new me was tough to say the least. At some point in time, I had to come to grips with the fact that the old me was gone, lost forever, with no chance of return. I didn't have the energy I once had, and my nervous system couldn't handle the stresses of life like it once did. I learned to cut the things out of my life that added no real value, and I try not to stress about the things I cannot control. Believe me, it's been very hard to comply, but you do what you must.

If you stop fighting it and learn to accept it, I believe the growing pains will lessen some. Your pain will never go away, but you do somehow learn to live with it. After awhile, the new you will start to emerge. I am not saying that I don't think about Dawn every minute of every day; however, I can't let it take me to the point of depression, which is a place I lived for a long time after her death. I fought hard to get out of that place; I don't want to go back.

My mission is to let other dads know that they too can get out of it. It will be the toughest fight of their lives, and it's scary— scary from the standpoint that you have to learn to reprogram the way you think and how you want others to perceive you. You have to let your defenses down and let yourself and others see you for who you really are. You have to learn to talk about what's on your mind and what's causing you to have a bad day. This was the hardest thing for me; I kept things bottled up inside before I lost my daughter.

You have to realize that some days are going to be easier than others, but tomorrow is a new day. At the beginning and end of every day, you have to remind yourself that your child wants you to keep living. She wants you to learn to smile, laugh, and love again. She doesn't want you to live in despair and depression. She wants you to live a life full of passion.

My writing is a result of my own realization that I must live a life of passion. My passion at this point in my life is to reach out to other grieving parents and help them back onto their feet—give them hope and let them know that there is light at the end of the tunnel. For some, it's a very long tunnel, and it's very dark and scary at times. If you try and keep a clear mind that your child is with you spiritually, then that can give you the extra strength you need to make it to the next day.

You must also realize that you will have days when you take three steps back and only one step forward. Just stand up, brush yourself off, and continue down that tunnel until you see the light and reach the other end. One last thing to remember is that our losses were due to different circumstances and are different. I understand the guilt and the "should haves" we place upon ourselves; however, we do have something very much in common. We lost a child.

Dad/Brendan

May 8, 2011

The death of a child is a pain unlike any other. It is an excruciating pain, because when you lose a child, you not only lose a part of your life but you also lose a part of yourself.

I lost my daughter in August 2009. Ten months prior, who would have ever imagined she would receive a diagnosis of terminal cancer? No one expected her to die—no one. Even under the most controlled environment with the most advanced, technological devices modern science and medicine had to offer, she still could not be saved.

So how did I survive? It was devastating and excruciating. I didn't know what to do. I didn't know how to continue living. All I knew was the pain was much too difficult to bear. In the days following Dawn's death, I found myself surrounded with family and close friends. Ironically, no one knew what to say or what to do, but at least they were able to give hugs and comfort. At the time, that's all I needed. Flowers were sent, cards arrived in the mail, and occasionally a gift basket of some sort was delivered. But none of those things helped the pain go away. I didn't know how to survive, only that I had to.

I must give credit where credit is due. I honestly believe I would not have made it if it weren't for my wife Cathy. Cathy was Dawn's "mother by marriage," as Dawn put it. It wasn't just the support from Cathy but the actual hands-on help she offered to care for Dawn.

After my daughter died, I realized I needed her strength to continue living. Everyone told me I was strong and brave, but I didn't feel it. I felt pain, anguish, and confusion. If I was strong, it was because my daughter helped me to be strong. She made me very proud during her ten-month battle with melanoma cancer. She struggled day in and day out and fought to live each day to its fullest. I would gain strength from her each day, and she would also give me courage to make it to the next day. She was so brave. She could be having her worst day, and then she would look at me and give me that beautiful smile. That smile gave me the courage and strength to endure the wrenching pain inside.

I had to figure out how to survive. I knew I would; I just didn't know how I would. I read books on grief and the loss of children. I read the Bible and visited the cemetery weekly. I tried to understand the circumstances of her death. I asked questions, talked to ministers and priests, and even sat in on counseling. None of these things gave me the answer as to how to survive.

After months of keeping a low profile—in other words, I was trying to hide from life in general—I realized that I had already survived. Despite the horrific pain I was feeling, I somehow managed to continue with life. Is there a secret or a magic formula that parents can use to survive? Is there a magic wand we can run across us? No. Sorry, there are none of those things. You have to learn to deal with it.

You must get involved in counseling, whether it's one-on-one or group. I found writing to be therapeutic. When I do have bad days, I go back and reread some of my earlier papers. It doesn't take long to snap out of that depression, because after reading my first couple of papers, I realize I don't want to revert back to the depressed days.

Find a hobby of some sort; you must keep your mind thinking and not wandering. Get outside and work in the yard. Start a garden in your loved one's honor. You can't just hide indoors all the time. It took me six months after Dawn died before I was brave enough to confront my pain and discover how to survive the traumatic loss. One February morning I had an eye-opening experience that let me know I wasn't alone. I wasn't climbing that imaginary mountain alone.

It took time, but eventually I learned to live with the pain. I learned to enjoy the simple pleasures of life. I learned to trust in God and the plan He set forth. I learned to accept my loss and to appreciate the blessings in my life. I will never forget my dear Dawn and the joy she brought into my life. I will never forget the twenty-eight wonderful years I spent with her. I will still feel the pain when I think about her and recount those precious memories. But the pain I feel today is dramatically different than the pain I felt when she died. You learn to tolerate the pain. The pain will never go away. The hole in your heart will never close. You learn to tolerate it.

If I hadn't made the effort to get involved with a hobby or other activities, I may never have learned to survive the death of my daughter. As I said, people cope with grief in very different ways. Your grief is different than mine. You need to learn to grieve so you can conqueror it. You also must remember that there is no timetable for grief. There is no rule that says you must be done grieving within six months to a year. Today I am that strong person that so many told me I was two years ago. Today I am a much more compassionate and cautious person. Today I can honestly say that I survived the death of my daughter, and somehow, in some strange way, I'm a better person because of it.

Dad/Brendan

May 15, 2011

All the papers I have written to date start after Dawn's death. I have had individuals suggest I start from the time Dawn found out about her illness. After giving it some thought, I decided to start with her first day of radiation treatment. Dawn was to receive fifteen treatments every day except Saturday, Sunday, and holidays. So here is the story from the beginning.

Friday, November 7, 2008, was Dawn's first scheduled full-scull radiation treatment. I prayed to God while Dawn and I were waiting, asking him to watch over her. I could see in her eyes she was scared. I also asked God to send my mother down to watch over Dawn and to be with her throughout her treatment.

A few minutes later, the radiology nurse came out and told Dawn it would be about fifteen minutes before she would be ready for her. I then told Dawn I was going to the restroom and would be right back. As I was heading back, I passed the gift store. I thought I would run in there for a minute and see if there was something I could get for Dawn to lift her spirits.

I didn't see anything in the gift store that struck my fancy, so I turned to this woman browsing beside me who was wearing an unusual hat covered with shiny pins. I told her that I was trying to find something for my daughter to cheer her up. I explained that she was starting her radiation treatment in a few minutes.

"I know just the thing for her," the woman replied, removing her hat to reveal a completely bald head. Her fingers moved quickly over her hat, and she selected an angel pin. "This was given to me by a friend recovering from cancer. Now I'm recovering myself, so please pass this on to your daughter. Tell her that healing is on the way."

This would be the perfect gift for Dawn, because she always loved angels. It was a message of hope from her guardian angel.

Dawn was always amazed with angels. As I was approaching her in the waiting area, I was so afraid for her. I sat down and told her I had something for her and then handed her the angel. She looked at it and said, "Daddy, I just prayed to God for him to send me an angel. Everything will be okay. Trust me."

That was the first of many times I heard those words come from Dawn, "trust me." About that time Dorothy, Dawn's nurse, came to get her. She asked Dorothy if she could pin the angel on her collar during the treatment. Dorothy told her it would be fine. Dawn was a hit with all the nurses. Every last one of them loved her. I was told that she would be back receiving treatment for about thirty minutes that first day. Each subsequent treatment would only be ten minutes. The reason it would take so long that first day was because they had to mark her head to make sure they were getting all eight tumors.

Every day for the next two weeks, Dawn was scheduled for her treatments at around three o'clock. Dawn's point of origin was her right groin area. She had a large tumor almost the size of a softball that had to be removed. On Friday, November 14, Dawn went under the knife to have the tumor removed, along with her Lymph nodes I kept thinking, *Let's hope this doesn't turn out to be a major surgery. Hopefully they can go right in and remove the area, and that's it.*

Once again, I could see the concern in Dawn's eyes. She didn't know what to expect. Dawn wanted me to be by her side until they took her to the operating room. I was sitting next to her for a while when I received a call. I had to go downstairs for a minute and told Dawn I would be right back. Dawn told me that she was going to pray while I was gone, and I told her I would pray also. The patient waiting room was full that day. The medical staff was rushing around the room in a blur of green scrubs, except for one nurse in a white uniform, whose job seemed to be to hold Dawn's hand. Within minutes, they were moving Dawn to the operating room with this nurse right by her side, holding her hand and telling her everything would be fine.

We got to the area where I couldn't go back with her. I kissed Dawn on the forehead and told her I loved her. The nurse in white was so kind and gentle. She looked at me and said, "She will be fine."

Later, after the surgery, I asked the recovery nurse who the nurse in white was. The nurse told me that there weren't any nurses in white. I told her that this nurse was holding Dawn's hand when they went into the operating room. The nurse looked at me and said, "Mr. Hoffman, no one is allowed in the operating room without being in scrubs."

I should have known there was something different about this nurse—very calm and gentle. She almost didn't seem real, but then again, she really wasn't.

Dad/Brendan

May 21, 2011

We will always grieve to some extent for our lost children. We will always remember our children and wish over and over again that we could hold them in our arms one last time. As time goes on, this wishing will no longer drain you of the will to live your own life. The pain doesn't go away; we just learn to tolerate it with each passing day. You see, grief will subside; however, sadness will linger.

Parental grief is devastating; there is nothing that can prepare us for its enormity or devastation. Parental grief never ends but only changes in intensity and manner of expression. Parental grief affects the head, the heart, and the spirit. It affects every part of the body, both mentally and physically.

We, as parents, will find out that the death of a child means coming to terms with untold emptiness and deep emotional hurt. Immediately after the death, some parents may even find it impossible to express grief at all, as many experience a period of shock and numbness. Believe it or not, but it is very normal to be in a state of shock. Even if you knew your child was going to pass, as a parent, you can never prepare yourself for that moment.

Each grieving parent must find ways to get through these most difficult times—not over it but enough for you to go forward with your life. Our lives must go on, and we are now forced to face life's journey in an individual manner. We, as grieving parents, often find ourselves in a sense of despair, a sense that life is not worth living, a sense of disarray and of sheer and complete confusion. Our pain may seem so severe and we so lack the desire to live that there is uncertainty about our own survival. Some of us feel that it is not right for us to live when our children have died. On the other hand, others feel they have failed at parenting and somehow should have found a way to keep their children from dying.

When you lose a child, a major part of you dies alongside him. More often than you realize, you have to adopt a whole new lifestyle—a new you. You must almost become a new and different person. The old you will be gone forever. You need to learn to be compassionate, gentle, and patient with others and yourself.

Grief is an emotionally devastating experience; grief is work and demands much patience, understanding, effort, and energy. Grief can and often does involve a vast array of conflicting emotions and responses, including shock and numbness, intense sadness and pain, depression, and often feelings of total confusion and disorganization. Sometimes we may not even seem sure of who we are and may feel as if we have lost an integral part of our very being. At other times, we may feel that what happened was a myth or an illusion or that we were having a nightmare.

Our reactions to our children's deaths can often involve emotional and physical symptoms, such as inability to sleep or a desire to sleep all the time, mood swings, exhaustion, extreme anxiety, headaches, or inability to concentrate. We can experience emotional and physical peaks and valleys. I always compared such emotions to being on a roller coaster—there are ups and your downs. We may think life finally seems to be on an even keel and that we are learning to cope when periods of intense sadness overwhelm us, perhaps with even more force than the first time. Believe me, it is not only like a roller coaster; it can be like a merry-go-round. It can return unexpectedly.

We, as parents, need to know how important it is to express our pain to someone who will understand and acknowledge what we are feeling and saying. We should be honest with others and ourselves about how we feel. We need to allow ourselves to cry, be angry, and complain. We need to admit we are overwhelmed, distracted, and unable to focus.

When will you know when it's time to live again? You need to make an effort. You do not need a list of events or anniversaries to check off. In fact, you are likely to begin living again before you realize you are doing it. You may catch yourself laughing. You may pick up a book for recreational reading again. You may start playing lighter, happier music. When you do make these steps toward living again, you are likely to feel guilty at first. *What right do I have?* you will ask yourself. *How can I be happy when my child is dead?* Yet, something inside feels as though you are being nudged in this positive direction. You may even have the sense that this nudge is from your child, or at least the feeling that she approves of it and wants you to move on with your life.

Always allow yourself time to mourn in your own way, and remember that there is no time frame. Grieving is unique for each one of us; we all grieve differently and timely. Take your time, because what just happened to you was devastating. Don't expect to follow a specific or prescribed pattern for grieving. This isn't something you experienced before, so this is a first-time challenge.

One very important thought you need to remember is that others may minimize or misunderstand your grief. Many don't understand the power, depth, intensity, or duration of parental grief. In some instances, we are ignored because individuals are not able to deal with the tragedy. They find the thought of a child's death too hard, too inexplicable, or too threatening. Many simply don't know what to say or do, and so they don't say or do anything.

You will experience great pain and distress deciding what to do with your child's belongings. You need to understand that this task will be very difficult and that different people make different decisions. We need to be encouraged to hold onto any experiences, memories, or mementoes we have of our children and find ways to keep and treasure them. These memories and mementoes are our legacies from the time we shared with our children.

Most grieving parents have or will experience a substantial amount of pain on special occasions, such as birthdays, holidays, or the anniversary of the death. You will need to find ways to cope with these events and should do what feels right for you, not what others think you should do. I had a celebration of Dawn's life on the first anniversary of her death. This helped me tremendously.

You must remember that we all will recover and reach a place of rest and hope. We will never forget our children, but rather, we will find ways to keep them as a cherished part of our inner selves forever.

We are all different, and we have ways to find our own comfort. Many grieving parents also find comfort in rituals. Funerals or memorial services have served many parents as beautiful and meaningful ways of saying good-bye, providing a sense of closure after the child's death. For others, sending announcement cards about the child's death, writing poems, keeping journals, writing down personal reflections or prayers, or volunteering with a parental bereavement group become ways to remember and honor the child who died.

By all means, grief is the natural response to any loss. We need to be reminded how important it is to process all feelings, thoughts, and emotions in resolving grief. Grieving parents must look within and be prepared to deal with the past and present. We need to talk about our losses, and others must acknowledge the loss. We need to tell others about what happened to our children and talk about our thoughts and feelings; these all need to come from the heart, not just from the mouth. Healing for grieving parents can begin to occur by acknowledging and sharing our grief.

Probably the most important step for parents on their grief journey is to allow themselves time to heal. We must come to the understanding that healing doesn't mean forgetting. We need to be good to ourselves and pardon ourselves from guilt. We need not be afraid to let grief loosen its grip on us when the time comes. Easing away from intense grief may sometimes cause pain, fear, and guilt for a while, but eventually, it usually allows parents to come to a new and more peaceful place in their journey. Allowing grief's place to become a less doesn't mean we think less of, nor are we abandoning, our child who died.

In the end, we, as parents, must heal ourselves. It was our child; it is our loss; it is our grief. We need to gain closure, to experience release, and to look to our new future.

Dad/Brendan

May 30, 2011

The death of a child is the most traumatic and devastating experience a couple will ever face. In most cases, mothers and fathers grieve differently when such a tragedy occurs. They grieve differently, because fathers are expected to be strong for their wives, to be the "rock" in the family. Comparing one another in this case is wrong. The father has a right to grieve the way he wants to. He can show his emotions and continue to be that rock. Who and what says he can't be?

All too often we are considered to be the ones who should tend to the practical but not the emotional aspects surrounding the death. We are expected to be the ones who should not let emotions show or tears fall outwardly, the ones who will not and should not fall apart. So many times I have been asked, "How is your wife doing?" But fathers are never asked how they are doing.

Death is an experience that is common to all of us, an experience that touches all members of the family. Death transcends all cultures and beliefs. There is both commonality and individuality in the grief experience. When a loved one dies, each person reacts differently. A child's death, however, is such a wrenching event that all affected by it express sadness and dismay and are painfully shaken. Such a devastating loss exacts an emotional, as well as a physical, toll on both the mother and father and the entire family.

This paper will be a little different from my others. I want people to know that all fathers are not alike. I want them to know that we can be the "rock" but still show our emotions. Does that make us less of a man? I believe it makes us more of a man, because you are not ashamed to show your true self. I have been to counseling sessions, and the majority of the time fathers look straight ahead with that stone-faced look. The wives do all the talking. I can tell you this: I know that the fathers hurt. Deep down, they want to let their feelings out but are afraid they will be looked down on as being weak. People who think this could not be more wrong.

These are my feelings, and I do not consider myself a weak father. When Dawn died, I felt that a part of me died, that a vital and core part of me had been ripped away. I honestly believed that the death of my daughter has been "the ultimate deprivation." The grief caused by her death was not only painful but profoundly disorienting. Your children are not supposed to die before you.

I was forced to confront an extremely painful and stressful paradox. I know now I am faced with a situation in which I must deal with both the grief caused by her death and with my inherent need to continue to live my own life as fully as possible. As a result, I had to face and deal with the contradictory burden of wanting to be free of this overwhelming pain and yet needing it as a reminder of her death.

Such expectations place an unmanageable burden on men and deprive us of our rightful and urgent need to grieve. This need will surface eventually if it is not expressed. It is not unusual for grieving fathers to feel overwhelmed, ignored, isolated, and abandoned as they try to continue to be caregivers and breadwinners for their families while their hearts are breaking. Fathers' feelings often stay hidden under layers of responsibility and grim determination. Most fathers feel they can't show grieving because it would make them less of a man. Grieving fathers often say that such strong emotions are very difficult to contain after the death of a child. Fathers must have a release, or it could one day rise up like a volcanic eruption. Much too often, fathers try to bury their pain with the child who died.

The idea of parental mourning has been a universal one throughout the centuries. In the literature on bereavement, writers repeat certain themes, thoughts, and reflections. They talk of the powerful and often conflicting emotions involved in the pain of grief and the spiral of mourning; the heartbreak at the heart of things . . . grief's contradictions. They speak of parents devastated by grief.

It is most important that a father's grief be verbalized and understood by his wife, other family members, professionals, coworkers, friends, and by anyone who will listen. Fathers need to try to free themselves from stereotypes and societal expectations about men and grief. Fathers repeatedly say that for their own peace of mind, they need to move away from this mind-set and allow themselves to grieve, as they are entitled.

I will, for the rest of my life, continue to be Dawn's father. I will always feel the empty place in my heart caused by her death. I will always be the loving father to Dawn. Yet, I have to accept that I will never be able to live my life with or share my love openly with Dawn. So I had to find ways to hold on to the memories. That is why I am doing what I am now, writing thoughts and feeling down and sharing them with other grieving fathers. You're not less of a man if you sit down and write. Deep down, you will love it. I am also writing a biography about Dawn, so her two beautiful children will know who their mother was and how she lived.

Dad/Brendan

June 9, 2011

The death of Dawn at the age of twenty-eight of melanoma cancer is indeed one of the cruelest blows that life has served us. The journey through this grief is a very long, dark, difficult, and painful one for Cathy and me.

In the early minutes, days, weeks, months, and a few months shy of the two-year anniversary of her death, we find ourselves in an all-consuming grief and pain beyond description. There are times we find it difficult to carry on our everyday lives or to think of little except Dawn's death. Even our once wonderfully happy memories that we shared with her while she lived at times bring us pain.

We, as bereaved parents, do not "get over" the death of a child or "snap out of it" as others seem to think we can and should. The death of Dawn was not an illness or a disease from which we recover. It is a life-altering change with which we must learn to live.

With the death of Dawn, we are forced to do the impossible— build a new life and discover a new normal for ourselves and for our family in a world that no longer includes our beloved Dawn.

It is important for other bereaved parents to know that they will experience a wide and often frightening variety of intense feelings after the death of a child.

It is also important for all bereaved parents to understand and know that all of the feelings they experience are very natural and normal under the circumstances. Equally important to know and believe is that as much as you cannot possibly believe it, you will not always feel this powerful and all-consuming grief.

Now, we must follow the instincts of our souls and allow our bodies and hearts to grieve. The grief resulting from Dawn's death cannot be skirted over, around, or under. We must go through it in order to come out on the other side.

We must learn to be gentle and patient with our family and ourselves. We must allow ourselves to cry, to grieve, and to retell Dawn's story as often as needed and for as long as we need to.

Eventually, we will smile and find joy again. We will never forget Dawn; she will be with us in our hearts and memories for as long as we all shall live.

Dad/Brendan

June 15, 2011

They say the death of a child is the greatest loss. I would say I believe that. The severe pain and grief that comes with the death of a child is more than you can ever imagine or try to put down in writing. Surviving the death of your child and the grief that comes with it becomes your new lifestyle.

I'm fifty-seven and come from a large family. When my mother passed away in October 1989, I felt the worst loss I had ever felt. Losing my mother was very hard—harder than I could imagine until I lost my daughter. The grief and the pain are so much different; there is no comparison. I'd like to, if I may, help you survive the unfathomable pain and grief that comes with the loss of a child—your own child.

It hasn't been two years yet since I lost Dawn at age twenty-eight. She missed her twenty-ninth birthday by only twelve days. Sometimes it feels like yesterday, but then other times it feels like ages since I last talked to her or held her hand. Day in and day out, the grief is so painful. My heart actually hurts. I have a huge hole in my heart that will never close up. I feel that I am only half a person. I have asked myself, "How will I ever survive?" What is wrong with this picture is that we are supposed to die before our children! It makes no sense.

For the longest time I would make comments like, "I hate you, death." Do you or have you ever feared death? You would be surprised to know how many people fear death. I guess I could say I was once like that. I looked at death as if it were something permanent. Oh, how wrong I was.

Death today doesn't scare me. Why? Because Jesus conquered death when he died on the cross for us so we may live forever with our children and loved ones. The Bible says you just have to believe Jesus is the Son of God, ask him to forgive you of your sins, and ask him to live in your heart forever. It's that easy. Faith is so important to have. So much opened my eyes with my loss. People think, *Oh,*

275

I'm still young, or *I'm pretty healthy. I have time.* You couldn't be any further from the truth. You must always be prepared to meet your maker. Faith—it is a must.

You're praying and asking God to help relieve this heavy load of pain. While you're praying, you're thinking, *God really doesn't understand this huge hole in my heart.* He does. He lost his only son. He watched his only child being beaten and nailed to a cross. Jesus died for us, and we will live again forever and ever with our children. The Bible says this life we now live is a vapor, a puff of smoke compared to eternity. Try and imagine that last statement—just knowing we will one day be reunited with our loved ones. How neat is that?

In the book of Revelations, the last book in the Bible, it describes heaven. I encourage you to read it. When I lost Dawn, so many people bought me books or recommended books to help comfort me. Each one that I read was outstanding. Prior to losing Dawn, the only books I would pick up were books that dealt with sports. After her passing, the only books I pick up are spiritual books. There is one book that does stand out. I enjoyed reading all of them, but this one book was like ointment to my wounds. It helped with the healing of my loss. It was *Within Heaven's Gates* by Rebecca Springer. "She clings to the hand of God to keep from going wild, while in his presence comes to know his other hand holds her child."

The book is about a lady who had a vision or dream of heaven while she was dying. I would close my eyes and try to imagine what she would describe. I wanted to know everything about the place where my girl now lives. If your child was a missionary in a foreign country and couldn't contact with you while he was there, you would get every book you could get your hands on that told you about the place he now lived. Why? Because it would comfort you and help you feel close to him. Read this book. It takes you away from your pain for the moment and helps you visualize heaven. It truly is a beautiful story.

Another thing that helps me cope with my loss is journaling. You can just write your thoughts and feelings down like I do, or you can write your child a letter and tell her all about how you are feeling at the moment and how very much you miss her. I've stained some of my journals with tears. When I first started my writings, I had many tears. These tears were tears of sorrow. I must admit that today when I write, my tears are more joyful tears because I do know where she is. As she once told me before her death, "Daddy, when you get to heaven, I will be your big sister." So I think of comments that will bring joy to me.

The healing process is a very long one, but together, we can make it. You really believe that there hasn't been any progress, and you don't think there ever will be. Believe me when I tell you that one day you will look back and come to realize that you have taken steps forward. One day I surprised myself when I walked outside and felt the warmth of the sun, saw the spring flowers, and said, "What a beautiful day!" I was shocked and then realized I had made progress. I ran inside, because I had to write it down. For the longest time, I typed things that were more sad and sorrowful. I knew I had to start writing positive things that were happening to me.

Change—it will happen, and you will be able to tolerate things differently; however, the pain will never leave. You will learn to tolerate it and continue to move forward. I would be lying if I didn't tell you that, yes, you will have days when you think you are reverting back. When I have days like that, I go back and reread some of my first writings. I was so mad and angry and also depressed. I don't want to be like that anymore. Rereading my papers brings me back to where I have worked so hard to be.

With the loss of your child, you have to start a new normal. You have to start a new path. The path you and your child were traveling on is no longer. That path is now a dead end, and you have to take the fork in the road. It's scary, very scary, traveling that path alone; however, there are two very important things that will help you make it on the path. The first one is faith that God will always be with you. He will not give you more than you can handle. The second thing is knowing that your loving child will be with you in spirit. On your new path you cannot keep your head down and be in a depressed mood. You must now keep your head up, so your loved one can see your face as she looks down from heaven.

Dad/Brendan

June 25, 2011

Words cannot describe the emotions and feelings that surround a household after a child has died. Since the passing of my daughter, I have read more than two dozen books on this subject. In most of these books, I have read that fathers feel the same emotions as mothers, but how they experience those emotions and how they deal with and express themselves is very different from how mothers grief.

Grief shows itself in many forms, including shock, despair, anger, and guilt. Fathers and mothers alike face these feelings. There is no set order for when they are felt; sometimes one feeling dominates all others. At times, we may feel guilty because we have not thought of our grief for a while—we may even have laughed at something—or we may feel guilt simply because we are numb and seem to have lost all the expected emotions.

Before I go any further, I would like to tell you a little about myself. I have always been the type of person who keeps things bottled up inside me. I spent twenty-one years in the military; I started my career in Vietnam and ended it in Desert Shield/Desert Storm. During that time frame, I served in five conflicts with Lebanon, Libya, Granada, Panama, and Iraq. I was the tough man. I've seen my fair share of death—more than I care to talk about. But I kept it bottled inside, because I am a man, and men aren't supposed to show emotions in public. A man is supposed to be the rock of the family. Everyone else is allowed to grieve, but not a father. If he showed emotions, people would think less of him; he wouldn't be a man.

Then one day I found out my daughter had terminal cancer. Right before my eyes I watched the expression on my twenty-eight-year-old daughter's face when the doctor told her she had six months to a year to live. All that macho, macho crap left my body. My girls were always my life. They were everything to me. At the time, I was leaning up against the bed, and my daughter was sitting in the chair. When the doctor gave her the diagnosis, I thought my legs were turning into rubber.

My daughter looked at me and said, "Daddy." And that was all it took. We both broke down and cried. I always knew my daughter was strong, but she showed me she was even stronger than I thought. We held each other, and all of a sudden she put her hands on my arms and stepped back. "Daddy, I am so sorry. I know how much you love me, and I know this will break your heart." Did you hear that? She'd just found out she had terminal brain cancer, and she was worried about me.

From that day forward, I carried my emotions wherever I went. I didn't care where I was or who I was with. I wasn't less of a man. I am the same person as I was before I found out about my daughter. For you men who are so adamant about not showing your emotions in public, I really feel sorry for you. I just wonder what my daughter would have thought about me if I didn't cry with her. Would she have thought I didn't care enough to even show my emotions?

I have heard men say at counseling sessions that they can cope with out shedding a tear. At one particular session, a man began to speak. "I am only here because my wife wanted me to come," he said. "I don't need this counseling. I have to remain strong for my wife, because she is grieving. I have to be strong for my other kids, because they just lost a sibling. I have to remain strong and in control, so no, I don't show emotions. I'm not weak." He then looked at me.

I raised my hand and asked if I could talk. The lady running the session said, "Sure, we love it when you talk."

The man who had referred to me as being weak just rolled his eyes. He'd lost a son in an auto accident. To me, it doesn't matter how; we still lost a child. I proceeded to tell the group what Dawn looked like when she was diagnosed. Then with all the medication and steroids she was taking to prevent the tumors on her brain from swelling, she blew up like a balloon. She lost all her hair from the radiation treatment. My girl went from a petite young lady to a balloon person. The pain she was in was unbearable, but she never complained, never complained at all—until the cancer went into her bones. "Daddy, I wish they would cut my arm off it hurts so bad," she said. You see, medication can't penetrate the bone. All that pain medicine didn't relive her pain. Then I mentioned her two little children and how they were now motherless. About that time, I looked over at this man, and he had tears running down his face.

I stopped talking, because he was looking right at me. When I stopped, he raised his hand and asked to talk. I couldn't understand a word he said, because he cried the whole time. His wife was in total disbelief. After the session, he came over to me, and I put my hand out to shake his. Instead of a hand shake, he gave me a hug and apologized. I then reach out and grabbed his arms, stepped back, and told him no apologies were needed. "We are here to help one another," I said.

As we were walking out for the night, he came up to me and said, "You were right. You really do feel better after a good cry."

Dad/Brendan

July 9, 2011

It's just so unforeseen: you expect to lose your parents at some point, maybe even your spouse, but you never expect to be standing beside your child's coffin.

The death of a child is so disturbing—a shock that forces you to survive with an absence in your life that irreparably changes the shape of your life forever.

When my daughter died, I felt guilty for surviving her, but I also believed that I had failed in my role as the father to protect her from everything. That is a normal feeling right after a loss. I don't believe that at all now. There was nothing I could have done to protect her from the horrible six-letter word *cancer*. Cancer does not discriminate with age, race, or sex.

I never gave it any thought before my daughter died, but the original meaning of the word *bereave* is "to rob," and it's this sense of deprivation that contributes to the unique grief felt by a parent over the death of a child. I guess this is the perfect meaning of the word. When you experience the passing of your parents, the isolation is felt when others try to sympathize with your loss; at least with the death of your parents, you have lots of memories to grieve with, whereas with children, this is exactly what you have been robbed of.

You could experience unbearable emotions that you didn't believe you were capable of feeling, such as lack of support from some family members. Support from your family is one of the key factors for strength. Without that support, you could form some bitterness toward those people. On top of that, you may have tension that could erupt with those family members who didn't show or give you support. After just losing a child, the last thing in this world you need is problems from your side of the family. Lots of the extreme feelings you are dealing with are a normal part of grieving.

Holidays and special occasions are still the hardest to face. I believe that no matter how many years I live, they will always be hard. You must plan around them. Do something special with your loved one in mind. Don't try and isolate yourself from others on those days, because you will be worse off. Spend those days with family and friends. They will be your support in making it through those times.

Individuals grieve differently, and that's why with this sort of grief, I found group counseling to help me the most. You could have more than a dozen couples in a session for the same reason, the loss of a child, but we all lost our children differently. I have learned so much from others, and I hope they have learned from me.

I have found The Compassionate Friends is the best fit for me. The Compassionate Friends is a society that was originated in England by two bereaved families. They now have regional groups across the UK, United States, and Canada. All major cities in the United Sates have a chapter. This is an organization that helps parents who have lost a child. They meet once a month. What I have found is you can always rely on support from others during the times you don't meet. We are all there for one another.

The benefit of a support group is that those present are not afraid to ask about the child who has died, allowing parents and families to talk about their child's personality and appreciate the individual that he or she was. This small, yet significant act is always available, no matter how long ago the bereavement occurred. This has helped me cope with life without Dawn.

You don't get over the death of your child. You have to find a 'new normal,' you adjust, and build your life around it.

Dad/Brendan

July 10, 2011

The loss of a child is something most parents cannot bear to even contemplate. It is such a horrible thought that most people do not and cannot envision it. All parents feel they will follow the normal path of everyday life. Their children will grow to adulthood, give them grandchildren, and then everyone will be happy and move on.

Sometimes life isn't as easy as we would like to think it to be. Have you ever heard the saying "We have to live with the cards that were dealt to us"? You can play those cards in several different ways, but you still have the final outcome. How we deal with it and live with it is another situation.

I lost my daughter Dawn to cancer at the age of twenty-eight. One day we were all sitting around telling jokes and cutting up. Life was good; life was fun. Then the next day my whole life was turned upside down with the news that my daughter had terminal brain cancer.

The one thing I hope is that you know you will see the light at the end of that tunnel. Grief is a process of healing, and there is no time limit for you to overcome your pain. However, you will see happiness again. There is help out there. Dawn was a gift given to me by God. If I had to do it all over again, I would raise her over again, because of how much I loved her. I would still do it all again and have the pain, because I had the love for her—that will never change.

I am living a parent's greatest fear, and that is losing a child. A day doesn't go by that I don't think of my daughter. The journey of this grief led me to writing this book. My daughter did tell me that writing my thoughts and feelings down would help me and others, so this is my way to share with you and try to help others. I have committed myself to try and help other parents cope with the horrific loss of a child. We must all remember that everyone grieves differently. There is no set time limit on when you should be done grieving. Don't let people tell you that you should be over it by now. What do they know? They are not you.

I am not a doctor or a counselor, but I have found that these ideas could assist those suffering from a devastating loss with coping in the days to come:

Don't try to rush your grief journey. Let it be in your own time. Everyone is different and grieves in his or her own way. Find what works for you at your own pace.

Do something special to honor your lost child. Plant a tree or a memory garden. These are the two things I did, and I love them so much. You could do monthly or yearly projects. Get other family members together and coordinate it. It can be anything that makes you feel closer to your child: you could set up a scholarship at their former school or college, scrapbook, or sent gift baskets to the elderly. There are so many different things you, as a parent, can do to keep your child's memory alive.

Some would think that this would be the last one listed, but in the grieving process, there is no order. You need to move forward. Find ways for you and your family to adjust to the loss. Get into some activities. If there isn't anything to join, start your own. Make it enjoyable.

Physical activity helps. Whether it is walking, biking, or swimming, these activities help you cope as each day passes. This truly is a must. You will feel so much better.

Helping others is the best way to heal yourself. Get involved in a selfless project. The satisfaction and gratitude you receive from helping others will soothe you.

Attend a grieving organization meeting. They are located in almost every city and state. They lend support and walk beside you in grief, because members have lost children also.

Sometimes the days will feel just too hard to get through, but with the help of family and friends, it will get easier (become tolerable). Develop a backup plan for these days. If possible, get out and go do something different. If you're at work, take a break and get some fresh air.

You are going to have good days and bad days. The love you have for your child will always be with you. It never goes away, but realize that you will experience happiness again. Do the best you can. Your grieving journey will teach you what is important in life: loving, showing concern for others, caring for others, and doing things without the possibility of benefit to help others. Through all these things, you will learn about hope, joy, and the things that are of real value.

Try to follow these ideas to cope with the loss of a child. There is no right or wrong method to learn to cope, and there is no time line to follow. Take your time; don't burden yourself with self-doubt about what should be normal. You will find your way, feeling hope and joy in your life again.

Dad/Brendan

August 21, 2011

The theme of parental mourning has been a universal one throughout the centuries. In the literature on bereavement, writers repeat certain themes, thoughts, and reflections. They talk of the powerful and often conflicting emotions involved in the pain of grief and the spiral of mourning; they refer to the heartbreak at the heart of things . . . grief's contradictions. They speak of parents devastated by grief.

It is a fact that the grief of bereaved parents is the most intense grief known to mankind. When a child dies, parents feel that a part of them died along with their child, that a vital and core part of them has been ripped away. As a bereaved father, I do feel that the death of Dawn is "the ultimate deprivation." The grief caused by Dawn's death is not only painful but profoundly disorienting—our children are not supposed to die before us. I am forced to confront an extremely painful and stressful paradox; I am faced with a situation in which I must deal both with the grief caused by Dawn's death and with my inherent need to continue to live my own life as fully as possible. Thus, I must deal with the contradictory burden of wanting to be free of this overwhelming pain and yet needing it as a reminder of Dawn, who died.

I will always continue to be the father of Dawn. I will always feel the empty place in my heart caused by her death. Yet, I have to accept that I will never be able to live my life or share my love openly with her, so I must find ways to hold on to the memories. I have come to learn that memories are the precious gifts of the heart. I need these memories and whispers to help create a sense of inner peace, a closure.

Sociologists and psychologists describe parental grief as complex and multilayered and agree that the death of a child is an incredibly traumatic event that leaves parents with overwhelming emotional needs. They also agree that this grief must be acknowledged and felt in its intensity. These experts repeatedly state that dealing with parental grief involves deep pain and ongoing work as the parents attempt to continue their journey down the lonely road of grief.

I am told that my grief is a lifelong process, a long and painful process, a process in which I try to take and keep some meaning from the loss and life without Dawn. After her death, I embarked on a long, sad journey that can be very frightening and extremely lonely—a journey that never really ends. The hope and desire that healing will come eventually is an intense and persistent one for a grieving father.

Dawn is considered a gift to me on loan by God. Unfortunately, I was forced to give up that gift. Yet, as a father, I also strive to let Dawn's life, no matter how short, be seen as a gift to others. I seek to find ways to continue to love, honor, and value the life of Dawn and continue to make her presence known and felt in the lives of family and friends. I often try to live my life more fully and generously because of this painful experience.

Death is an experience that is common to all mankind, an experience that touches all members of the family. Death transcends all cultures and beliefs; there is both commonality and individuality in the grief experience. When a loved one dies, each person reacts differently. A child's death, however, is such a wrenching event that all affected by it express sadness and dismay and are painfully shaken. Such a devastating loss exacts an emotional, as well as a physical, toll on you and your family.

Bereavement specialists point to the commonalities of our grief that may include an overwhelming sense of its magnitude, a sense that the pain will last forever, and a sense that the grief is etched into one's very being. They explain that it is also important for you to express your anger outwardly so that it will not turn inward and possibly become a destructive force in the future. These specialists say that although there are many commonalities in our grief, individual reactions often vary and the same people may even experience contradictory reactions. They also say that the two responses experienced most commonly by bereaved parents is a baffling sense of disorientation and a deep conviction that they must never let go of the grief.

But there are also many unique ways that we can express our grief. We can have several responses that are influenced by many factors, including our life experiences, coping skills, personality, age, gender, family, cultural background, support and/or belief systems, and even the death or type of death that occurred.

My grief is boundless. It touches every aspect of my being. The range of expression of my grief is wide. Some fathers will express tears openly, and I can be put in that category. Others will silence there expressions and grieve inwardly. Despite the volumes of work on grief, the experience of grief seems to defy description. Definitions touch the fringes of grief but do not embrace its totality or reach its core. Grief is a complicated, evolving human process. Grief is a binding experience; its universality binds sufferers together. More is shared than is different.

As part of the grieving process, I have experienced ups and downs and a literal roller coaster of emotions. For me, a personal history includes a past with Dawn and a present and future without her. For my grieving, it is vitally important to verbalize the pain, to talk about what happened, to ask questions, and to puzzle aloud, sometimes over and over.

It is the nature of grief that feelings, thoughts, and emotions need to be processed and that I must look into my heart and soul and try to heal from within. Everyone is different, and each person has to do this in his or her own way. I am a survivor, and each survivor travels this lonely and painful road in a way each maps out. In traveling this road, I often respond differently, learn to live with my grief separately, and express my sadness uniquely. I can and often do feel alone, disconnected, and alienated. I need to know that there are many ways to grieve; there is no timetable for grief's duration; there are no rules, boundaries, or protocols for grieving.

Moreover, those who seek to comfort me need to recognize and understand the complexities of my emotions and should avoid relying on preconceived ideas about the way I am supposed to grieve. Reactions of my grieving may seem overly intense, self-absorbing, contradictory, or even puzzling. For me, the death of Dawn is such an overwhelming event that my response may often be baffling, not only to others but to myself as well.

The death of Dawn is the most traumatic and devastating experience I think I will ever face in my life. Individuals grieve deeply when such a tragedy occurs, they grieve differently, and it is most important that each partner give the other permission to grieve as needed. This may be the greatest gift each can give the other.

There is no relationship like that of father and daughter. It is unique and special. The bond between a father and daughter is so powerful that its strength endures time, distance, and strife. No loss is as significant as the loss of a daughter. After losing my daughter, I feel less than whole.

A father's grief is overwhelming; there was nothing that could have prepared me for its enormity or devastation. My grief never ends but only changes in intensity and manner of expression. My grief affects the head, the heart, and the spirit.

My loss of Dawn means coming to terms with untold emptiness and deep emotional hurt. Immediately after her death, I experience a period of shock and numbness. I had all; I expressed the grief openly and was also shocked and numb.

I have to find ways to get through, not over, my grief—to go on with my life. I am forced to continue life's journey in an individual manner.

As a grieving father, I need to learn to be compassionate, gentle, and patient with myself and others. Grief is an emotionally devastating experience; grief is work and demands much patience, understanding, effort, and energy.

My grief can and often does involve a vast array of conflicting emotions and responses, including shock and numbness, intense sadness and pain, depression, and often feelings of total confusion and disorganization. Sometimes, I may not even seem sure of who I am and may feel as if I have lost an integral part of my very being.

Other times, I may feel that what happened was a myth or an illusion or that I was having a nightmare.

Typically, my reactions to Dawn's death involve emotional and physical symptoms such as inability to sleep, mood swings, exhaustion, extreme anxiety, headaches, or inability to concentrate. I have experienced emotional and physical peaks and valleys. You may think life finally seems on an even keel and you are learning to cope when periods of intense sadness overwhelm you, perhaps with even more force than before. Experiencing any or all of these reactions does not mean permanent loss of control or inability to recover and are usually part of the grief process. So I am told.

I do need to know how important it is to express my pain to someone who will understand and acknowledge what I am feeling and saying. I should be honest with myself and others about how I feel. There have been many time when family and friends ask how I am doing, and I tell them I'm fine, knowing deep down I'm not fine. Being honest is a very important step to healing. I allow myself to cry, be angry, and complain. I need to admit I am overwhelmed, distracted, and unable to focus or concentrate. I may even need to admit to myself and others that I might show some emotional symptoms that they don't want or can't even understand.

It is very important that we be allowed to mourn in our own way and time frame. Each person's grief is unique, even that of family members facing the same loss. I shouldn't expect or try to follow a specific or prescribed pattern for grief or worry if I seem out of sync with other grieving individuals.

I need to know that others may minimize or misunderstand my grief. Many don't understand the power, depth, intensity, or duration of a father's grief, especially after the death of a child. In some instances, you can't even ignore, because some individuals are not able to deal with the tragedy. They find the thought of a child's death too hard, too inexplicable, or too threatening. Many simply don't know what to say or do, and so they don't say or do anything.

I have and still am experiencing great pain and distress deciding what to do with Dawn's belongings. Yes, I gave the majority to

Kristie Lynn and told her to do with it as she sees fit. I also need to understand that this task will be the most difficult and that different individuals make different decisions. I should be encouraged to hold onto any experiences, memories, or mementoes I have of Dawn and find ways to keep and treasure them. These memories and mementoes—her legacy from the short time we shared with this very special person—will be affirming and restorative in the future. One day these items will be handed down to her two wonderful children, Tyler and Jordan.

I also experience considerable pain on special occasions, such as birthdays, holidays, or the anniversary of her death. I will need to find ways to cope with these events and should do what feels right for them, not what others think I should do.

You must find peace in your religion. Not only will your religious beliefs significantly alter the meaning that you give to life, death, and life after death, but it will also affect your grief response. If you have a religious background, you should be encouraged to express your beliefs if this is helpful. Some people without a formal or organized religious background may maintain spirituality or a personal faith that is also a part of their lives and gives them comfort. They too should be encouraged to express these feelings.

Seeking spiritual comfort in a time of grief does not mean repressing the grief. It is important, however, that others offering support to grieving individuals do not try to dismiss or diminish the grief by using religious or other platitudes or by forcing religion on people. I thank God every day for Dawn opening my eyes and bringing God back into my heart. I have been told numerous times that I will recover and reach a place of rest and hope. I will never forget Dawn, but rather, I will find ways to keep her a cherished part of my inner self forever. I have not and don't know when I will ever reach that level.

Grief is the natural response to any loss. I need to be reminded how important it is to process all feelings, thoughts, and emotions in resolving grief. I must also look within and be prepared to deal with the past and present. I need to talk about my loss, and the loss must be acknowledged by others. I need to tell others about what happened to Dawn; I need to talk out and through my thoughts and feelings from the heart, not just from the head. Healing for me can begin to occur by acknowledging and sharing my grief.

Probably the most important step in my grief journey is to allow myself to heal. I need to come to the understanding that healing doesn't mean forgetting. I need to be good to myself and absolve myself from guilt. I should not be afraid to let grief loosen its grip on me when the time comes. Easing away from intense grief may sometimes cause pain, fear, and guilt for a while, but eventually, it usually allows me to come to a new and more peaceful place in my journey. Allowing grief's place to become a lesser one does not mean abandoning Dawn.

Dad/Brendan

November 2011

I knew the day would come—the one I tried to avoid since Dawn's death. I believe most in this situation would do the same. I have known individuals who acted on this task right after the funeral, because they felt it was the best way to handle it. I know I couldn't do it that soon. In many of my papers, I've stated that everyone grieves differently. Well, here is a good example. I am talking about cleaning out the closet and/or bedroom of your diseased loved one. I guess the question to ask is when should you begin to tackle this job, a job that will be very emotional to complete?

Cleaning out the closets presents a significant challenge for most parents after losing a child. The overwhelming thought of going through my daughter's belongings and trying to decide what do with the items is by far one of the hardest pieces of fatherhood or (parenthood). For me, it was so overwhelming that it was easier to just leave everything as was until I was ready to clean it out. Others may want to clean things out immediately after the funeral. Everyone is different, and we should respect everyone's wishes.

I chose to leave Dawn's possessions alone for a couple of years after her passing. I found peace when I went into her room. I would go in and sit in the rocking chair glider and read a book. I always felt a part of her in the room with me. It is a personal decision of what works best for you. Many friends and family members have their opinions of what is right or wrong when it comes to cleaning out the closets, but the true right or wrong is in the eyes and the heart of the parent.

For some parents, an immediate reaction to the loss, especially if it was a sudden death, is to quickly clean out everything. The thought behind this approach is that you will feel better if you do not see the personal belongings. I have been told by some parents that the real truth is this will not make most people feel better; in fact, as time goes by, they will regret having cleaned out and given away the items so quickly.

After the funeral of my daughter, I spoke to my wife and asked her if we could leave Dawn's belongings alone. If you are not in need of that bedroom, then why rush in to something so emotional? As the realization of the loss slowly finds its way to your heart, you will want to savor every minute with each belonging. Be careful not to clean out or advise anyone to clean out the items too fast. There are many ways of approaching the cleaning and organizing when you are ready to attack it.

The million-dollar question is when should you start to clean and organize your child's personal belongings? And the answer is very simple—when you are ready! Some start the process when they decide to sell their home, and others wake up one morning and decide today is the day.

Before you begin, think of family members and friends who may enjoy special items from your loved one—maybe a scarf or a piece of jewelry. To a family member or friend, any item could have a very important sentimental meaning.

We decided to donate some things to our local Hospice Center. I always think of the not-for-profits in our community that can benefit from donations first—coats for the homeless and nicer clothes for the workforce initiatives.

The best way is to have your mind ready for this huge challenge. It will wear you out both mentally and physically. It will get emotional. You will stop and think things like, *I remember her in that.* Be sure you put something aside for yourself. The best suggestion is to make four piles—a pile of things you like, a pile of things to donate, a pile of things you don't know what to do with yet, and a pile for the trash. If you start this way, you have "an out" if you do not know what to do with some of the personal items—they would end up in the third pile.

Be sure to take the time to savor memories of each item that goes through your hands. If it is overwhelming, take a few items to a different room and go through them at your leisure. Once you start, you will find that you will develop a rhythm and a balance between feeling you are accomplishing the task and taking pleasure in reminiscing.

Parents often wonder what happens if they find an item that upsets them, such as a picture, journal, or letter. Up to a year after her passing, my wife and I found notes that our daughter had left us. I found them when I really needed a spiritual uplifting. I always loved looking and seeing my daughter, so we put a couple pictures of her throughout the house.

Be kind to yourself while cleaning out the closets. It is something you should do yourself, as it is a great way to work through your grief. Take your time, do not let yourself be overwhelmed, and cherish the memories. If you are not ready to go through the belongings, don't. Wait until you are ready. Each parent is different, and there are no set rules.

The box of possessions I could not discard is my memorial of Dawn's personal belongings that mean the world to me, as simple as it may seem. When I open the box, I can touch her, I can smell her, and I can see her.

Parents have the perception that if and when they get rid of their loved one's belongings, they are totally letting go. That is the furthest thing from the truth.

Dad/Brendan

CONCLUSION

OUR CHILDREN ARE valuable and precious symbols of what lies ahead. No matter the age of the children, they are considered the hope of our future. When a child dies, that hope is lost. When you lose a parent, you've lost your past. When you lose a child, you've lost your future.

It's interesting to note in other types of familial death, there is a term that denotes a change in relationship. When a wife loses her husband, she becomes a widow. When a wife dies, the husband becomes a widower. When a child loses his parents, he becomes an orphan. However, there is no word that reflects the change in status from parent to bereaved parent. It is a change that defies even our vocabulary.

I have heard many times that life is referred to as a journey down a curvy path. If you think in these terms, then before Dawn died, we were traveling together on one path. Most people have a sense of where they are heading on their paths. Unfortunately, with the death of Dawn, I now have to come to a fork in my path. At the fork, I'm forced onto a different path, heading off in another direction. This new path is not one of my choosing, and I'm not sure of what lies ahead. The path I was originally on is now closed and is no longer an option.

The challenge I now face is finding out how to make this new path as rewarding as possible, given that I wish I were still on my original path. Before I can do this, I need to pay attention to my feelings and work out what I have to do to express my loss and help myself adjust to living without Dawn. This new path I'm taking is what you call a new *normal*. I can never put my old normal back together.

For the individuals who have never experienced this, it is hard to understand. When your child dies, you become disoriented and confused, and letting go of a child is impossible. You will never forget the child who died. The bond that formed between Dawn and I will forever remain in my heart.

Being a father who survived, I will try to adapt to the new existence forced on me. I will try to pass on to others the love and other special gifts I received from my daughter Dawn. I will try to make Dawn a part of our lives forever. I will constantly try to honor Dawn, who should have lived. I will try and encourage others as we make this new journey. I will ask others to help me, and in turn, I will help them. This new journey is now my new *normal*.

What has happened has changed my life. I will never see life the same way, and I will never be the same person I once was. As I attempt to move forward, I must realize I am now a survivor, and I have been strong enough to endure life's harshest blow. There is nothing in this world worse than losing a child.

When I felt the depression coming on, I would read some of my beginning letters. I didn't want to revert back to that stage of grieving.

Even with this book being published, I will continue to do more writings. My thoughts and feeling will not end here. My girl will forever be in my heart. I will continue to pray to our Lord, our God, and I will ask him to please let this book help grieving parents. The pain is unbearable, and if God would let others see this and enable it to help them, even if it's a little, then it was worth writing.

CPSIA information can be obtained at www.ICGtesting.com
Printed in the USA
BVOW071123080412

287145BV00001B/76/P